The Hat and a Nice Old Lady

A Football Fan's Diary

Anthony Rubin

Copyright © 2022

All Rights Reserved

Table of Contents

Dedication i
Acknowledgements ii
About the Author iii
Chapter 1 - The Beginning 2
Chapter 2 - My First Live Match 3
Chapter 3 - The Beginning of the Italian Connection 5
Chapter 4 - 90th Anniversary of the FA and the 1954 World Cup 8
Chapter 5 - Luton Town in the 50s 10
Chapter 6 - My Adolescent Years 11
Chapter 7 - European Competitions 13
Chapter 8 - Matty and Arsenal 14
Chapter 9 - Further Education 15
Chapter 10 - The Real Italian Connection 16
Chapter 11 - Turin 18
Chapter 12 - Late Teens and Twenties 20
Chapter 13 - FA Cup Run 58/59 23
Chapter 14 - FA Cup Final 24
Chapter 15 - Ajax Amsterdam 26
Chapter 16 - Italians Again and a Trip to Sweden 27
Chapter 17 - European Cup Finals 28
Chapter 18 - Spurs in Turin 29
Chapter 19 - Soccer Magazines and Journalists 31
Chapter 20 - 1961 and Medicine 32
Chapter 21 - A First Overseas Football Trip 35
Chapter 22 - 1962 World Cup in Chile 37
Chapter 23 - An English Exodus 38
Chapter 24 - Lean Years 1961 to 1965 39
Chapter 25 - On the Move 40
Chapter 26 - Football on Television 42
Chapter 27 - A Base at Last 44
Chapter 28 - Season 1965/66 46
Chapter 29 - 1966 and the World Cup 48
Chapter 30 - World Cup Final Day 51
Chapter 31 - Seasons 1966/67 and 67/68 53
Chapter 32 - European Cup Final 1968 55
Chapter 33 - Season 1968/69 56
Chapter 34 - A Year's Sabbatical without Live Soccer 58

Chapter 35 - Continuing My Career 63
Chapter 36 - Season 1970/71 64
Chapter 37 - Season 1971/72 67
Chapter 38 - Season 1972/73 69
Chapter 39 - French Riviera OGC Nice and AS Monaco.. 72
Chapter 40 - Season 1973/74 and the World Cup... 74
Chapter 41 - Season 1974/75 76
Chapter 42 - Seasons 1975/76 to 1978/79 79
Chapter 43 - World Cups and England Managers 81
Chapter 44 - Referees.. 83
Chapter 45 - David Pleat... 84
Chapter 46 - Artificial (Plastic) Pitches 85
Chapter 47 - Three Foreigners at Juventus 88
Chapter 48 - Kidnapping and Terrorism in Italy 90
Chapter 49 - Ajax 1981... 91
Chapter 50 - Season 1981/82 92
Chapter 51 - 1982 World Cup in Spain 94
Chapter 52 - Season 1982/83 95
Chapter 53 - Season 1983/84 96
Chapter 54 - David Evans... 97
Chapter 55 - Argentinians... 98
Chapter 56 - VIP at Villa Park!... 100
Chapter 57 - Season 1983/84 102
Chapter 58 - Season 1984/85 103
Chapter 59 - Hooliganism... 105
Chapter 60 - European Championships 1980 108
Chapter 61 - Raddy Antic 110
Chapter 62 - Mick Harford 111
Chapter 63 - The Heysel Stadium... 113
Chapter 64 - I've Found a New Friend... 116
Chapter 65 - Sion and Aberdeen 118
Chapter 66 - Season 1986/87 119
Chapter 67 - 1986 World Cup in Mexico 121
Chapter 68 - Juventus 1986/87 122
Chapter 69 - Season 1987/88 125
Chapter 70 - Littlewoods Cup victory 127
Chapter 71 - 1988 European Championships 130
Chapter 72 - 1989 Another Cup Final.. 131

Chapter 73 - Season 1989/90 133
Chapter 74 - Turbulent Times 134
Chapter 75 - Forza Italia 139
Chapter 76 - Spectating in Style 140
Chapter 77 - 1990 World Cup in Italy 141
Chapter 78 - A Rare Semi-Final for England 146
Chapter 79 - Season 1990/91 149
Chapter 80 - Season 1991/92 152
Chapter 81 - Season 1992/93 157
Chapter 82 - Season 1993/94 160
Chapter 83 - Man Utd in Barcelona 162
Chapter 84 - Season 1994/95 163
Chapter 85 - Eric Cantona 164
Chapter 86 - A Semifinal with Man United 166
Chapter 87 - Season 1995/96 168
Chapter 88 - George Best's 50th Birthday 170
Chapter 89 - Foreigners in English Football and Another Turin Trip 172
Chapter 90 - 1996 European Championships 174
Chapter 91 - Season 1996/97 176
Chapter 92 - Season 1997/98 178
Chapter 93 - 1998 World Cup in France 179
Chapter 94 - AS Monaco 184
Chapter 95 - Season 1998/99 187
Chapter 96 - Season 1999/00 189
Chapter 97 - Season 2000/01 190
Chapter 98 - Season 2001/02 192
Chapter 99 - 2002 World Cup South Korea/Japan 196
Chapter 100 - Season 2002/03 Including Nantes 197
Chapter 101 - Football in Bucharest 199
Chapter 102 - Another Turin Visit 201
Chapter 103 - 2003 Champions League Final 203
Chapter 104 - Season 2003/04 204
Chapter 105 - A Champions League Match in Monaco 207
Chapter 106 - FIFA 100 208
Chapter 107 - A final in Cardiff 209
Chapter 108 - Season 2004/05 211
Chapter 109 - Season 2005/06 214
Chapter 110 - Why do I go to away matches? 216

Chapter 111 - Keith Keane 218
Chapter 112 - Season 2006/07 220
Chapter 113 - A French League Cup Final 221
Chapter 114 - Calciopoli scandal 222
Chapter 115 - 2006 World Cup in Germany 224
Chapter 116 - More Drama 226
Chapter 117 - New Wembley Stadium 227
Chapter 118 - Season 2007/08 228
Chapter 119 - An 80th birthday outing 231
Chapter 120 - Season 2008/09 233
Chapter 121 - Trophy victory 234
Chapter 122 - Conference years 236
Chapter 123 - Chelsea versus Juventus 237
Chapter 124 - Watching Juventus on TV in England 239
Chapter 125 - 2010 World Cup in South Africa 241
Chapter 126 - Season 2010/11 246
Chapter 127 - Season 2011/12 250
Chapter 128 - Season 2012/13 252
Chapter 129 - Alessandro Del Piero 254
Chapter 130 - Yet another Turin trip 255
Chapter 131 - OGC Nice and Season 2013/14 257
Chapter 132 - Season 2014/15 260
Chapter 133 - 2014 World Cup in Brazil 262
Chapter 134 - Season 2015/16 264
Chapter 135 - Season 2016/17 266
Chapter 136 - Season 2017/18 268
Chapter 137 - Season 2018/19 272
Chapter 138 - Season 2019/20 274
Chapter 139 - Season 2020/21 277
Chapter 140 - Season 2021/2022 279
Chapter 141 - In Memoriam 280
Chapter 142 - My Favourite Quotes 281

Dedication

For Gillian,

and for my daughters Deborah and Esther

and my six grandchildren Thomas, Lily, Alice, Issy, Harvey and Daisy

and in memory of my late parents Henry and Lily.

Acknowledgements

I would like to thank Roger Wash, Luton Town Historian and Chairman of Hatters' Heritage, for helpful advice.

Publications that I have dipped into or read include:

- Alan Adair. 1,2,3,4,5 5 Decades of devotion to Luton Town FC
- Steve Bailey, Brian Ellis, Alan Shury. The Definitive Luton Town F.C
- Timothy Collings. The Luton Town story 1885 - 1985
- Timothy Collings. Luton Town A Pictorial Celebration of their Cup History
- Robert Endeacott. The Gigante
- Giampiero Boniperti con Enrica Speroni. Una Vita A Testa Alta
- John Foot. Calcio A history of Italian football
- Robert Hadgraft. Luton Town Staring into the Abyss. Minus 30 the Coldest place in Football
- Alexandra Manna and Mike Gibbs. The Day Italian Football Died Torino and the Tragedy of Superga
- George WH Jackson. Luton Town FC A Season by Season History 1885 - 2018
- Many Newspapers and Magazines including L'Equipe, Nice Matin and La Gazzetta dello Sport
- Barry Moss. Give it to Joe, A biography of Joe Payne, footballer.
- Newspaper Headlines Luton Town A History from 1931
- Paul Rance. Luton Town FC in the 1970s
- Herbie Sykes. Juve! 100 years of an Italian Football Dynasty
- Roger Wash. Luton Town at Kenilworth Road. A century of Memories
- Roger Wash and Simon Pitts. Luton Town Football Club The full record 1885 - 2010.
- Wikipedia. Many entries
- World Soccer Magazines

About the Author

Anthony Rubin is a retired consultant anaesthetist with a passion for football as well as for France and Italy.

Chapter 1 - The Beginning

I came into the world on Monday 20th September 1937 in a house on Wembley Park Drive. This could have been significant because it was within earshot of Wembley Stadium. I might well have been affected positively by the frequent roars from the stadium as I lay in my pram on the porch outside the front door.

It was also just four days after the BBC had shown its first live football match, which featured a specially put on friendly match between Arsenal and Arsenal reserves. It was only available to a small number of homes close to Alexandra Palace, where the BBC had a transmission site, one of the oldest in the world. The score is not recorded, but the Arsenal team contained such luminaries as goalkeeper George Swindin, George Male, who made 318 appearances for the Gunners, Cliff Bastin, third-highest Arsenal goalscorer of all time and with 21 England caps, Eddie Hapgood with 30 England caps, Ted Drake, Alex James, and the Compton brothers. Ted Drake is remembered for the seven goals he scored in a match in 1935, which is still the English top-flight record. Of course, the overall football league record for most individual goals in a match still rests with Luton's Joe Payne, who scored ten against Bristol Rovers on Easter Monday 13th April 1936. Alex James was a Scots inside forward who got eight international caps. The Compton brothers, centre half Leslie and left winger Denis, were, of course, both internationals in soccer and cricket, although Leslie was probably slightly more successful at soccer and Denis at cricket. Apart from his fame as a sportsman, Denis was famous for his absent-mindedness and his ability to run out his fellow batsman. Trevor Bailey, a contemporary cricketer, famously said, "A call for a run from Denis should be treated as no more than a basis for negotiation." Denis, along with Stanley Matthews, was also one of the first sportsmen to make a substantial living by using their fame to advertise and endorse products. In Denis's case, it was famously the hair care product Brylcreem. Denis was also well known for his social life, several times coming into the dressing room in the morning still in his dinner jacket!

Chapter 2 - My First Live Match

We were evacuated during the war to a small Bedfordshire village called Kensworth. We and an assortment of near relatives lived in a small cottage that didn't have running water and with the only loo at the bottom of the garden. My education started at Kensworth school, where I acquired a splendid Bedfordshire accent. My parents then bought a much larger weekend house there in 1944, and the local football team was Luton Town, affectionately known as the Hatters after one of the main industries in the town. They had been founded in 1885, making them one of the oldest league clubs. My father had little interest in football, preferring boxing and indeed one night took me to a Leicester Square cinema to watch a transmission of a Cassius Clay (as he was then) fight at two in the morning! In 1949, however, I did persuade him to take me to a Luton match who were at the time in the second division. The occasion was a fifth-round FA Cup tie against Leicester City, at that time also in the second division, on Saturday the 12th February 1949.

We arrived at the Kenilworth Road stadium just before kick-off to find the Oak Road end gates closed as that end was already full to capacity. We were told that there was a small possibility of getting in at the opposite Kenilworth road end, where there was a large uncovered terrace (standing, of course, in those days) behind the goal. We ran as fast as we could around to the other end along a very narrow and hazardous path. The path was called the Beech Hill Path and is still there today. One is used to the announcement during the second half of contemporary matches that "the Beech Hill Path will be closed at the end of the game to assist the police with crowd dispersal"! We gained admission, but by the time we had got into place ten minutes into the game, three goals had already been scored! Being a shortie, I could only catch glimpses of the play but remember very vividly that every time a goal was scored (and there were ten), there was a surge from behind, and we finished up lower down. By half time, we were somehow nearer the front than the back, and my view had improved considerably. The match had many ebbs and flows and finally ended 5-5 after extra time, Leicester equalising in the very last minute! No one should be surprised that I was hooked. The attendance was 26,280 in the same stadium that now has a maximum capacity of 10,356! The gate receipts were a then-record £4,678.

The Luton goalkeeper was Bernard Streten, who with Ron Baynham was one of two England International goalies on Luton's books at that time. Streten was 5'9", very short for a goalie by today's standards, but he made up for it by amazing agility. Another renowned player in the team was Bob Morton, a local boy born in Aston Clinton, who was equally at home at wing-half or centre forward. He played for Luton from 1946 to 1964 and holds the record to this day of the most appearances for the club, with 495 in the league and 562 overall. He also scored 55 goals in all competitions.

A certain Don Revie was in the Leicester team! He was one of the first deep-lying centre-forwards. This was a few months before he moved on to Hull City for a transfer fee of £19,000, later moving to Manchester City, Sunderland and most famously Leeds United. Incidentally, Leicester won that 5th round replay 5-3 and went on to the final at Wembley, where they lost 1-3 to Wolves! Two of the Wolves' goals that day were scored by Jesse Pye, who, having earned one England cap, was later transferred to Luton at the age of 33 for a fee of £5000. He played from 1952 to 1954 for Luton scoring 36 goals in 61 appearances. He was a great help to the maturing Gordon Turner playing alongside him in those years.

Next month we signed Bud Aherne, a Northern Ireland international left full back who cost £6,000! He earned 15 caps and played 288 times for Luton. He always boasted that he had kept Stanley Matthews quiet whenever they were in opposition! Walter (Wally) Shanks was a very reliable midfield player who played 276 games for the Town from 1946. His wages at the time were reputed to be £8 in the season and £6 in the off-season. He later did some coaching for the club, and in 1959, he opened a successful sports shop in Bury Park Road very close to the Luton ground and was later joined in running the shop by Gordon Turner, a Luton goalscoring legend who played from 1950 to 1964.

Chapter 3 - The Beginning of the Italian Connection

On 4th May 1949, one of the worst aviation accidents involving a football team took place in Italy. A plane carrying 31 passengers, including the players of the Torino club and a four-man crew, crashed in very foggy weather on a hill just outside Turin, their home city and close to the Basilica of Superga, which is at an altitude of 669 metres. The very experienced pilot had been advised that he should delay landing or divert to Milan. However, he felt that he knew the landing path sufficiently well to proceed at a speed of 180 kph with the disastrous consequences that the plane crashed without survivors. At the time, that team known as il Grande Torino had a majority of the Italian international team, and this tragedy had a very adverse effect on their chances of winning the 1950 World Cup to be held in Brazil. Understandably the replacement Italy team refused to fly to Brazil only going by boat, a journey that took 15 days.

On 30th November 1949, England had played Italy at White Hart Lane and beat them 2-0. The attendance was 71,797 for a 2.15 pm kick-off. Incidentally, in that match, Luton's Bernard Streten was the substitute goalkeeper behind Bert Williams of Wolves. The match was only of interest to me in hindsight because it was the first time I had heard of 21-year-old Giampiero Boniperti, who was one of five Juventus players in that Italian team. Boniperti went on to earn 38 caps for Italy in total, 24 as captain. He had made his debut for Juventus in 1946 at the age of 18 and has always said that was when his life started! Although I didn't know it at the time, he was to feature very largely and very happily in my football life. Juventus were the best known and overall most successful Italian team and based in the Northern Italian City of Turin. I later found out that Boniperti would play in two World Cups, the 1950 and 1954 versions, in the latter as captain.

In the 1950 World Cup, Italy lost to Sweden 3-2 in one of their group matches and were eliminated. England managed by Walter Winterbottom won their first match 2-0 against Chile but were eliminated after losing 1-0 to Spain in the famous 200,000 capacity Maracana stadium in Rio de Janeiro. Before that, they had lost 1-0 to the USA in Belo Horizonte. That was one of the World Cup's greatest shocks ever, considering the famous names in that England team led by Billy Wright. England did not play the USA again in a World Cup until 2010, a match that ended in a 1-1 draw. Uruguay won that 1950 World Cup defeating Brazil in the final in the Maracana stadium in Rio de Janeiro 2-1 in front of a paid attendance of 173,380 but an estimated actual attendance of around 205,000!

The next year 1951, Juventus had taken part in the Copa Rio, an International eight club tournament played in Brazil, and in which Boniperti also featured. Juventus had only been invited when the Italian champions AC Milan declined. For the tournament, the organisers had invited the champions of the following top state or country leagues: Rio de Janeiro, San Paolo, Portugal, Spain, England, Scotland, Italy and Uruguay. English clubs did not accept and were replaced by Austrians represented by Austria Wien. Similarly, OGC Nice from France got in when others declined to participate. Nice is another team with whom I developed close connections and interest later on. Unfortunately, there were serious troubles on and off the field associated with Juve's semifinal 1st leg with Austria Wien. The Austrians had a strong team, including the very well known Ernst Ocwirk. In the last few seconds, the referee awarded the Austrians a penalty for an alleged but probably non-existent handball which they converted. A great rumpus and widespread fighting broke out on and off the field, and police were needed to try and re-establish order. In the chaos, two Juventus players, Viola, the goalie and Muccinelli, a forward, were actually arrested and taken to the police station. Juventus did beat Austria Wien 6-4 on aggregate in Sao Paolo, the first leg ending 3-3 with that non-existent penalty leading to the equaliser. And the second 3-1 to Juve with a Boniperti goal. The next day the whole Juventus delegation, including the players, were asked to leave their hotel and left under armed guard. In spite of all this, Juventus did play in the two-leg final, where they lost a bad-tempered match to the Brazilian club Palmeiras of Sao Paolo. The scores were 1-0 to Palmeiras in the first leg played in Sao Paolo, and a 2-2 draw in the 2nd leg played in the Maracana. Juventus at the time had the famous Danish trio: John Hansen, Karl Aage Hansen and Carl Praest in their team. Boni scored one of the two Juve goals in that second leg, and at one point, Juve were leading 2-0 and looking likely winners. Boniperti won the player of the tournament award and announced himself to world football as a superstar. He has always said that he felt intoxicated by playing at the Maracana stadium in Rio on a par with Wembley and the San Siro in Milan. Juventus were invited to participate in the 1952 Copa Rio as well withdrew in favour of playing in the Latin Cup, often seen as the predecessor of the European Cup, which was of course later renamed the Champions League. The Latin Cup featured only club sides from southwest Europe. In that year, Juve took 3rd place behind winners Barcelona and 2nd placed Nice, Boniperti scoring three goals in all, and enhance his reputation further. Juventus did not play in any other episodes of the Latin Cup, although it lasted from 1949 to 1957. Sadly Italian football at that time was beginning to get a bad reputation for dubious tactics, constantly harassing referees, fouling cynically, and diving.

The highlight of that period for me was the Luton team captained by Syd Owen, an excellent centre half, as they were called in those days. He played three times for England, unfortunately once against Hungary, the mighty Magyars. In the first match against them on 25th November 1953, England (without Syd Owen) had lost 3-6 at Wembley, their first defeat at home to a foreign team. I was taken to see it by a very dear friend of the family, Matty, who was an avid Arsenal supporter, and about whom there is plenty to tell later.

The Hungarian team included the likes of Puskas, Hidegkuti, Czibor, Koscis and Bozsik. Puskas scored a hat trick and Hidegkuti two goals. While England played in the well established but rather outdated WM formation, pioneered by Arsenal's manager Tom Whittaker, the Hungarians played in a different 3-2-1-4 formation allowing much greater fluidity and movement of the outfield players. The novel features were the deep-lying centre forward, Nandor Hidegkuti and a sweeper-keeper, Gyula Groscis. It is no exaggeration to say that they were a revelation. In 30 matches, they had only lost once, which sadly was to be the 1954 World Cup Final! It was my first international and my first visit to Wembley stadium. The attendance was 105,000. The Magyars manager was the legendary Gusztav Sebes, who was in charge from 1949 to 1957 and is considered to be the pioneer of those different formations as well as an early version of "total football". The Hungarian team was led by Ferenc Puskas, who amazingly scored 84 international goals in 85 matches. Puskas famously said, "I could feel the ball as a violinist feels his instrument". The England side that included Stanley Matthews, Stan Mortensen, Billy Wright and Alf Ramsey was considered to be very strong!

Afterwards, on the 3rd May 1954, in a warm-up game for the 1954 World Cup, Hungary consolidated their victory over England at Wembley by beating us 7-1 in Budapest, not the sort of score a talented centre half like Syd Owen, picked for that game, would have been proud of.

Chapter 4 - 90th Anniversary of the FA and the 1954 World Cup

England internationals Gil Merrick, Alf Ramsey, Billy Wright, Stanley Matthews and Stan Mortensen, among others, were to clash again with Boniperti in the England versus Rest of the World match in October 1953 at Wembley, where Boni memorably scored two first-half goals. The match was to mark the 90th Anniversary of the Football Association. I am not sure why the opposition was not called the Rest of Europe as all the players were from that continent! The game ended 4-4 with England rescued by a controversial last-minute penalty given by Welsh referee Mervyn Griffiths after Stan Mortensen had been challenged. It was duly converted by our right back Alf Ramsey. Griffiths was later often accused of bias and a keenness to help England maintain their up to then-unbeaten home record against foreign teams!

Walter Winterbottom, who was manager of England continuously from 1946 to 1962, was asked after the game, "What would it take to strengthen your team?" He replied 11 Bonipertis. Little did I know that I would meet Boniperti later, and that he would become a lifelong friend.

The next World Cup in 1954 in Switzerland is noted for the rise and fall of that great Hungarian team who were the overwhelming favourites, being unbeaten for 4 years. The Hungarians had a squad that still included goalie Grosics, midfielder Bozsik, and forwards Hideghuti, Koscis and Puskas. Hungary had been very high scorers in the group matches, winning two of the matches 9-0 against South Korea and 8-3 against West Germany. However, it took a playoff for the Germans to beat the Turks 7-2 and qualify for the quarters. The Hungarians were obviously fulfilling their promise.

Boniperti was captain of Italy then, and he scored a goal, but Italy went out having been beaten by Switzerland in a group match and later in a playoff to decide which one of them qualified for the quarter-finals.

The England team topped their group ahead of Switzerland but lost to Uruguay 4-2 in the quarter-finals and were eliminated. The infamous World Cup match in that 1954 tournament was the "Battle of Berne" when Hungary was playing Brazil in a quarter-final which they won 4-2, but there was fighting and mayhem among the players. Brazil had scored six goals in two group games, while Hungary had scored 17! All the darkest arts of football were unfortunately on view, and the troubles continued long after the final whistle. Arthur Ellis, the English referee, sent off three players, two from Brazil, but overall failed to control the players who continued to brawl in the dressing rooms after the final whistle. He said afterwards that if he had followed the letter of the law, he would have had to book and send off so many players that the match would have had to be abandoned. He had really wanted to avoid that.

Meanwhile, the Germans beat Yugoslavia 2-0 in the quarters and then Austria 6-1 in the semis and so entered the final. In the semis, the Magyars beat Uruguay, who were reigning world champions also by 4-2 after extra time and so joined the Germans in the final expected to win against them. By contrast, the final was one of the finest games ever seen, although the result was totally unexpected. By the 8th minute, Hungary were 2-0 up courtesy of goals from Puskas and Czibor. What was more of a surprise was that West Germany then came back to be level by the 18th minute through Morlock and Rahn and then scored an 84th-minute winner by Rahn, his second of the match. As Puskas's 86th 'goal' was disallowed for offside, Rahn's goal turned out to be the winner. That unexpected 3-2 win was always known as the Miracle of Bern. It was the second time that Hungary had been runner up. In 1938 they had lost 4-2 to Italy in France. Sandor Kocsis was the 1954 tournament's top scorer with 11 goals, a little way short of the record 13 scored by Juste Fontaine in 1958 in Sweden, a tournament won 5-2 by Brazil with 2 Pele goals over the hosts. The Miracle of Bern is often considered to have had a big impact on post-war history, giving West Germany international recognition after losing the 2nd world war, and for Hungary unhappiness with the communist regime which preceded the Hungarian revolution in 1956.

Things were definitely changing in Italy. Torino were never again a force, only winning one more title in 75/76, and indeed the scudetto went to one of Juventus, Inter Milan or AC Milan on 54 occasions out of the 67 after that. The others were shared between Roma (3), Verona (1), Napoli (1) and Sampdoria (1). It became obvious that Juventus had massive support throughout Italy, whereas Milan and Inter and especially Torino had much more local support.

Chapter 5 - Luton Town in the 50s

From 1949 to 1955, Luton had maintained their Division 2 status very calmly, only being close to relegation in 49/50 and 50/51 and to the top in 52/53. In only one season 51/52, Dave Sexton played for Luton, his first professional club. He went on to make his name as a coach and manager, being at clubs like Chelsea and Manchester United and in charge of England under 21 team in two spells. In 1951 a certain Ron Baynham had joined Luton as a goalkeeper from Worcester City. He went on to make 434 appearances in 15 years and earned three caps for England. 1953/54 season saw the arrival of inside forward George Cummins from Everton. He scored 30 goals in 209 games for the Hatters and won 19 caps for the Republic of Ireland. He was to be in the later FA Cup final team.

In January 1954, there was an extraordinary Cup tie against Blackpool the holders, Stanley Matthews and all! A home draw made Blackpool hot favourites, but the first game finished 1-1. Blackpool only qualified after the fourth match. All we had to show was two goals by Cummins in the four matches. In those days, the first replay was at the home ground of the team playing away in the opening tie; then, further replays were at neutral grounds. In this case, the first replay at Luton ended 0-0, the 2nd replay at Villa Park 1-1, and in the 3rd at Molineux, we lost 2-0. No penalty shoot-outs or golden goals in those days! Four games with a total between both teams of 6 goals doesn't sound like great entertainment, does it?

In 54/55, we finished in 2nd place and so were promoted to Division 1, largely thanks to Gordon Turner's 32 goals. The end was very exciting with Birmingham City, the Town and Rotherham United all on 54 points, and the final positions worked out only on goal average. On that basis, Rotherham were the ones to miss out. All the familiar players of the period were featured. The goalkeeper duties were shared almost equally between Baynham and Streten. Fullbacks Dunne and Aherne played all the games, Syd Owen most of them. Syd was that cultured centre half who had earned 3 England caps. Bob Morton missed only 3, and Wally Shanks 3 in that season. Add to them Gordon Turner and George Cummins, and you have the nucleus of the team. In that season, we also got to the 5th round of the FA Cup, where we lost 2-0 at home to Manchester City. It was to be the first time Luton featured in Division 1, and in their first season 55/56, a final position of 10th was very creditable.

Chapter 6 - My Adolescent Years

The next few years after the Leicester Cup tie, I was not considered old enough to go to Kenilworth Road on my own, so my attendance at the matches was very rare. It was probably a wise decision, having been "propositioned" by a man on a motorcycle while cycling between St Albans and Redbourn. Never before had anyone pedalled so fast until I reached the relative safety of the Redbourn Police Station forecourt.

I did play football at my preparatory school, Colet Court, but showed little promise in my chosen position of inside left. Any statistics on goal scorers would have seen me in the lower reaches, but I did enjoy it. My senior school St Pauls did not support soccer, so I had to play rugby. Being small and slight, the only sensible position was scrum-half. In spite of being regularly trampled on by the bigger boys, I did manage to score a few points as one of the penalties and conversion kickers.

In the summer term, I played tennis rather than cricket as the school had an arrangement with Queen's Club, which was very close by. There was the annual tennis tournament then, as now played just before Wimbledon. It was, of course, much more amateur in all senses of the word. I remember on one occasion in 1955, they were short of umpires, and one of the coaches, who, of course, knew us schoolboys well, asked me if I would be willing to umpire a men's doubles match. I readily agreed. It is difficult to imagine a more nerve-wracking experience than to be in charge of a match with the great Lew Hoad and Ken Rosewall (Australians) on one side and Budge Patty and Gardnar Mulloy (Americans); on the other! At the end of the second game, Mulloy, well known for his fiery behaviour towards officials, marched up to me and said, "Buddy, I suggest we call the lines, and you just keep the score!" I was embarrassed but indeed relieved rather than upset.

It wasn't long before I was finding my own way to Luton, using the infrequent public transport and enjoyed the matches and atmosphere very much. I was always an avid collector of autographs waiting outside the Kenilworth Road exit for the players to emerge! In those days, the programmes often had a different player on each cover, and I wanted to get them all signed.

Of course, I missed quite a few because I didn't get to all the matches and also some of the players, especially if they had cars came out at the Maple Road end where there was and still is a large car park. Later, I would always head for the Dunstable crossroads to await the arrival of the Luton News Green'un, which amazingly by 5.30 had a report of the match up to about the three-quarter mark.

Thinking of journalists, one has to remember Brian Swain, who was a legend as a football writer for the Luton News and Dunstable Gazette and later programme editor, commentator, and founder and vice-chairman of the Supporters Club. He covered a phenomenal 1629 consecutive Luton matches, and it is difficult to think of anyone else who contributed as much to the club over so many years. He had a happy retirement with his wife, Rosemary, in Falmouth and occasionally came up to Luton to see a game and meet up with old friends. Sadly he died in 2017 at the age of 78.

In 1953, floodlights had been installed at Kenilworth Road but were, generally, of poor intensity so that some clubs would not play under them, and evening matches had to be rescheduled to the afternoon. At Luton, there was no room in the corners, so the lights had had to be placed along the sides. Another strange feature of our ground is that the dugouts are now placed on the opposite side of the ground to the player's tunnel, so the staff and substitutes have to cross the pitch to get to their positions. Also, the dugouts are in full sunshine, if there is any, and many very strange arrangements are seen to keep the sun out of their eyes.

In 1953, the year of Queen Elizabeth's coronation, I met the son of a Dutch colleague of my father, roughly 16 years old, the same age as me. He was called Berri, and I discovered that he was a keen Ajax supporter. At a party that my parents held that coronation evening, Berri had far too much to drink, and when he emerged late next morning, he was famously heard to say, "Last night, I was so ill that I wanted to suicide myself!" More about him and Ajax later.

Chapter 7 - European Competitions

June 1st 1955, was the day that the European Economic Community was formed later to be designated the European Union. It was then that the European Cup was launched and I believe that the first match was between Sporting Club de Portugal, Lisbon based and Partizan Belgrade. The first leg played in Lisbon ended in a 3-3 draw, the 2nd leg a 5-2 result, which meant Partizan won 8-5 on aggregate. No marks for guessing who won that inaugural European Cup and the next four. Yes, it was Real Madrid. In the 60s, Benfica won two in succession, a feat repeated by Inter of Milan. Celtic were the first British team to win it, overcoming Inter in 1976, and the next year came the famous Manchester United victory over Benfica, to be described later. Ajax and Bayern Munich had runs of three wins in the 70s, and Liverpool and Notts Forest each won two in succession. Real Madrid had a run of three wins from 2016. Reference to many more matches will be given further in the book as in the order they happened!

Suffice it to say that I always saw the European competitions as the best football as it was contested by the top club sides in Europe, used, of course, to playing together as highly co-ordinated and skilled teams. That was why I tried to see as many of those matches as I could.

Chapter 8 - Matty and Arsenal

In my teen years, my connection with and love of football took me frequently to Arsenal, then playing at Highbury. This was courtesy of a family friend, Matty, who was a regular attender, standing behind the goal at the Clock End. Again, inevitable crowd movement meant that even if I started at the back of the terrace, I would finish up much further forward and, even on occasions, was passed right down to the front and allowed to sit on the grass on the perimeter of the pitch. In no time, my faithful guardian had become a season ticket holder in the East stand. When we went together, we would go in his old mini with a parcel on the passenger seat, destined for an address in the street very close to the ground. Waving this at the police and telling them that he was just delivering it, he always passed through the various controls until close enough to park conveniently near the ground. He was completely deaf, following an infection in childhood, and although he could lip read well, he seemed always to fail to understand what any policeman or official was saying to him! He would give me his season ticket entry counterfoil with the location of his seat, so I got in easily. Somehow, I never knew how he would appear soon after at my side and always found a vacant seat!

Chapter 9 - Further Education

In 1955, I went to Gonville and Caius College in Cambridge to start my medical studies. Soccer was again an option, thank goodness! I was selected for the College 2nd XI, and I went back to my number 10 position, but again, I did not excel, scoring the occasional goal if I was unmarked, the ball was within the goal area, and the net was unguarded! It was very clear that I wasn't another Bobby Charlton in the making, but I did enjoy it. In addition, I wanted to row but being small and light; I was chosen to be the cox of what was known as the College "Medics" boat. We were quite successful, but I disgraced myself and cost the college a fine by having a minor collision with the Blues (University) boat also out training. Yes, the one that competes with Oxford annually on the Thames! In those days, there was a shortage of girls at the University, and Caius was all male. However, as medics and with apparently more to learn than most other disciplines, we had to do an extra term called the long vac term, which partly filled the summer break. At first, I rather resented it, but then I realised that Cambridge in the summer was full of foreign language students, mostly female. Hence, I saw the advantages. Unsurprisingly, I rapidly developed a penchant for the Swedish girls who seemed to be ahead of us in many respects! I will always remember one, Susie, as my first real love! She re-appeared for the next summer but by then had transferred her affections to a Swedish boy. I was devastated!

Chapter 10 - The Real Italian Connection

One of my favourite holidays was the one that involved skiing. In the early days, the lifts and facilities were more basic, but one had the advantage of clean air and wonderful mountain scenery. Another advantage was the absence of motor cars and phones! Of course, the mobile phone has changed all that!

One such trip when I was in my late teens involved going to Kitzbuhel in Austria with a fellow school friend. For the first and last time, I managed to suffer an injury. Normally I was too nervous and cautious to risk injury, but on this occasion, I lost my nerve and skied into a bank of snow lining a narrow path and hurt my ankle. I went to the doctor's surgery and was awaiting my turn and found that on the same bench was an Italian man who seemed to be a bit older than me. Although I didn't speak more than a very few words of Italian, and he didn't speak any French or English, we seemed to have the same type of injury, so there was a sort of bond between us. I didn't think any more about it until that evening in an apres-ski venue I spotted him, his name was Eugenio and he was with a whole group of his family and friends across the room. In no time at all, one of the girls who spoke good English came over and invited us to join them, which we did. They all seemed to be members of an extended family.

It transpired that they were mostly from the Turin area and more usually skied at Sestriere. Sestriere is a well-known ski resort fairly close to Turin, built by the Agnellis and belonging to the Fiat empire. Anyone who knows it will recognise the two high tower buildings which were at the time two of the hotels. Before we all left Kitzbuhel, they had suggested that we might like to join them in Sestriere next year, which I was very keen to do.

Not wanting to go on my own, I had little difficulty in persuading my best friend Richard to come too. He decided that he should bring his then-girlfriend as well, which I was a bit apprehensive about. We all went by train and were met at Oulx (Ulzio) station by our new Italian friend Eugenio. We all stayed at the very elegant and comfortable Duchi d' Aosta hotel, which is the largest of the two towers and served great Piemontese food. If one was foolish enough to return to the hotel for lunch, there was no way one would have been able to go skiing again in the afternoon! What struck me particularly about the Italian group? I would say their elegance, impeccable manners and ability to really enjoy themselves without resorting to much alcohol. All went well until the younger members of the group discovered that my friend and his girlfriend were sharing a bedroom. This really shocked them, and Eugenio, who turned out to be seven years older than me, would remind me of this many times afterwards! I don't think that they were too impressed by her rather provocative style of dancing either!

What has all this got to do with being a football fan? You are about to discover! During the weekend a newcomer joined our party. He turned out to be the most famous Italian footballer of his day and probably any day, Giampiero Boniperti. Giampiero was born in 1928 in a small Piemonte town called Barengo, 50 miles northeast of Turin. When he was signed by the Juventus owner Gianni Agnelli, always known as the "avvocato", the lawyer, he was promised a cow for every goal he scored. When he went to collect his reward, having scored two goals in his first league match, he made sure to pick the two who were in calf, hence doubling his reward. Coming from farming stock, he understood these things!

He was a good friend of Eugenio, who himself was, in fact, an executive member of the Juventus football club. Juventus were one of the top two Turin clubs, the other being Torino. While Juventus was the club of the bosses being owned by the Agnelli family, Torino was very much the club of the workers. It meant that most of the Torinesi supported Torino while Juventus had its support from throughout Italy and even abroad.

The footballer, who had joined Juventus in 1946, had made his league debut at the age of 18. He was treated as you would expect a sporting icon to be treated and given extra-large portions of food. Of course, he was not allowed to ski for fear of a costly injury. In spite of the relative language barrier, he was immensely friendly, very interested in what I knew about football, and always keen to discuss football players and tactics at length. It was apparent that he had huge respect for British football, helped by playing alongside John Charles, who had recently joined Juventus from Leeds United. Little did I know or imagine that more than 60 years later, we could or would still be good friends!

Chapter 11 - Turin

The next step was to arrange a visit to Turin. I was invited to stay in Eugenio's family house on the outskirts of Turin and was very well cared for by his mother, a typical and very possessive and protective Italian mamma. Eugenio ran a very successful company involved with the transport of Fiat cars across Italy. Three of us, Eugenio and myself, accompanied by Lelio, a friend of his, went to a Juventus match at the Stadio Communale where they played in those days. It seemed to be the norm for the matches to be played on Sundays, the day starting with a mass in the church, then a good lunch with the family and finally on to the match for the afternoon kick-off. Undoubtedly one of my lasting memories was of the trio of forwards, Giampiero Boniperti, the local boy through and through, Omar Sivori, an Italian Argentinian and the wonderful Welshman John Charles. The three were known as "il trio magico". Each of them individually would justify a whole book, and, in fact, several have been written about each one. It is impossible to imagine three more different characters who merged together to form such a formidable strike force. All three were incredibly skilful, although with very different talents. From their different backgrounds, Sivori and John Charles both came to Juve in 1957. While Sivori liked to play up front, both the other two were more versatile. Boniperti was best known as a centre forward but was just as effective playing behind the main strikers or on the right-wing, while Charles could play centre forward or centre half equally brilliantly. John Charles was also as effective with his head as with his feet, and his calmness meant that he rarely missed a chance. Charles, known in Italy as the "il gigante buono" or "the good giant", had the record of never being booked or sent off during his five years and scoring 108 goals in his 155 appearances for Juventus. He would jump for the ball with his elbows by his side, never deliberately harming his marker or trying to gain an unfair advantage. In fact, Giampiero always said that when he suggested to John that he might be more physical, keep his elbows up and retaliate more, John replied. "I can't. You do it for me". His sportsmanship was exemplary, and international referee Clive Thomas said: if you had 22 players of John Charles's calibre on the field, there would be no need for referees, only timekeepers! Apart from his prowess as a footballer, he had the Welsh gift of singing and recorded a 45 rpm disc with Love in Portofino on one side and Sixteen Tons on the other. He also joined a Juventus teammate Umberto Colombo in opening a smart restaurant called "Kings". Many years later, in a chat with David Pleat, I asked him who he thought was the greatest player of all time, and without a moment's hesitation, he said John Charles.

Omar Sivori had all the skills, speed, and tricks that one associates with Argentinian footballers. He was a prolific goalscorer scoring 167 goals in 253 games for Juventus. He was characterised by always playing with his socks down around his ankles, without any form of protection, to show he wasn't frightened of defenders. Although Argentinian-born and winning 18 caps and scoring 9 goals for Argentina, his later Italian nationality and a ban from the Argentina federation for playing abroad allowed him to play for Italy, for whom he made 9 appearances and scored a further 8 goals. With others of his compatriots like Maschio, who went to Bologna, and Angelillo, who went to Inter, they were known "as the angels with dirty faces". This was because of their dubious style of play and their reluctance to train hard. Omar was very short, 5 ft 4 in but technically very gifted. He was very fast with amazing dribbling skills and frequent use of the nutmeg ("tunnel" in Italian) where the ball is passed deliberately between an opponent's legs. He was very professional in the worst sense of the word, being very volatile, provoking opponents and referees alike and frequently pulling rather than ruffling opponent's hair. He was always keen to try and humiliate opponents. He earned the appropriate nickname El Cabexon, meaning the pig-headed one. The result was over 30 suspensions and 10 red cards while at Juventus. Later on, he was dubbed by the press as "the Maradona of the Sixties". In 1961 he had been elected the "Ballon d'Or" (Golden Ball), an honour created by France Football magazine in 1956 and first won by Stanley Matthews. Undoubtedly Boniperti was the perfect link between two such diverse personalities and contributed massively to their and the team's success. Sivori described Boni as "a playmaker with very clear ideas and who directs the traffic"! However, when Boni retired in 1961 and Charles went back to Leeds, it was not the same for Sivori, who ended his playing career in 1969 after three turbulent years at Napoli. There he helped them to 2nd place, their highest finish until the Maradona era. Sadly his last game, coincidentally against Juventus, was marked by him receiving a red card and a theoretical six-game ban. It persuaded him to return to Argentina, where he was coach of several club sides, and from 1972 till 1974, the Argentina national team. He was in charge when Argentina played in the 1974 World Cup in West Germany, where they lost to Poland 3-2, drew with Italy 1-1 and beat Haiti 4-1 to qualify for the next round in second place. However, in the second round group matches, they lost to the Netherlands 4-0, to Brazil 1-2 and only drew 1-1 to East Germany to be eliminated. He then became a chief scout for Juventus in Argentina, although history does not record many Argentinian players in Juventus squads until much later when I think of Mauro Camoranesi, also with a very poor disciplinary record, Gonzalo Higuain, and currently Paulo Dybala. Very sadly, Omar died of pancreatic cancer in 2005 at the age of 69.

Chapter 12 - Late Teens and Twenties

A real highlight was Luton being promoted to the 1st division in 1954/55, the season-ending with them being 2nd behind Birmingham City. We beat Rotherham into third place on goal average, with Leeds only one point behind them. Dally Duncan was the manager from 1947 to 1958, and I remember that they went on to hold their own for a few seasons in the top flight thanks in large part due to the skills of Bob Morton, the goals of Gordon Turner, the wing play of newly acquired Northern Ireland international Billy Bingham, and the strength and skill of Scottish forward Allan Brown.

There were a lot of boardroom changes at Luton at that time, including the resignation of Hugh Woods, who lived two doors down from us in Kensworth and with whose daughter in law we are still very friendly. Another director was A F (Bertie) England, who also lived very close to us. I remember him for managing to have a head-on collision with his wife's car in their long drive at Kensworth House, no mean feat. Luckily neither were seriously injured. It was about then that Tommy Hodgson was invited on to the board. Of all the six directors, he was the one most connected with football, and he did a lot of scouting. He later rose to chairman and finally president and earned the honour of leading the team out at the 1959 FA Cup final in Wembley in the absence of long-serving manager Dally Duncan who had left for Blackburn Rovers in October 1958 after 11 years at the helm of Luton. Strangely the club was without a manager until Syd Owen was appointed in May 1959, just after that final.

Luton had been founded in 1885 and were elected to the football league in 1897 but resigned three years later. They later rejoined in 1920, but in 1922, their main stand was destroyed by fire. It was replaced by a stand thought to have been bought second hand from Kempton Park racecourse. It now has an upper-tier with seats and a lower one in the enclosure, with backless seats, which was originally all standing. Luton remained in the league from 1920 with many promotions and relegations until 2009, when they spent five years in the non-league Conference. They were then promoted back to the Football league and have since reached the Championship (2nd tier).

I remember 1955 as the year when, as well as celebrating promotion to the top league, I first heard that we were to build a new stadium. Several projects since then have come to nothing, although we do now have planning permission for a stadium in the Power Court area of central Luton, near to the Mall shopping centre and St Mary's Church. It is expected to have an initial capacity of 17,500 and was originally to open for the start of the 2021-22 season. However, it has been held up by planning appeals, especially by the owners of the Mall Shopping Centre, who saw competition from the nearby stadium and the development of a mixed-use industrial estate called Newlands Park near Junction 10 of the motorway on land belonging to the club. The sale of this asset would be essential to finance the new stadium. Unfortunately, the advent of the coronavirus pandemic and further objections has meant that all the plans are on hold, although our chief executive Gary Sweet has made reassuring noises about the future prospects. Just when I thought the road to the stadium was clear, an application to site an Aldi close by has thrown the latest of many spanners into the works, and so we go on waiting and hoping.

A new signing in July 1955 from the Vauxhall Motors club, who were, of course, Luton based at the time, was Tony Gregory. He was at Luton for five years, and that had enabled him to feature controversially in the FA Cup final team in 1959. He made 74 first-team appearances and scored 24 goals before being transferred to of all teams Watford!.

The 55/56 season included a new competition, the Southern Professional Floodlit Cup. It was open to teams from London, the south-east and a small number from the midlands. The first year it featured ten clubs, and for some reason, Luton were not one of them. The next year it was increased to thirteen clubs and included Luton, who won it, beating Reading away 2-1 in the final. By 59-60, it included eighteen clubs, but there were no more finals for us, and it ended at the end of that season. It proved to be the forerunner of the Football League Cup becoming open to all the football league clubs and which we famously would go on to win in 1988.

1958 was the year of the tragic Munich air crash. The plane taking the Manchester United "Busby Babes" team home from a European Cup match in Belgrade crashed on takeoff from a slush-covered runway in Munich, killing 23 people and injuring a further 19. Twenty-one people did, in fact, survive, and what was left of the team with a few newcomers got to the FA Cup Final, where they lost 0—2 to Bolton. The crash had a huge effect on everyone connected with the sport and reminded Italians of the Superga crash of 1949. Among the famous players were Bobby Charlton and manager Matt Busby and they were two of the survivors, but the very promising 21-year-old midfielder Duncan Edwards and centre forward Tommy Taylor were sadly two of those who lost their lives.

In 1958 the European Nations Cup was launched much later to be called the European championships and played every four years between World Cups. The ability to watch the best European sides and their players was very welcome and dramatically widened our knowledge of how the more successful teams did it and where on the continent they played. The advent of foreign players and managers hastened the progress of the British players, who now play more like continentals at the top level. The EU has only about 6% of the world's population but is undoubtedly football's superpower. Not since 2002 has any country from outside Europe won the World Cup.

Chapter 13 - FA Cup Run 58/59

We finished 8th in the top flight in 1958 and finally reached the FA Cup final in 1959. In that competition, in the 3rd round, we beat Leeds United 5-1 and then Leicester 4-1 after a 1-1 away draw. In the 5th round, we beat second division Ipswich 5-2 away. I well remember the 6th round tie with Blackpool, which after a 1-1 draw at Bloomfield Road, the Town won 1-0 in front of a record 30,069 fans. The match was played in the afternoon as the tangerines would not agree to play under Luton's floodlights. I somehow managed to get the time off from medical school to get down to Kenilworth Road. It was perhaps inevitable that the winning goal should be scored by ex-Blackpool and Scotland forward Allan Brown, who played for Luton from 1956 to 1960 and scored 51 goals in 151 league appearances. He was undoubtedly the star of that amazing Cup run in which he scored 5 goals, one behind Billy Bingham, one ahead of Tony Gregory and 2 ahead of Bob Morton. Brown later became a successful manager for us from 1966 to 1968, leading Luton to the 4th Division title in 1969/70 before he was replaced by Alec Stock. In the semifinal, we were drawn against Norwich City, then in the third division. The semifinal was played at a neutral ground, in this case, White Hart Lane, the home of Spurs. The match had been switched from Chelsea's home Stamford Bridge because Norwich believed that Luton would have had an unfair advantage as they had played there the week before in the league! The match on March 14th 1959, ended in a 1-1 draw with an Allan Brown header being cancelled out by ex-Hatter Bobby Brennan. This necessitated a replay on March 18th at another neutral ground, in this case at St Andrew's Birmingham. Again my professional commitments prevented me from going, but it ended in a 1-0 Luton victory with a Billy Bingham blockbuster meaning a managerless Luton were in the FA Cup Final for the first and up to now only time in their history.

Chapter 14 - FA Cup Final

In April, we had a dress rehearsal against Notts Forest, in which we won 5-1 with Allan Brown scoring four goals! Maybe that gave us false hope and a bit of complacency. Syd Owen, our captain, was in his last season and ended his playing career with the Cup final on May 2nd 1959 and the Footballer of the Year award chosen by the Football Writers' Association. He went on to manage Luton for the next season, 1959-1960.

Of course, I wanted to go to the Cup final, but then tickets for that match were at a premium even at a rather thinly supported club like Luton. Indeed as Luton were only allocated 16,000, there was no way I could have got one through the usual channels, especially not having the time to get down to Luton and to join the long queues all the way down Kenilworth Road or taking one's chance in a ballot set up for non-season ticket holders. A few extra appeared later, but they were mostly acquired by Touts, who were happy to sell them on with a vast mark up. Indeed it has been told how 3s6d (17.5p in today's currency value after decimalisation in 1971) tickets were going for about £4. Interestingly the prices for 2019's Cup final were from £45 to £145. Now that's what I call inflation! Luckily my father had a business colleague Charles Pratt who was on the board of the Chelsea Football Club at the time, and he managed to get us the two required tickets. The match was a real anticlimax for all Luton supporters. As stated before, the club was without a manager, Dally Duncan, having left in October 1958 after 11 years in charge and in spite of getting the club promoted to the first (then top) division! Without a manager, the team was led out by Tommy Hodgson, one of the directors. He had at least been a Luton player in the period 1930 to 1933 before becoming a director and indeed later chairman. All decisions, including team selection, were made by the directors with some input from Captain Syd Owen! Tom Hodgson claimed that he had wanted to pick Gordon Turner, who was such a prolific goalscorer but was overruled. It was felt that as Tony Gregory had featured in all the preceding Cup games and scored four goals, he should be chosen for the final as well. Indeed most unusually, Luton had fielded the same team in all nine FA Cup matches! After a presentation to the Duke of Edinburgh and, for the first time, an exchange of banners, the game kicked off. In the tenth minute, Forest scored the first goal and another in the 14th minute. Oh, dear! Luton seemed to be completely out of their depth and couldn't find their usual fluent football at all. As Bob Morton put it afterwards, we all had an off day and just could never get going. A glimmer of hope was felt for the Town as in the 32nd minute, the unlucky Roy Dwight, cousin of Elton John, had to leave the field with a broken leg. Severe injuries seemed to be a relatively common occurrence in those days due perhaps to the very lush turf at Wembley. This was at a time before substitutes were permitted. Although Dave Pacey the Luton left half reduced the arrears by 62 minutes, no further goals were forthcoming, and it was Forest that had played most of the football. There was a final hope when in the last few minutes, Allan Brown almost scored with a header which would have forced extra time, but it was not to be, and the better team on the day deservedly won and received the FA Cup from the Queen. The Queen was reputed to have replied to the question from Sir Stanley Rous, the secretary of the FA "ma'am who do you think was the player of the match" replied "the band". Team selection had clearly been a factor, being that it was in the hands of a committee of directors. Another star of our side had been Billy Bingham, a mercurial winger and Northern Ireland international who scored 10 international goals in 56 appearances and 27 in 87 games for Luton, including that winner in the semifinal against Norwich. The celebratory dinner at the Piccadilly Hotel had been a very subdued affair. Another Luton hero of the time had been Gordon Turner, who scored 276 goals in 450 games in all competitions. The one down in his career was having been left out of the 1959 FA Cup final team. He had been out for a while with injury but was to be fit in time for the final. He could not displace Tony Gregory. Tony, as we would say, was a nice guy, but nothing exceptional as a footballer and the omission of Gordon proved to be very costly. Very sadly, Gordon was later smitten with Motor Neurone disease and died at the really young age of 46.

The following season Syd Owen was appointed manager, and in his one season at the helm, 1959/60, the Town were sadly bottom and relegated to division two. Syd left the club over many disagreements with the board, especially about policy and transfers. He remained in coaching, having posts with Leeds, Birmingham and Manchester United. He was replaced at Luton by Sam Bartram, the ex-Charlton goalie who lasted two years.

You might well ask how Luton could go on to fall from the 1st division and Cup final in 1959 to the 4th division in six seasons? You've seen the beginning, but there is much more of that to come!

Chapter 15 - Ajax Amsterdam

My father with my uncle ran an international antique furniture business. They had contacts in many European countries but especially Holland. He frequently visited Holland to make purchases and was remembered for many things but especially for the fact that he was the first antiques dealer to charter a plane to bring back his recently purchased furniture to London. Very novel in the early 60s. My father, in fact, went to Holland so often that we all believed that he had a girlfriend there! We often saw one particular Dutch family in London and Amsterdam. I remember the father Moutje well as he was pint-sized, very jovial and married to a very tall girl called Lucy. He really enjoyed life and, on many occasions, came out with his classic saying, "what a life like millionaires"! Berri, short for Barendt, was their son and was a keen Ajax supporter. Ajax, in their traditional half red and white shirts, were the most famous Dutch club, and he agreed to take me to a match sometime in the future. When it happened, I don't remember who they were playing or the score. My main recollection was going in his car and asking how he was going to find a parking space as Ajax drew full houses. Don't worry, he said reassuringly. He parked his car about a mile from the stadium, got two-fold-up bicycles out of the boot, and we peddled happily right up to the stadium, where we locked the bikes to the stadium railings. For some reason, I remember that striker Piet Kaiser was definitely playing and maybe Johan Cruyff and Ruud Krol as well. At that time, Ajax played in the De Meer stadium with a rather small capacity of 29,500. Their biggest matches were transferred to the Olympic stadium. Later in 1996, they moved to a new stadium soon after to be renamed the Johan Cruyff Arena or Amsterdam Arena with a capacity of 55,500. As happened to me often, I developed a soft spot for Ajax and since then have always followed their results. They have been ranked the seventh or eighth most successful European club.

Chapter 16 - Italians Again and a Trip to Sweden

On May 6th 1959, England drew 2-2 against Italy and again, I was able to go with my Italian friends Eugenio and Lelio, who had come over, especially from Turin. Again a good lunch was had, this time at Mario and Franco, the first of the Italian trattorias that were to become so popular. I never found the Italians very adventurous when it came to trying other nations' food, but they really didn't need to as their own was so varied and good!

The preliminaries at Wembley were characterised by the organisers making a blunder by getting the band to play the wrong, indeed fascist, wartime national anthem, Giovinezza, instead of Il Canto degli Italiani, also known as Inno di Mameli after its creator, and still the national anthem today. Far from being annoyed, my Italian friends thought that it was very comical! I don't remember anything about the match except that, for some reason, Boniperti, in the twilight of his international career, was not playing, presumably due to injury. He had scored 179 goals in 459 league matches and 8 international goals in 38 matches. He had played for Italy from 1947 to 1960 and from 1952 had been captain of the national side.

The next year 1960, was memorable for one match. It was a Division 2 match against Middlesborough on November 19th, and Luton won 6-1. Remembered by me as my mother then aged 50 came with me, the only match she ever came to in spite of living to 90 years of age! I think she thought that all football matches had that sort of score. Of course, women spectators were very much in the minority in those days, so it was not surprising really that she didn't appreciate the rarity of such a score.

Talking about my mother reminds me of a family holiday in Scandinavia. I was excited as I thought it was a chance to find again my first real girlfriend who was Swedish from Stockholm! While in Stockholm, I found my way to a match at Djurgardens IF. I have no recollection of any detail, but sadly I can say that Swedish football obviously did not excite me, and Djurgardens did not become a team whose results I followed. I next surprisingly heard of Djurgardens when Malcolm Macdonald spent the last two months of his playing career there in 1979! No, not surprisingly, I never did find Susie the Swede!

Chapter 17 - European Cup Finals

The European Cup was first played in 1956 when Real Madrid played and beat Reims of France. Chelsea had been eligible to enter but were barred from participation by the Football Association. Real went on to win the next four European Cups.

Undoubtedly the most memorable of the five was the last one with Real beating Eintracht Frankfurt 7-3 in front of 127,621 spectators at Hampden Park, Glasgow on May 18th 1960. The Real goals were scored by Hungarian Puskas with 4 and Argentinian Alfredo Di Stefano with 3. Other Real stars at the time included Jose Santamaria, who played for both Uruguay and Spain, Luis Del Sol, who was later to join Juve, and Francisco Gento, who were both Spaniards. To think that the game only went ahead after Puskas was made to apologise for remarks made about the German team taking drugs in 1954. Undoubtedly that match enhanced the ever-increasing interest in foreign football that followed. Those first four European Cups featured victories over Reims, Fiorentina, AC Milan and Reims again. Reims had famous French players such as Raymond Kopa, who was integral to the French national team of the 1950s, winning 45 caps and being the first footballer to be awarded the Legion d'Honneur, the highest French order of merit. He indeed himself later played for Real Madrid in between two spells with Reims. Another famous Reims player was Just Fontaine, who had a 6-year spell with them, and who to date holds the record for the most goals in a single World Cup, 13 in 6 matches in the 1958 edition. In season 55/56, Hibernian had been the first British club to enter the European Cup, followed one year later by Manchester United, who had defied the Football Association. However, it took United eleven more years to actually win it. Real are still the most frequent champions with 13 victories, while Juve hold a rather unwanted record of being the most frequent runners up with 7!

Chapter 18 - Spurs in Turin

On Wednesday, May 25th 1960, Juventus played an end of season friendly against Spurs in Turin. I don't know whether I just happened to be in Turin at that time, but I suspect it was not an accident! The Spurs team managed by Bill Nicholson was pretty well the one that in the following season would win the double and become the first club to win it since Aston Villa in 1897. Spurs included such as Maurice Norman, Danny Blanchflower, Dave Mackay, Bobby Smith and Cliff Jones. The Spurs team were put up at the Principe di Piemonte, one of Turin's best hotels in the centre of town. We stayed there ourselves on many occasions after, and it later became the hotel where the Juventus team was locked away on the nights before their home matches. On one such occasion many years later, when we were in Turin for a Boniperti family wedding, we met Claudio Ranieri in the lift of that hotel at the time he was managing Juventus. He had left Chelsea a few years before, so that was the obvious topic of conversation! In England, he had been nicknamed "Tinkerman" for his habit of rotating his players all the time. His English seemed limited in spite of his time in England but more than enough for a short time we were together in the lift! The Italians were, I think, one of the first to realise the importance of keeping the players away from temptation on the nights before games! Many years later, of course, in season 2015/16, Ranieri managed Leicester City to the Premier League title, one of the great shocks of that or any other season. He is still active and has managed to date at least 20 other clubs, but that may not be the final total! The latest seems to be of all clubs, Watford!

The Spurs party visited the Juventus headquarters in the city centre above the renowned Caffe Torino in the famous central square in Turin, the Piazza San Carlo. They were very palatial facilities, with extensive offices, games rooms and restaurants. I had the pleasure of spending time there myself on many occasions afterwards. They were also taken on a tour of the Fiat works, Mirafiori, which at the time employed about 80,000 people, and were introduced to the Juventus president Gianni Agnelli. The kick-off was not until 9.30 pm, very welcome as it had been a very hot day. There was an amazing crowd for a friendly of around 35,000. Boniperti, in what was his penultimate season as a player and captain, played, and it was considered to have been a high-quality game. Juve won 2-0 with goals from Omar Sivori and Bruno Nicole. After the match, we all gathered at Giampiero's flat, which was in a wide boulevard almost opposite the stadium that they played in at that time, the Stadio Comunale. I especially remember meeting the Juventus chaplain, who was always seemed to be there after games and was a really lovely man. I also met Giampiero's charming wife, who he had married in 1954. He had met her at a party organised by a fellow Juve player called Carlo Parola and held in Finale Ligure. Finale has always been known as the summer retreat for the Torinese, being well placed on the Ligurian coast and one of the nearest to Turin. Obviously, over the years, I got to know her better, and she always struck me as the perfect superstar's wife, rather in the background but fully supportive of everything that Giampiero did in his long and varied career. When Giampiero came back, one of the first things he asked me was to translate two English words he had heard Dave Mackay and Bobby Smith frequently utter during the match and which were f…ing hell! That led to an interesting discussion about expletives in both languages. I remember learning especially Vaffanculo (f..k off) and Porca Miseria (literally Miserable pig, but it means dammit or holy shit). It was about then that I learnt that Boni had earned the nickname "Marisa" on account of his rather feminine head of golden curls! The next day Boni took me to Sisport, a sports complex in Turin where Juventus did a lot of their training. Another important venue was Villar Perosa, a magnificent residence southwest of Turin belonging to the Agnelli family. The extensive grounds have a football pitch which is used pre-season for friendlies and training. It usually holds an annual friendly between the Juventus first team and the Primavera, the youngsters. Unfortunately, I was never invited to visit it.

Chapter 19 - Soccer Magazines and Journalists

The first soccer magazine that I remember reading regularly was Charles Buchan's Football Monthly. Famously from September 1951, he edited it, and it was always a good read. Buchan had been a very successful footballer, especially with a 14-year spell with Sunderland and afterwards a 3-year spell with Arsenal. The first issue had the note, "Our objective is to provide a publication that will be worthy of our National game and the grand sportsmen who play and watch it". I think he succeeded completely, as confirmed by the monthly sales figures which at their peak were 250,000. It was going strong until its demise in 1974, although it continued under the name of "Football Digest" and "Football" until it was sold in 1997 to, guess who, Ken Bates of Chelsea! Its 247 issues have really chronicled the changes and trends from the importance of the FA Cup and Internationals, as well as amateur football, to the ever-growing importance of the top league and European competitions. It finally stopped publication in 1999 when it was sold to Football Monthly Archives, which featured electronic reproductions.

In October 1960, another magazine was launched called World Soccer. I have been a subscriber since June 1967 and have kept all the issues! It has always had excellent contributors, and I especially enjoyed reading the contributions by Brian Glanville, who wrote for it since 1963. Incidentally, Brian was the son of our family dentist who practised in Portland Place in London. He must be one of the most prolific and greatest sportswriters of all time with a multitude of novels, short stories and plays. He has been described fittingly as the doyen of football writers. As he spent much of his early life in Italy, especially Florence and Rome, he is also an expert on Italian football, which of course appeals to me! Inevitably he contributed to daily Italian newspapers as well, especially Corriere Dello Sport, which is Rome based, and the nationals La Stampa (Turin based) and Corriere Della Sera (Milan based). Another notable thing was that he was responsible for setting up the Chelsea Casuals, an amateur soccer team made up of a motley collection of actors, artists, journalists, LSE alumni, and friends. They played on various sites, especially Hackney Marshes and Wormwood Scrubs. Other well-known contributors to World Soccer include Keir Radnedge, former editor and another prolific author, and Tim Vickery, who was based in Brazil and consequently specialised in South American football. I am happy to mention again Brian Swain, whose contributions to Luton Town were legendary.

Chapter 20 - 1961 and Medicine

On January 28th 1961, there was an FA Cup match at Luton that I went to and will never forget and nor does Denis Law, I suspect. It was a tie against Manchester City, and in addition to Denis Law, there was Bert Trautmann, a German goalkeeper who famously played on for City in the 1956 Cup final in spite of breaking his neck. Trautman had overcome prejudice against him for having been part of the German Luftwaffe. He had later in the war been captured by the British and famously had refused repatriation. Going back to Denis Law, he was one of the greatest Scottish players of all time. On this occasion, he was playing in that FA Cup tie and had scored six goals in front of 23,727 fans. At around 70 minutes, the match was abandoned because of heavy rain and an exceptionally muddy pitch. The result and everything that went with it, including Denis's six goals, were expunged from the records. It cost him his place as the record goalscorer in a single match in favour of Ian Rush! Ian Rush had scored his five in a match at Anfield in October 1983 for Liverpool against Luton in a 6-0 thrashing! In three days' time, although the pitch was no better, the match was replayed, and inevitably, in spite of Denis scoring, City lost 3-1 and were eliminated.

From 1958 to 1961, I was at Medical School at the London Hospital in Whitechapel, and the nearest professional club was Tottenham Hotspur, so I developed a serious interest in them and went to many matches in the late 50s and early 60s. What a team they had then! Who could forget the elegant Danny Blanchflower, surely one of the greatest wing halves of all time and Dave Mackay, a ferocious tackler? Upfront, there was Bobby Smith, a typical bruising English centre forward, Cliff Jones, a flying winger and the cultured John White at inside forward. What a huge tragedy when John was killed by a lightning strike while sheltering from a storm under a tree at Crews Hill Golf Club. He died at the tender age of 27, leaving a 22-year-old widow and two very young children.

1961 was also the year that Boniperti was to surprise everyone by announcing his retirement from playing at the age of 32. He had helped Juve to lift five Serie A titles and two Italian Cups. He had spent his entire playing career with Juve. During Boniperti's playing career, he scored 179 goals in 443 league appearances. He held these records until Alessandro Del Piero overtook the goals scored one in 2006 and the appearances one in 2010.

It was a special year in that soon after stopping playing. The Bonipertis had their first child. A son was born to be followed soon after by another boy in 1963 and a daughter in 1964. Looking far ahead, we were honoured to be very kindly invited to two of their weddings which we were delighted to attend.

Umberto Agnelli, the owner and president at that time, kept Boni on in a variety of roles and later, in 1971, he was elected chairman of the club. It was a post he held until 1990 when he became Presidente Onorario (honorary president), remaining as such until his sad demise in 2021. He was awarded the Grand Officer of the Order of Merit of the Italian Republic and was the first to be inducted into the Italian Football Hall of Fame when it was inaugurated. As well as playing all his career for Juventus, he had been captain of Italy from 1952 to 1960, making 38 appearances and scoring 8 goals. A long-serving board member from 1960 a vice president from 1970 was Vittorio Chiusano, a lawyer. He went on to become the 23rd president in 1990, a post he held until his death in 2003. A few days after his death, Juve won the Supercoppa in the Giants stadium in New York, beating AC Milan 5-3 on penalties after a 1-1 draw. In opposition, not for the first or last time, were Marcello Lippi for Juve and Carlo Ancelotti for Milan. The victory was dedicated to Chiusano.

Franzo Grande Stevens was another honorary president. He was the principal lawyer for the Agnelli family. He was, therefore, commonly known as the avvocato del avvocato! As well as a long history of looking after Gianni Agnelli, he has continued to look after his grandson and heir, John Elkann, who was to become chairman of Exor, the holding company of the Agnellis.

By 1961 I had qualified as a doctor and was looking for a specialty as I wanted to stay in hospital medicine. I had flirted with Plastic and Reconstructive Surgery, having been inspired by a lecture from Sir Archibald McIndoe. He was famous for his work at the Queen Victoria Hospital in East Grinstead, Sussex, in reconstructing the burnt faces of serving airmen. A whole system was created to get them integrated back into society, and the famous Guinea Pig Club was formed. However, by the time I might have trained to become a plastic surgeon, it seemed that the reconstructive work had been largely overtaken by cosmetic surgery, something that did not appeal to me. So my next choice was to be Obstetrics and Gynaecology. At the London, the most prestigious third house job was called the resident accoucheur and was usually awarded to the student that won the O & G prize. I worked very hard in preparation for it reading large tomes normally reserved for specialists in the discipline. I felt I had done well with very detailed answers but later discovered that the examiner was famous for the brevity of his examination answers, and so I did not get it. Anyway, I would not have been wanted to be called any time in the 24 hours to deliver babies as I got older and wasn't sure that Gynaecology appealed either. I always remember the anecdote of the patient undergoing a gynaecology examination who said to the consultant, "Does your mother know what you do for a living!" So finally, I settled on training to be an Anaesthetist, a decision that I have never regretted. In fact, one of my main interests became the use of epidurals to provide painless childbirth, so I remained involved with many births and night calls after all.

Chapter 21 - A First Overseas Football Trip

One of my first overseas football trips was to follow Spurs to Benfica in Lisbon with an unknown group of fellow Spurs supporters. It was the occasion of a European Cup semi-final, and Benfica, the reigning European champions, who were managed by the legendary Hungarian Bela Guttmann. Guttmann was Jewish but had somehow survived the Holocaust in spite of spending time in a Nazi slave labour camp where he was tortured. He had pioneered the 4-2-4 formation with fellow Hungarians Marton Bukovi and Gusztav Sebes, innovative at the time. Sebes, in particular, will be remembered as the coach of the wonderful Hungarian national teams of the late 40s and 50s.

I remember prior to boarding the plane at Gatwick in the very early morning of Wednesday, March 21st 1962, very large amounts of beer had already been consumed by the majority. Although I had learnt to drink beer as a medical student, there was no way I could keep up! I felt a bit out of it. I remember well that on arrival in Lisbon, there was no mention of visiting any museum or other cultural or historical sites. The taxi driver was asked to take us to "the Girls", and it seemed he knew the best addresses. Another first (and perhaps last?) for me!

A club stadium, Estadio da Luz, with an attendance of well over 60,000 and a capacity of up to 120,00, was a novelty for me, and the atmosphere was electric. Unfortunately, Benfica took an early 2-0 lead with goals from Jose Aguas and Jose Augusto, and Spurs lost 3-1 to a team containing the great Eusebio, a Mozambican striker, Mario Coluna in midfield, wingers Simoes and Jose Augusto, and goalie Costa Pereira to name just a few. Anyway, in the second half, Bobby Smith headed a Blanchflower cross into the net to raise hopes that we might get something out of the game, but the hope was soon extinguished when Jose Augusto scored. That really put the game out of Spurs' reach in spite of them having a goal ruled out for a very dubious offside call. Dave Mackay had managed to keep Eusebio in his first season as a Benfica player very quiet. The return flight was uneventful if understandingly very subdued.

The return leg two weeks later ended in a 2-1 win for Spurs but not enough for them to qualify for the next round. After 15 minutes, Benfica had scored through their captain Aguas. Greaves had a goal disallowed for offside before Smith equalised on the night. In the early second-half, Spurs were awarded a penalty when White was fouled by Mario Coluna, and Blanchflower duly dispatched the spot-kick. Only one goal behind now, but no more goals were forthcoming. It was considered to have been a thrilling game, and fittingly Benfica went on to win the trophy in

Amsterdam against the previously mighty Real Madrid by 5-3! Puskas scored all three Real goals, Eusebio two for Benfica.

Chapter 22 - 1962 World Cup in Chile

The 1962 World Cup was held in Chile, who qualified as host and included defending champions Brazil. In May 1960, a very powerful earthquake struck, centred on Valdivia in Chile. It caused 50,000 casualties and was the largest ever recorded in the world at a magnitude of 9.5 and led to several changes in calendar and venues. The most notable match was the so-called "Battle of Santiago" when Chile played Italy in a first-round match. The name came from the violence in the game, the fact that there were several punch-ups and the need for police intervention four times. Chile won 2-0 with goals in the last 16 minutes. The referee was Englishman Ken Aston, who, in spite of the violence all around him, only sent off two players, both Italian, the first as early as the 8th minute.

He became a senior member of the referees' committee for the 1966 and 1970 tournaments. David Coleman was the TV commentator who described the match as "the most stupid, appalling, disgusting and disgraceful exhibition of football, possibly in the history of the game". By coincidence, the two met again in the 1966 tournament at Sunderland, this time Italy winning 2-0 and the match passing peacefully and uneventfully. In 1962, Italy and Argentina were eliminated in the first round, and England by Brazil 3-1 in the first knock out stage. Surprise finalists were Czechoslovakia, who beat Hungary and Yugoslavia but who lost to Brazil 3-1 in the final. Some consolation for Chile was winning the third-place match 1-0 over Yugoslavia. One of the features of the tournament was the shift towards predominantly defensive tactics. It resulted in that the average goals per match fell to 2.78 the first time it had been under three, where incidentally, it has remained ever since. Maybe that was the explanation for the fact that the top goalscorer only scored four, but there were six of them sharing that number. No English player scored more than one goal.

Chapter 23 - An English Exodus

The success of John Charles in Italy had led several Italian clubs to follow that example and sign British strikers. One of the first was Jimmy Greaves, who signed for AC Milan from Chelsea in June 1961. His stay in Italy was unhappy. He never learnt the language properly, drank far too much and couldn't cope with Italian defenders or the constant intrusion by the press. He only made 14 appearances and only scored 9 goals. He didn't get on with the AC manager Nereo Rocco, not taking to the very strict standards of behaviour demanded nor the coaches' very defensive tactics. Indeed Rocco was one of the first coaches to use catenaccio (door bolt) defences together with the sweeper, libero, in Italian. Similarly, Jimmy's wife Irene was constantly harassed and equally unhappy. So after just one season, he was transferred to Spurs for £99,999, a figure meaning that he was spared the burden of being the first £100,000 player. His further career is well chronicled, and he remained an ace marksman. Of special note is how after losing his wife due to his alcoholism, he finally overcame the drinking issues, and after stopping playing, he forged a new career as a journalist co-hosting the immensely popular Saturday morning TV show Saint and Greavsie, which ran on ITV from 1985 to 1992. The Saint was, of course, Ian St John, a Scotsman of Liverpool fame. It was taken off the air as the advent of the Premier League had led to the TV rights being lost by ITV and contracted to Sky Sports. His wife returned to him, and indeed they were re-married later on, and she remained faithfully at his side after he had two serious strokes, the latter making him almost speechless and wheelchair-bound.

At the same time as Greaves joined AC Milan, Torino signed Denis Law from Manchester City for £110,000 and Joe Baker from Hibernian for £75,000. Both were 21 years old and probably too immature to cope with their new situation. Law was a success on the pitch making 28 appearances and scoring 10 goals but was very unhappy with it. Again he couldn't really hope with the enhanced discipline, the tactics of the defenders and the press. He and Joe spent a lot of their time hiding in their Turin apartment. At the end of one season, Law left for Manchester United. Baker led a flamboyant lifestyle, noted for fighting paparazzi, crashing a new Alfa due to driving on the wrong side of the road and running up huge debts. He also left after one season, Arsenal paying £70,000 for him. Another 1961 import that was much more successful was Gerry Hitchens signed from Aston Villa by Inter for £85,000. In a nine-year stay in Italy, Gerry also played for Torino, Atalanta and Cagliari. He won 7 caps for England, but once he went abroad, he was rather forgotten. There were many more exports to Italy who will be described as they happened.

Chapter 24 - Lean Years 1961 to 1965

In the days before the arrival of agents, Boniperti was responsible for negotiating players' contracts. He was very tough, and the negotiations were mostly in one direction. I often felt as I sat in his office that I was sitting in the chair that so many famous Italian and foreign superstars must have sat! The walls of his office were covered with fascinating memorabilia of his career. He was especially proud of a photo taken with our very young Queen when he was invited to the 100-year celebration of Liverpool FC in 1992. In Italy, he was characterised by mostly leaving the games immediately the half time whistle blew and rushing home to keep up with the game from the tranquillity of his home. The year after Boni's retirement as a player, a great addition to the Juve squad was the great midfielder Luis Del Sol signed from Real Madrid and who stayed for 8 years, 1962 to 1970, before going on to Roma. He was the first Spanish player to play for Juve. He played in Sivori's number 10 shirt and was one of those players one always looked forward to watching him play. For Juve, he made 292 appearances and scored 29 goals,

At the end of the 61/62 season, manager Sam Bartram left Luton, as they so often say, by mutual consent. Luton had finished in a respectable mid-table 13th place, Gordon Turner scoring 21 goals to be top scorer. Sam was succeeded for one week by Jack Crompton, our former trainer who immediately left on so-called medical grounds but showed up at Manchester United straight after! The next choice was Bill Harvey, who in his first managerial post at least lasted two years! However, at the end of 62/63, the Town was relegated to Division 3, where we only lasted 2 seasons before dropping further into the 4th division. 1963 was marked by the sale of prolific Welsh striker Ron Davies to Norwich City for £35,000. As well as his 21 goals for Luton, he scored nine goals for Wales in 29 appearances. He was compared by some very flatteringly to John Charles for his heading ability. At the end of that season, we avoided relegation at the death thanks to 22 goals in 23 appearances from a fresh John O'Rourke. John was an Arsenal youth player, and after a short time without an appearance for Chelsea, this elegant centre forward came to light up the Town. He scored 54 goals in 84 appearances, many of them headers in spite of his being under six feet tall. I recall him scoring a quartet at Brentford in an amazing 6-2 win.

Sadly relegation to the bottom tier of the football league meant that we had dropped all the way from the top to the bottom in 5 years!

Chapter 25 - On the Move

Working at the London Hospital and inspired by Matty's successful parking at Arsenal, I would tell the police on my visits to the Spurs ground that I was a doctor on call, only occasionally true. Normally that was enough to get through, and I could park close to the ground! Never being the fittest nor the most energetic, car parking was usually a need at most away matches and the nearer the ground, the better! Of course, many grounds have their own parking, very convenient on arrival but usually meaning a long and slow queue to leave! Amazingly in spite of all the matches I attended, only rarely was there any damage to my car, and while I often struggled to find a legal space, I somehow usually succeeded. In view of the traffic leaving the area of grounds, the temptation was to leave a little bit before the end, but that was risky as a match went on for at least 90 minutes, and it was just as likely that something exciting would happen in the last 5 minutes as in the other 85!

My usual treat at the Spurs ground was a little pot of cockles. They had such a lovely fresh taste, and to this day, I still get them wherever I see them. Most often, I find them in the fishmonger at Southwold port near where my elder daughter and her family live.

My most memorable Spurs match in that era was against Manchester United on March 21st 1964, in front of 56,392 spectators. Spurs had Jimmy Greaves, Cliff Jones and John White, while Alan Mullery was making his debut. United had the famous trio of Best, Charlton and Law playing! A match not to be missed under any circumstances! I can't remember the details, but I know that I went to the match from St Margaret's Hospital, Epping, where I was on call as an anaesthetist. In those days, you did not have to remain in the hospital when on call, but I don't think being packed into a football stadium some 20 miles away from the hospital was what the authorities would have had in mind. I believe that I even took the duty theatre sister with me so, further reducing the possibility of any surgery being carried out and my being needed!

I would point out that this was before the advent of long-range bleeps or mobile phones. So, to be called, the hospital would have had to phone the ground and get a message broadcast on the public address system! I could add that at that time, the loudspeakers were not very efficient, so I don't know if I would even have heard it! Anyway, it was a memorable game with 5 goals, Spurs scoring through Laurie Brown, one of the several to have played for both Spurs and Arsenal, and a Jimmy Greaves penalty, United replying through Bobby Charlton, Denis Law, and Graham Moore. You might ask who managed both Arsenal and Spurs, and the answer is Terry Neill and

George Graham? And some of the players to play for both? They include Willie Young, Pat Jennings, Sol Campbell, William Gallas and Emmanuel Adebayor.

Talking of public address systems, I enjoyed an incident at Wembley when the announcer made the famous pronouncement (I only remember that the message was addressed to a person with an obviously Italian name) that he had just become a father and was to be congratulated. At the other end of the spectrum was the rather sick joke about the man at a sell-out match who had an empty seat next to him and, when asked by a man behind why it was empty, said, "My wife recently passed away."

"I'm very sorry to hear that," replied the man. "Couldn't you have invited one of your friends to come with you to fill the seat?

"Oh no," the man replied. "They are all at the funeral".

Chapter 26 - Football on Television

The first FA Cup final to be televised was the 1938 game between Preston North End and Huddersfield Town won by Preston with the only goal scored from the penalty spot by George Mutch in the last minute of extra time. The actual attendance of 93,497 was nearly ten times the TV audience watching at home! The first international televised was the England Scotland match also in 1938 and won by the Scots 1 - 0 with a 6th-minute goal. The first broadcast of an FA Cup tie that wasn't a final was in 1947 and was a 5th round tie between Charlton and Blackburn. In 1954 the World Cup was broadcast live for the first time, and in the next year, ITV started to show matches from the newly created European Cup while the BBC had matches from the top English league in a show called Soccer Special. Later on in 1960 came ITV coverage of league matches, starting with Blackpool versus Bolton. Sensibly they were screened at 7.30 pm so as not to conflict with attendances at the 3 pm matches.

In August 1964, a soccer-related television show called Match of the Day (MOTD) was first screened in black and white on BBC 2. It was shown late on a Saturday evening without any prior information as to which match was to be shown. The first goal shown was scored by Roger Hunt of Liverpool against Arsenal after 11 minutes. In 1969, the first colour edition was put on featuring Liverpool and West Ham. Slow-motion replays were used to help elucidate controversial or special moments. From 1970 the famous theme tune written by Barry Stoller was added and served to summon the fans from other programmes or activities! The amazing success of Match of the Day has been helped by the fact that in nearly 60 years, the show has only had five lead presenters, namely Kenneth Wolstenholme, David Coleman, Jimmy Hill, Desmond Lynam and Gary Lineker! More recently, MOTD has sprung several additions, such as showing complete matches, the first being Manchester United versus Tottenham Hotspur in December 1983. It was a good choice as it ended 4 - 2 to United. While most people wanted to see goals, the connoisseur and the fanatic could usually find much of interest even in a goalless draw! 1992 saw the arrival of the Premier League and the new commercial broadcaster Sky. The deal was reputed to be worth £304 million. 1997 saw the arrival of MUTV, the first channel devoted to a single club, in this case, Manchester United. It was soon followed by others.

Also, MOTD 2 appeared on Sunday evenings in 2004, reflecting the fact that more matches were played on Sundays. I remember that there became a great competition between the BBC and ITV, the latter screening The Big Match on Sunday afternoons with Brian Moore as the presenter and Jimmy Hill as the commentator. It ran from 1968 and was also characterised by a catchy opening tune. Another frequent contributor to it from 1980 was Jim Rosenthal, who, in addition to covering many different sports, was also prominent in broadcasting FIFA World Cups since 1982. Later on, came the era of pay television with providers such as Sky, Eurosport, BT, Premier sport, among others, all competing for the rights. Another innovation in 2007 was the landmark appearance of the first female commentator Jacqui Oatley. She was obviously a success as today there are as many women as men in all the roles of sports broadcasting on TV. The "red button" concept now allows one to frequently choose to watch one of several matches on offer at any given time. Look where soccer on television is now, fought over by many broadcasters and with multiple games shown on TV at the same time almost every day. Who could have foreseen the numerous camera angles, action replays, pundits and interviews that now accompany matches?

Chapter 27 - A Base at Last

In the autumn of 1964, I was appointed to the Charing Cross Group of Hospitals, working first at the old Fulham Hospital in Fulham Palace Road. Local teams, of course, were Fulham, Chelsea and Queens Park Rangers. Even I couldn't support three teams, although I did have reasons to see some matches of all of them. I transferred my allegiance to Chelsea even though Luton always stayed closest to my heart. Chelsea stars at the time included Peter Bonetti (the cat), the goalkeeper, Ron Harris, known as "chopper" for his aggressive tackles from full-back, George Graham, John Hollins and Terry Venables in midfield, and forwards Peter Osgood, Barry Bridges and Bobby Tambling. On one occasion, their orthopaedic surgeon, who I worked with, asked me if I would like to deputise for him on a European trip which he couldn't make. I pointed out that I really didn't have the expertise to diagnose and deal with strained muscles, nor damaged bones or joints. "Don't worry," he said, "you will only have to deal with stomach upsets, hangovers and sexually transmitted diseases"! I declined the offer! Thanks to him, I gained entry to the Directors lounge at Chelsea, where I mixed with the so-called elite of football, including Ken Bates, the owner at the time. He had made his fortune in the haulage industry as well as quarrying ready mix concrete and dairy farming. His Rolls Royce with a personalised number plate was always prominently parked at the stadium! Any mention to him of Luton Town was greeted with a tirade against David Evans and his schemes at Luton. Amongst others I managed to natter with included Bobby Robson, then Ipswich manager, and our own Ray Harford, manager of course, over the period of our two Littlewoods Cup finals.

Luton, meanwhile, had been facing relegation to division 4 in 1965, a season when Ron Baynham and Dave Pacey, the last remaining two of the Cup final team, retired.

In 1965 I went to the Cup Winners Cup Final at Wembley between West Ham United and TSV 1860 Munich. I don't know why I decided to go or how I got the tickets, but it was an exciting match with the Hammers managed by Ron Greenwood winning thanks to two goals from Alan Sealey in the second half. Sadly Sealey broke his leg in a cricket match, which forced his early retirement at the age of 29. The three England players soon to become heroes in 1966, Moore, Peters, and Hurst, were all playing in that final! Johnny (Budgie, as he chatted all the time) Byrne could not play because of injury. Recently 1860 have slipped down the leagues since 2017, so now I believe they are in the 3rd Bundesliga. Johnny Byrne went to South Africa in 1969, where he did a lot to promote South African football and to finish his career playing for a year for Durban City alongside Johnny Haynes. Sadly Budgie died after a heart attack aged only 60. Johnny Haynes was considered to be Fulham's greatest player, playing there for 20 years in spite of never getting nearer to winning a trophy than two FA Cup semifinals. As an inside forward, he still managed to score 146 league goals and won 56 England caps. The maximum wage of £20 having been removed in 1961, he became notorious for being the first to earn £100 a week. As chairman of the Professional Footballers Association and also a Fulham player, Jimmy Hill was the leading light in the campaign to remove the maximum wage. He was also known for a letter to the Times in 1958 with Johnny Haynes in which he opposed apartheid and defended the principle of racial equality. Apart from the abolition of apartheid in the early 90s, has there been much change?

Chapter 28 - Season 1965/66

In 65/66, substitutes were allowed for the first time, initially only for injuries. However, two years later, they were allowed for tactical reasons as well. Over the years the number allowed has risen to three or even five in some competitions and sometimes a further one in extra time. Now the whole declared squad can sit on the bench and the allowed ones chosen from them all as the need arises. A new addition allows another one if a team want to substitute a player for a concussion injury. We are in an era where there is concern over a link between heading or severe head injury and dementia. Could heading be reduced or even become outlawed in the future? I don't believe that to be only speculative. I think it highlights the improvements in the management of severe injury or illness, including the mandatory presence of designated doctors and the availability of paramedics and other first aiders. Among the many dramatic moments of particular note were the cardiac arrests suffered by Patrice Muamba of Bolton and Christian Eriksen playing for Denmark in the Euro 2020 match against Finland. In Patrice's case, he was probably saved by the fact that in the crowd was a fan who was a qualified cardiologist. His heart was restarted after an extraordinary 78 minutes and multiple defibrillator shocks. By contrast, Christian only needed one. Sudden cardiac arrest in young, screened, and apparently healthy athletes is a well-recognised phenomenon, the cause of which is not totally understood.

In 65/66, John O'Rourke, who had been signed from Chelsea in 1963, scored 32 league goals but the Hatters narrowly missed promotion up to the third division, finishing in 6th place. O'Rourke stayed until 1966, earning England under 23 recognition before he was transferred to Middlesbrough for £18,500, and we obviously would need to replace his firepower and talent, although we did have Bruce Rioch. We even used Tony Read, a goalkeeper, as a striker, and he scored 12 goals in 20 outfield starts, including one hat-trick! Then the goals dried up, and he returned to his former goalkeeper role before retiring. In 1965 we had signed winger Graham French, although he was known to have a suspect temperament and a liking for all the things unacceptable in a professional sportsman, especially alcohol. In spite of it, he helped Luton to two promotions, and he scored 22 league goals, several memorable. A particular one in the 68/69 season was against Mansfield at home when he got the ball in his own penalty area and dribbled past any opposition player in his path before rounding the goalkeeper and scoring! French was definitely aided by a parallel decoy run by Brian Lewis, which took defenders away from him. It was the third goal in a 4-2 win and maybe should be considered as Luton's greatest individual goal ever.

A shooting incident at the Unicorn Pub involving the winger earned him a three-year prison sentence, and although the Town gave him a chance to resurrect his career after his release, it never worked out. He was, however, thought of by some as the poor man's George Best. During his time at Luton, he did help them with two promotions.

Around the same time in 1964 that Bruce Rioch signed his first professional contract at Luton, we also signed a clever winger from Nottingham Forest called David Pleat, who played for Luton for 5 years and scored 48 goals. Little did we know the impact he would have on the club in the next years, although his playing career had not been helped by a broken leg in his first season. Then Bill Harvey resigned as manager, replaced by former player Charlie Watkins and soon after by George Martin. Believe it or not, Ron Baynham, the goalkeeper who had played in the FA Cup final in 1959, was still playing brilliantly at 34 years of age but finally retired in 1965. At the time of writing, Baynham, at the age of 92, is the oldest member of the 1959 Cup final team and the oldest England International to be still alive! One of Martin's successful ideas was to move Bruce Rioch with his very strong left foot shots from centre forward to a more withdrawn position. Alan Slough, a local boy and goalscoring wing-half, also started to make a name for himself.

An outstanding signing was Scotsman John Moore, a no-nonsense centre half who made 306 appearances and stayed until 1973. He came from Motherwell and became another of my heroes. At that time, the never to be forgotten goalie Ron Baynham and Colin Tinsley, his understudy, were succeeded by Tony Read. Tony is remembered for the number of games he played at centre forward and for the 12 goals he scored as well as the ones he had saved. In 67/68, Allan Brown led the Hatters to the 4th division title thanks largely to 24 league goals from Bruce Rioch, and the next season we just missed out on a further promotion as they finished 3rd, Rioch only managing 10 goals compared with Brian Lewis with 22. Brian Lewis was a bit of a character with lots of cheeky daring play and an uncanny ability to earn penalties. I saw him as a real crowd pleaser! In one match, he started in his usual inside forward position, dropped back to left-back and then finally was goalkeeper to cover for injuries!

Chapter 29 - 1966 and the World Cup

1966 was a momentous year in my life. I was dating a very nice petite staff nurse who worked in the operating theatres, but honestly, I didn't see any long term future in the relationship. One evening I followed a pre-war Austin Seven Ruby saloon (1937 vintage) into the hospital car park. What a fabulous little car, I thought. Out of that fabulous little car came the most beautiful girl. So I always said that I married the car and the girl came too! We went out for four years before I succumbed and married her. What has all that got to do with football? I knew it would help our potential future life together if she showed an interest in football which up to then she had not! So I took her to a Chelsea - Liverpool match. Her comments related to the brightness of the strips (the blue and the red) and the quality of the players' legs (the shorts were very short at that time!). I remember having to rush her back to Fulham Hospital, where she was on night duty. I also took her to England - Mexico. I forgot to tell her about national colours so inevitably she appeared in a glamorous top in a bright green colour with white trousers. Green just happened to be Mexico's colours, so I was a bit apprehensive as to our safety sitting inevitably among the England supporters. Luckily England won 2-0 with goals from Bobby Charlton and Roger Hunt, so the locals were happy and peaceful. So the seeds of an interest in football were sown, but they sadly never really germinated.

1966 was the first World Cup to have a mascot. The mascot was called World Cup Willie, and there was a stirring song to commemorate him. He was an anthropomorphic lion, a symbol of England with a Union Jack jersey and the words World Cup on it. It started me on a collection of World Cup key rings and stamps, both sadly very incomplete!

I had managed to get tickets for all the England games, including the final, and of course, it was all amazing. I saw the first match, which was England - Uruguay and had ended 0 - 0, not a very auspicious start. France then drew with Mexico 1-1. I remember the Uruguay - France match being played at White City stadium because Wembley had a contract with the Greyhound Racing Association and would not cancel the dog racing even for a World Cup football match! Uruguay then beat France 2-1 while we beat Mexico 2-0. The final group matches ended England 2 France 0 while Mexico could only draw 0-0 with Uruguay. So we topped our group with 5 points, a point ahead of Uruguay. Both of us thus went into the quarter-finals, where fearsome Argentina awaited us and West Germany would await Uruguay. Clearly, the defence was up to scratch, but what about the attack? Alf Ramsey had played a narrow formation known as the "wingless wonders", about which there was considerable scepticism among the pundits.

The stars of the group stages were Portugal, who won all their matches and included Eusebio, known as "the black pearl", in their ranks. One shock of their group was the elimination of Brazil, who had lost to Portugal thanks in part to many over robust tackles on Pele.

The real shock of the Group stages was the elimination of Italy beaten by the Soviet Union and, amazingly, North Korea at Middlesborough in front of fewer than 18,000 supporters. On their arrival back in Italy, the players were greeted at the airport by volleys of missiles, especially ripe tomatoes. North Korea nearly caused another shock, leading 3-0 after 22 minutes against Portugal in the quarters. However, Portugal fought back to win 5-3, with Eusebio scoring 4 more goals.

England's next match, now in the knockout stage, was, therefore, to be against Argentina, who had been pipped by West Germany for the top spot in their group. They had a fearsome reputation, having been cautioned by FIFA for repeated foul play in the group matches. Not unexpectedly, the Argentinians demonstrated most of the dark arts of the game, and every free kick awarded against them, and there were many, was followed by the captain Antonio Rattin and several other players having a long aggressive discussion and indeed dispute with West German referee Rudolph Kreitlein. It was always said the Kreitlein did not speak a word of Spanish which maybe didn't help. However, after several such disputes, in the 35th minute, Kreitlein sent off Rattin, who memorably refused to go, apparently demanding an interpreter. Their manager threatened to take the whole team off but was persuaded to leave them on; otherwise, Argentina would have immediately had to forfeit the match and been eliminated from the tournament. After about 10 minutes of discussion, Rattin finally left the field. In fact, we were all very pleased that they did go out thanks to Geoff Hurst, a replacement for the injured Jimmy Greaves, scoring an unanswered goal in the 78th minute. After the match, the England players were not allowed by Alf Ramsey to swap shirts, famously calling the Argentinians "animals". It has always been believed that yellow and red cards were then introduced in time for the next World Cup in Mexico as a direct result of Argentinian behaviour in 1966. Sadly afterwards, Greaves was not able to regain his place, Geoff Hurst and Roger Hunt keeping the shirts for the rest of the tournament.

The semifinal was against Portugal, with Eusebio upfront. Eusebio was one of a host of Portuguese players born in Mozambique, then a Portuguese colony, and was a quite outstanding footballer as well as being a really sporting and friendly guy. Other stars included some of the Benfica players that I had seen in Lisbon in 1962, viz Mario Coluna, the captain in midfield, Jose Augusto on the wing, Antonio Simoes on the other wing and Jose Torres upfront. It was a close match with Bobby Charlton scoring two spectacular goals, the second in the 80th minute. Eusebio scored a lone reply in the 82nd minute from the penalty spot, but it was not enough, and England had qualified to meet old rivals West Germany in the final. Unlike the quarter-final against the Argies, the semifinal had been played in a real spirit of sportsmanship, a delight to see! Eusebio finished the tournament as a top scorer with nine, three ahead of Helmut Haller.

Chapter 30 - World Cup Final Day

What a day it was, the 29th of July. The final turned out to be the highlight of any English football supporter's life. Giampiero had come over from Turin and accepted my invitation to come with his wife Rosi to lunch in my parent's house in Kensworth near Luton. Among the other guests were Celia and Matty (the deaf Arsenal supporter), my good friend Richard (of Sestriere fame!) and maybe others I cannot recall. I did record the lunch menu, which consisted of Prawn Cocktail, Chicken Kiev and Apple Meringue, no doubt washed down with something nice for those who were not driving. We thought there was no point in trying to offer Italian food to Italians as they would surely do it better!

I had acquired a further ticket, presumably through Giampiero and which I had earmarked for Matty. We managed to keep it quiet from him until it was time to leave for the stadium. I will never forget Matty's face when he realised he was to come with us to Wembley rather than watch it on the very small TV screen. It was still in black and white in England at that time, but the match attracted over 32 million viewers, a record.

The story of the match is well chronicled. The England team was unchanged and played in red shirts to avoid a colour clash with the white-shirted Germans. The Germans were captained by Uwe Seeler and included Franz Beckenbauer (Der Kaiser, the Emperor), then 21 years of age, who as a midfielder scored 4 goals in the tournament and earned the Best Young Player award. He went on to win the Ballon d'Or twice, one of the few defenders to win it ever. He was also the only player to have won the World Cup as a player (1974) and as a manager (1990). The match started badly for England. A misplaced headed clearance from Ray Wilson in the 12th minute was dispatched into the net by Helmut Haller. Incidentally, Haller joined Juventus two years later, where he played for five years. Their lead was short-lived. In the 18th minute, Bobby Moore took a free-kick from near to the halfway line. It was aimed at a space in the penalty area. The delivery was very accurate, the ball meeting Geoff Hurst's head and landing into the German net. So 1-1 at half time with Bobby Charlton and Franz Beckenbauer rather cancelling each other out. The second half was fairly even until, in the 78th minute Martin Peters volleyed home from close range. It looks as though England had done enough to win, but calamity struck in the 89th minute. The ball was pinging about in the England penalty area and fell conveniently to Weber, who stroked it into the net. There was a feeling, led by Gordon Banks that there had been a German handball in the build-up, but that was certainly not seen by the officials. So we were heading for extra time when Alf Ramsey famously told his tired players, "you have won it once, now go out and win it again". The first period of extra time was memorable for one of the most controversial goals in football history. In the 101st minute, Geoff Hurst struck a shot that cannoned down off the bar. Had it crossed the line or not? Hunt, close to the goal line, raised his arm to celebrate the goal, but the Germans protested vehemently that the ball had not crossed the line. There followed a long debate with the referee, Gottfreid Dienst, a Swiss, the Russian linesman Tofiq Bahramov and many players until, after what seemed like an eternity, the goal was awarded. The Germans always believed that they were robbed! Of course, at that time, there was no goalmouth technology, so we will never know! It looked as though all we needed was the final whistle, but famously, in the last minute, Geoff Hurst broke away, and as the Germans defence receded, he struck the ball forcibly into the top corner, hence 4-2 the final result. As Hurst was running towards the goal, famously, the TV commentator Kenneth Wolstenhome was saying, "there are people on the pitch, they think it's all over," and as the ball hit the back of the net, "it is now". Inevitably celebrations galore in the England camp. Who can forget as he was going up to collect the Jules Rimet trophy from Her Majesty, Queen Elizabeth, Bobby Moore wiping his hands on the velvet-covered ledge so as not to dirty the Royal gloves? Prior to the match, the Cup had been stolen, and a replica had been made. But later, it was found in a hedgerow by a dog called Pickles. Everyone remembers a toothless Nobby Stiles doing a frenetic dance during the lap of honour and Bobby Charlton sobbing in his brother's arms! We had to wait a while for the Bonipertis as he had been hijacked by the Italian media, who wanted him to reproduce his two goals scored in 1953 in England - Rest of the World 4-4 game at Wembley. Then we had to go back to the Park Lane Hotel for him to face more interviews with the Italian press. Finally, we managed to extricate him from his duties and take him and his wife back to Kensworth for dinner. I remember us watching the highlights, and Boni was particularly struck by the skill and amazing energy of Alan Ball, then just aged 21. I thought he might find his way to Juventus, but he went to Everton and later Arsenal instead.

I got the Bonipertis safely back to their hotel, and I safely got back to Bedfordshire. I could finally try and relax but continued to relive the most amazing day.

Chapter 31 - Seasons 1966/67 and 67/68

In 66/67, Luton went on a spell of twenty-three away matches without a win, so it was no surprise that they could only finish in 17th place with only Bruce Rioch just reaching double figures with 10 goals. The lack of real success with Luton only finishing 17th led to the departure of George Martin at the end of 1966 and his replacement by former favourite Allan Brown, six years after he had finished playing for the Town.

In 67/68, his second season back, he led the Hatters to the 4th division title, and the next season they just missed out on a further promotion as they finished 3rd. No playoffs till 1986! Laurie Sheffield finished with 19 goals and Brian Lewis with 22. Wealthy people joined the board, including Tony Hunt and Reggie Burr, owners of insurance giant Vehicle and General who made a loan of £100,000. Generous bonuses of £5000 were offered to the players if they gained promotion from the 4th division, which of course, they did. And there were many improvements to the facilities. A massive spending spree on players followed, which encouraged many more supporters to buy season tickets.

In December 1968, Allan Brown was to leave the Town after applying for a vacant manager's post at Leicester, which incidentally he didn't get. He was sacked for "disloyalty" and replaced by Alec Stock. Stock was a very experienced manager, having been one since 1946 and whose clubs had included AS Roma for a year but especially Queens Park Rangers, where he stayed for nine years and formed a successful duo with forceful chairman Jim Gregory. They got QPR to the 1st division for the first time, having won the League Cup as a third division club in 1967, beating top league West Bromwich Albion. He managed some interesting characters, especially Rodney Marsh, who went on to Manchester City. Another was Mark Lazarus, one of the few Jewish sportsmen choosing football over boxing and scoring the winner in the 1967 League Cup Final. It took Alec just two years to get Luton back to the second division, having been 3rd in his first season and then 2nd in his second. The promotion was largely due to Malcolm Macdonald, whom he had converted from a full back to a centre forward with the result that he scored 25 league goals.

1967/68 had been a momentous season as Luton became 4th Division champions. In that season, they had a run of 12 successive home wins. The undoubted star player who became one of my all-time favourites was again Bruce Rioch. Bruce scored 24 league goals in 44 appearances, many of them spectacular and most with his left foot. Luton clinched the championship in April with a 4-0 over Crewe, Rioch scoring two more goals. I was heartbroken when he was sold to

Aston Villa for £100,000, where he went on to win 24 caps for Scotland. In that team was another of my heroes. John Moore was a no-nonsense Scottish central defender who made 274 appearances for us. Obviously, as a centre back, he was less flamboyant than some but immensely solid and, alongside captain Terry Branston formed a formidable barrier. John spent almost his whole career with Luton and was to become another of my favourites. He continued to keep links with the club, being appointed manager in 1986 in succession to David Pleat and later doing some coaching. He stayed on Luton's staff until his 60th birthday in 2003 and still does some summariser work during the coverage of Luton on Beds, Herts and Bucks 3 Counties radio to this day. I often see him as we both park in the same car park, and he is always up for a chat as long as you keep moving at his pace! I have to give thanks to 3 Counties radio which still keeps me informed during the many Luton matches that I cannot attend. A much later media addition was the subscription EFL iFollow with audio and visual streaming coverage of many of our matches.

Chapter 32 - European Cup Final 1968

I remember 1968 for being able to go to a wonderful European Cup final at Wembley between Manchester United and Benfica. Benfica had already played in 5 finals, winning two of them, so Manchester United, who had yet to win one, were the underdogs. For manager Matt Busby who had survived the Munich air crash, it was the chance of a lifetime. It was a surprise that we had a goalless first half with one team having Eusebio and Torres and the other Charlton and Best. It came to life in the second half when Bobby Charlton scored with a rare header. His goal was, however, equalised by Jaime Graca taking it to extra time. Nobby Stiles had really kept the shackles on Eusebio. George Best couldn't really get into the game, and the treatment he received led him to become petulant and bad-tempered. The match was won by United with three extra-time goals. The first was a Best special after a great dribble including rounding the goalie, the second a Brian Kidd header and the final one a Charlton thunderbolt. Matt Busby described it as "the most wonderful thing that happened to me in my life". So they became the first English team to win the European Cup, following Celtic, who had been the first British team to win it the year before with a squad of 15 players, all born within 30 miles of Celtic Park and managed by Jock Stein. How times have changed! The top teams are truly international now, with players from most of the different continents. Celtic were afterwards known as the Lisbon Lions for their 2-1 victory while Internazionale were vanquished, clearly missing their midfield maestro Luis Suarez who was out injured. In spite of Inter being among the pioneers and masters of catenaccio (the door bolt) defence under their famous Argentinian coach Helenio Herrera, Celtic breached it twice. While then it meant playing with a sweeper (libero in Italian) behind the back four to add to the defence, today, a five-man defence more often means three in the centre of the defence with two attacking wing-backs. If one wing back goes forward, the other stays back, so there was always "a back four" as well. Interestingly Juventus, who were hopelessly outdistanced in the middle of that season, finished up beating Inter to the title by one point, their 13th title. "Parking the bus" became a frequent tactic in Italy, especially for the away team, and 1-0 was the most frequent and favoured score.

Chapter 33 - Season 1968/69

Allan Brown only lasted a further six months and was replaced by Alec Stock, recently sacked by Queens Park Rangers in spite of leading them from the third to the first divisions in successive seasons! His asthma was cited as a reason, but there was more frequently a fall out with QPR chairman Jim Gregory. Alec Stock is best remembered for signing Malcolm Macdonald from Fulham for £17,500 and converting him from a full back to a prolific centre forward. Malcolm is remembered for his stocky physique and explosive shooting, especially with his left foot. For Luton, he scored 58 goals in 101 appearances and was one of those players who was always likely to do something spectacular. He stayed at Kenilworth Road until the summer of 1971, when he signed for Newcastle United for £180,000, a large sum at that time and a big profit for the Hatters. His personal life was rather sad and complex and has been well documented elsewhere.

1968/69 was a nearly season, the Town finishing 3rd and thus just missing out on promotion. I took my wife to one away match in that season at Orient, a club in Leyton whose stadium was quite difficult to find and characterised by having a block of flats along one side of the pitch!! The match was dire, ending in a 0-0 draw, and the man behind us was repeatedly shouting out "rubbish", a sentiment with which we had to agree! My wife was not impressed, and it made her wonder how I could love soccer so much. One of the most renowned players of the era was a seriously extrovert forward called Brian Lewis, renowned for a collection of tricks and an ability to obtain free kicks and penalties out of nothing. Alec Stock also had bought Mike Keen from QPR. I thought he was very underrated, being a very skilful and productive wing-half who could always spot an effective pass forwards. The last match of the season was at home to Watford, and although it concluded with a 2-1 Town win, it was marred by horrific crowd violence, and sadly the Town were pipped by Swindon for the second promotion place. We did make it in the following season, finishing second when the 25 goals of that other hero, Malcolm Macdonald, gave us the boost we needed.

That year Manchester United, as European Cup winners, played the Argentinian South American Copa Libertadores champions, Estudiantes de la Plata, in a two-leg final. They lost the away leg 1-0 with Nobby Stiles being sent off, and three weeks later came the return leg. I went with an uncle who loved football as well, and I remember him doing the driving, both journeys just before and after the match. It was the first time that I went to Old Trafford and was, of course, very impressed with its grandeur and the support given to United, especially from the Stretford end. The bad relations between the teams and countries, unfortunately, persisted into the second leg, where both George Best and Jose Hugo Medina were dismissed. The result was 1-1, Juan Ramon Veron scored the Estudiantes goal in the 6th minute, but Willie Morgan equalised in the 90th minute, giving the Argentinians the overall victory, but certainly no new admirers in England.

Chapter 34 - A Year's Sabbatical without Live Soccer

June 1969 was another special month for me. My future wife, Gillian, having retired from nursing to become an air stewardess with British United Airways (BUA), had survived an air crash outside Milan on 14th January when soon after takeoff, a loud bang was heard. The pilot of the BAC 111 identified the problem but then shut down the fuel to the wrong engine necessitating a forced glider like landing. The plane just avoided hitting a motorway and many buildings, posts and pylons. Undoubtedly the landing was helped by the field being covered with snow. The plane was a write-off, but although 2 miles from the end of the runway, there were no fatalities, and out of the 33 occupants (seven crew and 26 passengers), there were only two serious injuries. Fortunately, my girlfriend was not physically injured but suffered a degree of post-traumatic stress disorder, undoubtedly aggravated by the crew being detained and locked up together in a hotel for several days. I remember how she had to have space around her and would walk down the pavement pushing people out of the way with her umbrella. Luckily she was very well treated by a psychiatrist colleague at Charing Cross Hospital. For a while, she was understandably seriously nervous about flying, which was a problem as we had complex plans to get married, to go to Brazil on honeymoon and then on to Seattle, USA, for a year of further anaesthetics training. On 13th June 1969, we were married in the Houghton Regis registry office and then prepared for the wonderful honeymoon and the year in Seattle. Gillian had made it clear that she would not come to Seattle with me unless we were married, which I quite understood and with which I complied willingly.

Gillian had worked for a year with the airline, and so we were entitled to honeymoon flights at ten percent of the normal fare and had chosen Brazil as the most exciting of the airlines' destinations. We had already booked the wedding and flights when I discovered that England were playing a friendly in the famous Maracana stadium in Rio de Janeiro just three days before our arrival. What bad planning! In that match, Colin Bell gave England the lead, and Gordon Banks then saved a penalty from Carlos Alberto before goals from Tostao and Jairzinho gave Brazil the victory. The match was played in front of 135,000 spectators, making it even sadder that we had missed it. The wedding day went according to plan, and the next day, there was a further gathering for those who had not been able to come to the Registry Office.

So departure for Rio via Las Palmas in a British United Airways VC10 on the 16th. We stayed in a hotel used by the aircrew right on Copacabana beach. We noted that several of the aircrews had what seemed to be an excess of baggage, and it turned out that there was a big demand for

Marks and Spencer knitwear in Brazil! In exchange, we all bought fashionable clothes, especially skirts and tops made of suede and other leather goods. What struck me immediately was the huge number of youngsters practising their soccer skills on the sandy beach. No wonder Brazil produced and continues to produce so many wonderful footballers. Although we had missed the England match, a visit to the iconic Maracana stadium was a must! What a wonderful stadium, a real soccer stadium with the fans fairly close to the pitch on all four sides. It had been re-built for the 1950 World Cup. World Soccer featured what they saw as two of the greatest games played there. Firstly the 1950 World Cup final when Brazil lost to Uruguay 2-1. At that date, the gate was an amazing 199,854, almost all standing. Secondly, in the 2014 World Cup Final when, after beating Brazil by an astonishing 7-1 in the semifinal, Germany went on to beat Argentina 1-0 in the final after extra time. By then, the stadium had become an all-seater with a capacity of only 78,000, but it remains the largest stadium in Brazil.

Another exciting trip was a visit to Ipanema beach, which had been made famous by the bossa nova (a style of samba) and jazz song "The Girl from Ipanema", sung originally by Pery Ribeiro in 1962 in Portuguese. It was made even more successful when recorded by Astrud Gilberto in English with the famous tenor saxophonist Stan Getz in 1964. Since then, it has been recorded by almost everyone from Frank Sinatra to Amy Winehouse and is probably the second most recorded song after the Beatles' "Yesterday"! We took a taxi to get there, and it seemed quite a long way from Copacabana, with the driver taking many turns all the time warning us of the danger of pickpockets and particularly to watch our camera. When we explored the beach a bit, we discovered that it was the next beach to Copacabana and an easy walking distance back!

A few days later, we flew on to Sao Paolo, where on arrival, we discovered that our checked-in luggage had gone on to Santiago, Chile, with all the crew luggage! You could say you don't need too many clothes on your honeymoon and anyway it was returned to us on the next flight back from Santiago. Luckily there was a match featuring Sao Paolo against Santos on the 21st, both very famous teams. Santos was the team that Pele played for, and wonderful that he was playing in that match. The hotel concierge got us the two tickets, probably with a considerable markup. Another large stadium with about 63,000 people present. It was the first time I had witnessed the widespread use of flares and firecrackers; quite impressive but a bit frightening. Santos played in black and white stripes very similar to my Juventus of Turin. It was essential for a football fanatic to have seen Pele in the flesh, although I don't have any specific memories of the match, which sadly ended 0-0. What I do remember was on exiting the stadium, there were lines of coaches as far as the eye could see. Very efficient therefore was the evacuation from the stadium and the dispersal of the large crowd. It meant that there was really no reason to drive there.

The next day we rented a Volkswagen "beetle" and drove to Santos, a lovely seaside town and, of course, home of Pele's team. It was about 75 km from Sao Paolo and had a seven km stretch of beach. It also has a famous coffee museum. We managed somehow to lock the car with the keys inside, but a passer-by showed us how easy it was to open a locked car without a key and without causing any damage! Years later, I had become friendly with a Brazilian anaesthetist who was based in Santos and knew Pele well. He always said that if we came to Santos in the future, he would get us to meet Pele. Unfortunately, it never happened, and I had to settle for a number ten black and white Santos shirt. I kept it until last year when a soccer-mad granddaughter acquired it and wore it often!

That ends the football part of the story for a while as we were leaving Sao Paolo and heading for Lima, Peru, Los Angeles and Seattle. Flying with Varig, the Brazilian airline, we had to take a small six-seater plane from one Sao Paolo airport to another to connect with the international Varig plane. I remember soon after takeoff, the pilot reached under the seat of his very small plane and produced a bottle of whisky which he passed to us. The bar was open, but luckily he didn't partake! The transfer to the Varig plane was uneventful. Lima was just a stopover, and although it was the middle of the night, I remember the duty-free shop was very large and very active. Then on to Los Angeles, a three day stop which included Disneyland, the Hollywood areas and Santa Monica.

There was no professional soccer club in Seattle at that time, so we had to show interest in American football, baseball, basketball and our favourite ice hockey. The Seattle Totems were in the Western Hockey league, and we loved the speed and physicality of the game. They finished 4th in our year there and reached the semifinal of their cup, where they lost to the Portland Buckaroos from the next state to the south.

In October 1969, I got the news that Boniperti had been recalled to the Juventus board, at first shadowing and then replacing Vittorio Catella, a former Fiat aircraft engineer who had been on the board since 1962.

So no live football for me for over a year, although, of course, there was the 1970 World Cup in Mexico to follow as well as keeping an ear on the goings-on at Luton who were in Division 3 at that time.

Eric Morecambe became a director in March 1970 and did a huge amount to publicise and improve the image of the club with regular references to it on the Morecambe and Wise show. He remained a director for five years but sadly died in 1984 after his third heart attack at the age of only 58. Later one of the hospitality rooms at Luton was named after him and is used for corporate hospitality, meetings and social events. The season 69/70 ended with Town in second place, meaning promotion to Division 2, but of course, I missed the whole season. Viv Busby, having joined in January 1970 and scored 3 very valuable goals in the last four games alongside the prolific Macdonald's twenty-five league and three Cup goals. He undoubtedly had a big influence on Matt Tees, who, although slight of physique, was very strong and a great header of the ball. Sadly, Tees, like so many others, developed dementia in later life, possibly largely due to repeated heading of the ball over a long period of time.

So we came back to England to be supporting a Division two team. Malcolm Macdonald scored another twenty-four league and six Cup goals in that next season in which we finished 6th and had been ever-present in the league in both seasons!

The build-up to the 1970 World Cup finals in Mexico was noted for the arrest of Bobby Moore in Bogota, Colombia, for allegedly stealing a bracelet from the hotel's jewellery shop. He was detained for five days before being released. Although the truth was never fully established, it was widely believed that he was innocent. Later he was indeed acquitted and played in all the final games for England. It was the first World Cup to be shown on colour television and was about the time that the penalty shootout was introduced as a way of settling drawn games. Referee Ken Aston had introduced cards focused on yellow and red. If you used these two colours on the football pitch, they would beat any language barriers and show players and spectators that they had either been warned or sent off.

The group matches for England included 1-0 wins over Romania and Czechoslovakia and a 1-0 loss to Brazil. During the Brazil game, Gordon Banks made one of the greatest saves of all time in keeping out a powerful and very accurate header from Pele. The shirt swap at the end between Pele and Bobby Moore was an iconic moment of friendship and mutual respect.

So England and Brazil both reached the last eight where England played West Germany, again! Five of 1966 final eleven played in that game in Leon, but the most significant change was the absence due to a stomach bug, known as Montezuma's revenge, of Gordon Banks and his replacement by Peter Bonetti of Chelsea.

Sadly Peter Bonetti was blamed for errors that contributed to the defeat. England had led 2-0 in the 50th minute through goals from Alan Mullery and Martin Peters and looked to be on course for victory. Then Alf Ramsey also got a lot of criticism for his decision to substitute Bobby

Charlton with Colin Bell just after Beckenbauer's 68th-minute first German goal. Presumably, his thinking was to stiffen the defence and try to hold on to the 2-1 score, but it sadly backfired, and in spite of Norman Hunter also replacing Martin Peters in the 81st minute, the Germans scored three goals, one each by Franz Beckenbauer and Uwe Seeler in normal time to force extra time, and then a characteristic close range volleyed goal by Gerd Muller in the 108th minute to knock England out. Muller was one of the most prolific strikers of all time, scoring 566 goals in 607 games for Bayern and 68 international goals in 62 appearances. He scored 10 goals in six matches in that 1970 tournament, but his two goals in the semis could not prevent Germany from being knocked out by Italy, who lost to Brazil 4-1 in the final. The final was memorable for Italy, equalising a Pele goal but then a rampant Brazil playing wonderful football scored three more times to take the trophy. Over 100,000 had watched the match in the Azteca stadium in Mexico City.

The Italy squad was unusual in that it only had one Juventus player, Beppe Furino and even more surprisingly, six from Cagliari, a team from Sardinia who that year had won their one and only Scudetto! The best known of the Cagliari players were probably goalie Enrico Albertosi and striker Luigi Riva.

Chapter 35 - Continuing My Career

We were back in England after the start of the 1970/1971 season. My most important task was to obtain a consultant post in anaesthetics. My preference was for the London area, but I wanted a post that allowed me to pursue my particular interest in obstetric anaesthesia. Especially to study and promote the use of epidurals in painless childbirth and, later on, awake Caesarean sections. I was unsuccessful in several applications for London Teaching Hospitals, the posts going to local candidates. So I also looked at several vacancies around the country and came close to applying for a new post in a brand new hospital in Wolverhampton. Would I have been able to transfer my allegiance to the Wanderers? We'll never know. However, I did some research, and at the time, Wolves had some well-known players such as Phil Parkes (not to be confused with the QPR one, although curiously, both were goalkeepers), Kenny Hibbitt, Derek Dougan, Bobby Gould and John Richards. Historically Wolves were one of the top clubs and one of the first English clubs to play friendlies in 1954 against foreign clubs such as Moscow Dynamo and Honved, the Budapest army side that contained several of the national team that had beaten England 3-6 and 7-1 in the past. The Wolves team included Bert Williams and Billy Wright, and their entire squad, apart from one Welshman and one South African, was English! A fourth-place finish in 1971 allowed them the entrance to the newly formed UEFA Cup. In 1972 they lost the UEFA Cup final 2-1 on aggregate to Tottenham Hotspur, the first leg in Tottenham being refereed by Tofiq Bakhramov of 1966 World Cup final fame. Tofiq was always remembered as a Russian, but I believe that he was actually from Azerbaijan. Tofiq is the only referee, as far as I know, to have had a stadium named after him. It is in Baku, the capital of Azerbaijan, and had previously been called the Vladimir Lenin stadium!

Somehow I always looked forward to matches against the Wolves, standing out as they did in their old gold shirts. Clearly, my roots were in the south, and that's where I hoped to be for the rest of my life and preferably not more than 30 miles from Luton!

Chapter 36 - Season 1970/71

The 1970s were years when as a junior doctor and later Consultant, I worked very long hours and most days and so going to football had to take second place.

A memorable match in 70/71 was Luton against Birmingham City. While we had Supermac, they had teenage prodigy Trevor Francis, 16 years of age at the time! Luton were 2-0 down but came back to win 3-2. Trevor will always be remembered as the first million-pound player when Brian Clough famously signed him for Forest. His header to win the European Cup final against Malmo from Sweden is one of the most famous headed goals of all time. Trevor was another who later joined the Italian exodus playing for four years at Sampdoria, one of the Genoa teams, and then a year at Atalanta of Bergamo in Lombardy. At Sampdoria, he played alongside Graeme Souness, who is, of course, is still going strong as a pundit and analyst.

Luton stayed in Division 2 from 1970/71 to the end of 1973/4, finishing in 6th, 13th, 12th and finally 2nd. We finished 15 points behind Middlesbrough, but it gave us promotion to the 1st Division, at last, thanks in large measure to Barry Butlin's 17 league goals. Sadly we only lasted in Division 1 for that one season, finishing in 20th place. Another star in the early 70s was central defender Chris Nicholl, signed in 1969 from Halifax Town. He left for Aston Villa in 1972, going on to win the League Cup with them and earned 51 caps for Northern Ireland. He organised the Aston Villa Old Stars, a team of ex Villa players who play in charity and testimonial matches.

At Juventus, there was a need for a top-class goalie, and to fill that gap, Dino Zoff was signed from Napoli in 1972. At club level, he made 330 appearances for Juve as they won the Scudetto six times, the Coppa Italia twice and the UEFA Cup once. He proved to be outstanding, winning 112 caps and helping Italy, captained by Inter's Giacinto Facchetti, to victory in the 1968 European Championships and in 1982, the World Cup at the age of 40 in a team that he captained himself. At the time, Dino was the oldest player to feature in a World Cup final, although now he only ranks sixth. In a poll at the time, he was elected the third best goalkeeper ever behind the Russian Lev Yashin and Gordon Banks. He was quiet and modest and never showed off. He very rarely missed a game and broke records season after season. He later managed both Juventus for 3 years and 8 years later the National team also for 3 years.

The collapse of Luton's major financiers, Vehicle and General Insurance, in 1971 didn't help as it necessitated bringing in money by transferring some of their best players. Tony Hunt of V & G resigned as chairman as the club entered into unofficial receivership. That was when Malcolm

Macdonald was sold to Newcastle for £180,000 and Chris Nicholl to Aston Villa for £90,000. Chris was replaced by John Faulkner, often known as Max, and a very steady and reliable centre half. The finances were balanced to some extent by Robert Keens, a knowledgable accountant. The ground advertising was increased, a lottery was introduced, and an executive area named the Century Club was opened.

Mention has to be made of the Ibrox stadium disaster in January 1971. At the end of an old firm derby with Celtic attended by over 80,000, there was a crush on exit stairway 13, and tragically 66 died, and over 200 were injured. It did not seem to relate to violence but was just a tragic accident compounded by poor stadium design, the stairway being too steep and narrow.

One exciting trip for me was to Elland Road Leeds on the 3rd June 1971 for a second leg Inter-Cities Fairs Cup final against Juventus, which ended 1-1. I was glad that I had not been able to go to the first leg in Turin as it was abandoned in the 51st minute at 0-0 due to heavy rain and a waterlogged pitch. Two days later, Leeds got a 2-2 draw in the replayed first leg, Bettega and Capello scoring the Juve goals. I remember the return game in Leeds for two things. Firstly the plethora of stars in both teams, and secondly, the frequent flare-ups between the players. The Leeds team had so many top-class players on view that I think it is worth naming them all: Gary Sprake, Paul Reaney, Terry Cooper, Billy Bremner, Jack Charlton, Norman Hunter, Alan Clarke, Mick Jones, Johnny Giles, Paul Madeley and Peter Lorimer. However, manager Don Revie had Leeds playing in a very fierce and provocative fashion. Juventus had, amongst others, Anastasi, who scored their goal in the second leg, Bettega, Causio, and Fabio Capello (yes, he did have a long playing career, including six years with Juventus before those 3 years as their manager. Lastly, the German Helmut Haller is remembered by all English supporters of the time for his 12th-minute opening goal in the 1966 World Cup final. So Leeds won the Cup on away goals! It was indeed the only time the Cup had been won on the away goals rule and the last Fairs Cup before it was renamed the UEFA Cup, and later again the UEFA Europa League. Roberto Bettega has been known variously as "la Penna Bianca (the White Feather)" due to his hair colour and Bobby Gol for equally obvious reasons. He was a striker and one of the greatest Juve players playing 490 games and scoring 179 goals for them between 1969 to 1983. He won seven Serie A titles, the 1977 UEFA Cup, and a Coppa Italia. For Italy, he won 42 caps and scored 19 goals. He played in the 1978 World Cup and the 1980 European championships.

He finally left Juventus to play for a year in North America with the Toronto Blizzards. He, unfortunately, had missed the 1982 World Cup win due to injury. In 1994 he became vice-chairman of the Juventus board of directors and stayed till 2006. In 2009 he was recalled as deputy director-general but only remained in that post for a year. He was then replaced by Giuseppe Marotta, who was general manager and CEO for eight years at Juve. His appointment was the first to be made by new president Andrea Agnelli. He is currently with Inter. Another name at the time was Fabio Paratici, who was head of technical affairs and sporting director at Juventus had come with Marotta from Sampdoria and remained in that post for eleven years.

Chapter 37 - Season 1971/72

In the close season in 1971, our first child was born. I was secretly hoping for a boy as I thought that would give me a better chance of the baby growing up to be a football fan like his father, but no, it was a girl as was our second born three years later! I think I was heard to express my disappointment publicly, perhaps not the most tactful thing to do, but it seems I was quickly forgiven. At least they both later married football fans, so Hull City would come into my life as well as Spurs once again!

I obtained my coveted consultant post finally in 1971 at Charing Cross Hospital, soon to be relocated to Fulham Palace Road and so still close to the threesome, Chelsea, Fulham and Queens Park Rangers.

News about developing our stadium or moving the club out of Luton were frequent. Milton Keynes was put forward as a possible location, a suggestion never well received. The only people in favour seemed to be those who lived in the Milton Keynes area. When the MK stadium finally opened in 2007, the Milton Keynes Dons (the old Wimbledon club) moved in there. I think we did lose quite a few supporters to them, including some good friends. I did visit it secretly and was very impressed with it. Especially the ease of access, good car parking and the comfort and excellent views. I'm afraid it made Kenilworth Road seem like a real slum. Of course, our ground was still of the old fashioned type right in the city centre and surrounded very closely by numerous houses. Inside, cramped leg room and many restricted views due to large posts didn't make for a wonderful experience. So many other clubs had moved into new purpose-built stadia out of town. In spite of its deficiencies, the 10,000 full capacity Kenny and especially under the lights, can still create a great atmosphere which is worth a few extra points per season to the Hatters! The club shop is a small portable building in the stadium forecourt, although it has been supplemented recently by a much larger one in Park Street in the town centre. The noisiest and most intense home supporters tend to be in the main stand end of the Oak road stand if it is open to them or, conversely, the Oak road end of the main stand when the Oak Road end was totally given to away supporters.

I don't remember anything particular about the 1971/72 season, except it is recorded that we finished in 13th place but narrowly avoided relegation by five points and that it was followed by the resignation of Alec Stock and his replacement by Harry Haslam. Our top goalscorer was Peter Anderson with 10, followed by Don Givens with 8, which rather sums it up. There was an FA Cup 3rd round at West Ham when we lost 2-1, and hooligans and particularly skinheads surfaced. Sadly

1972 was the year when Glasgow Rangers supporters, despite winning 3-2, invaded the pitch just before the scheduled end of the European Cup Winners Cup final against Dynamo Moscow in Barcelona. They also rioted in the streets outside before and after the match. It was the first time that a full-scale British riot was seen live across Europe. This led to British fans being banned from Europe for two years. Segregation with fences began to be put in place with only limited benefit and made trouble outside the grounds more prevalent.

In 1971, Luton had played in the Watney Mann Invitation Cup a pre-season tournament open to the two clubs from each division who had scored the most goals. They had to be clubs that had not won anything in the previous season or earned promotion. I only know that we only played in it the one season and didn't progress, losing 1-0 at Colchester United in the first round and that the final was between Colchester and West Bromwich Albion and finished 4-4, Colchester winning a penalty shootout 4-3. After 4 years, it was discontinued. Maybe it should be remembered for a trial of a change to the offside law moving the line from the halfway line to the edge of the penalty area. Presumably, it was not a success as it lasted only one season! It was the first tournament to include penalty shootouts and was also the first soccer competition to bear a sponsor's name.

1972 was the year of the Euros and played in Belgium. For some reason, only four teams took part in the actual finals, which therefore consisted only of the two semifinals, a third-place match and the final itself. There had been obviously many earlier matches played in a variety of venues. England had been knocked out by West Germany at Wembley in a pre-tournament quarter-final, with our nemesis Gerd Muller scoring a last-minute goal as Germany won 3-1. They went on to win the whole thing with wins over Belgium in the semis (2-1) and the Soviet Union in the final 3-0. Of the five goals scored by the Germans, 4 were scored by Muller. The third-place match was won by Belgium (2-1) over Hungary.

Chapter 38 - Season 1972/73

In the 72/73 season, we finished 12th and got to the FA Cup sixth round, having beaten Crewe 2-0 at home, then Newcastle away 2-0 with Aston the double goalscorer. Next came Bolton, the future division 3 champions, where we won 1-0, but we then lost 2-0 away to Sunderland, also in the second division like us and to be the eventual winners.

By another coincidence, in May 1973, we were in Amsterdam and were able to watch that English Cup final in Berri Groen parent's flat. Joining us apart from his parents was Piet Romer, an actor who famously played the son of Steptoe on Dutch TV. Piet became a good friend, and if one went out with him, he would always be accosted by a large number of autograph seeking fans. I remember the match well in spite of imbibing large amounts of Dutch Genever Gin, characteristically sold in stone bottles and drunk neat! The final was Leeds, one of the top teams of the era, against second division Sunderland. The highlights were the only goal scored by Ian Porterfield for Sunderland in the 32nd minute and a string of wonderful saves by goalkeeper Jimmy Montgomery, one of which has been compared to Gordon Banks save from Pele in that Mexico 1970 World Cup match. Who could forget manager Bob Stokoe, the Sunderland manager, in a trilby hat and elegant raincoat, rushing across the pitch at the final whistle to embrace Montgomery and to start the celebrations for the underdog who had beaten the favourites?

1973 was a season when we entered the Anglo-Italian Cup, the one and only European competition in which we were able to compete. The Cup had been created by Gigi Peronace, a Calabrian born agent. He is famous as one of the first football agents and was involved in most of the transfers of British players to Italy. He was foremost in the transfers of John Charles. Liam Brady, Jimmy Greaves, Joe Baker and Denis Law. He had also acted as interpreter for successive English Juventus managers William Chambers and Jesse Carver and had negotiated the move of Alec Stock to Roma as manager for the season 57/58. Violence was frequent in the Anglo-Italian Cup, and the first final in 1970 involving Swindon Town and Napoli in front of 55,000 people in the San Paolo stadium actually had to be abandoned in the 79th minute because of serious disturbances from especially the Napoli fans who made two pitch invasions in protest to their sides poor showing. The police responded with tear gas, and then a whole array of missiles were hurled onto the pitch. At least 40 policemen and 60 demonstrators were injured, and £20,000 of damage was done to the stadium. In spite of the match not being concluded, the Cup was awarded to Swindon, who had been leading 3-0. Incidentally, it was a golden era for Swindon, who had won the 1969 League Cup and that previous year's Anglo-Italian Cup. In the League Cup, they surprisingly had beaten the mighty Arsenal 3-1 after extra time in spite of being in the 3rd division. Their victory was in part due to an excellent performance by winger Don Rogers who scored two goals in extra time.

In the Anglo-Italian Cup, we played Bari (4-0) and Fiorentina (1-0) at home and Verona (1-2) and Lazio (2-2) away. However, we did not get past the group stage. For some reason, I don't remember going to any of the matches, surprising in view of my love and great interest in Italy and its football. I don't think I was excited by the Italian teams, mostly from Serie B, the Italian 2nd division and the long history of violence. Also, most crucially, I didn't really have anyone wanting to go with me. For the record, we never got past the first group stages. We might have played in the UEFA Cup in 88-89 after winning the League Cup, but English clubs were banned from Europe following the Heysel disaster.

Central defenders Paul Price and John Faulkner had come to Kenilworth Road. The former came from local non-league side Welwyn Garden City and stayed till 1984 when he was transferred to Spurs for £250,000. He was a member of the Spurs team that got to the League Cup final and lost 3-1 to Liverpool in 1982. He won 25 caps for Wales. John Faulkner spent almost his entire career at Luton coming from Leeds United. Another surprising but very successful signing was John Aston Jr. from Manchester United. He was Jr. because his father had the same name and had also been a professional footballer and had indeed played for United in the years after the 2nd World War. John Jr. had a wonderful pedigree, having been part of Manchester United's 1968 European Cup final victorious team against Benfica and having been selected as man of the match. He was at the Town for 5 years.

An infamous player at the time was full-back Don Shanks, son of Wally. He is remembered as one of Stan Bowles's regular betting, womanising and drinking partners and for dating Mary Stävin, the 1977 Swedish Miss World. In addition to acting, Stävin released the exercise album Shape Up and Dance with George Best.

Harry Haslam, as manager, lasted almost six years, during which time we were Division 2 runners up in 73/74 and therefore promoted to the top division but had more financial problems and indeed only lasted that one season in the top flight. Another important signing at the time was Bobby Thomson, an England left-back who became the club captain and played every game in that promotion season, as did fellow defender Alan Garner. The Bobbers Stand, which was opposite the main stand, had by then been converted to a seating area, obviously reducing the capacity. Later that same stand was converted to 25 executive boxes, which have always looked a bit odd and are so low that balls are constantly being kicked out of the ground on that side. Most are collected and returned, but some finish up as presents to members of the local population. The Bobbers Club under the Oak Road end is a members-only club and is also responsible for the Bobbers Travel Club, which arranges travel to all the away games. For a time, there was another group called Town on Tour, which also took fans to away matches in, it was claimed, a slightly more upmarket fashion!

The seventies seemed to me to be the era of continuing hooligan issues that really dominated the game. I have clear memories of witnessing violence caused by marauding groups of fans at away games at Cambridge and Leicester, as well as a home game against Bristol Rovers when this peace-loving supporter finished up with a black eye. At that time, there were special trains put on for fans, but again violence and damage meant that they were curtailed. They always had the disadvantage that there was often quite a walk from the stations to most grounds exposing the supporters to the local gangs. In the end, the away fans had to have police escorts, be marched to the grounds, and the whole atmosphere was very hostile. It was not long before the trains were replaced by supporters' coaches that could get right up to the ground and obviously broke up the away fans into smaller groups.

In April 1973, Brian Clough brought his Derby team to Turin for a European Cup semifinal 1st leg. It ended 3-1 to Juve, with the German referee awarding 42 free kicks to Juve and only 19 to Derby. Helmut Haller was seen to go to the dressing room at half time with the referee Gerhard Schulenburg. Clough saw these facts as evidence that Juventus had bribed the referee and told the expectant Italian reporters: "I will not talk to any cheating bastards". John Charles was visiting but declined Clough's invitation to mediate and speak to the Italian press, a duty that was given to Italian based English sports journalist and author Brian Glanville. Clough asked him to "tell them what I said, Brian"! The second leg was noted for the absence of two suspended Derby players, Roy McFarland and Archie Gemmill, who had been booked controversially by the referee in the first leg and were therefore not eligible for the second leg. Although Derby scraped a 0-0 draw, they went out on the 3-1 aggregate score. The final in Belgrade was won by Ajax 1-0 with a 5th minute Johnny Rep goal. It was a famous Ajax team including Johan Cruyff as captain, Ruud Krol, Johan Neeskens, Arie Haan and Piet Keizer among others. The win was the third successive win for Ajax, who, therefore, could keep the Cup. Juventus finally got a final win over Ajax in Rome in 1996, as you will read later.

Chapter 39 - French Riviera OGC Nice and AS Monaco

In 1973 we decided to buy a large caravan that was permanently sited on a campsite in the south of France, an area that I was very fond of, having spent a lot of summers there in my teens. We were never very keen on camping/caravanning, but this caravan belonged to another antique dealer friend of my father, who was always immaculate in his appearance. We assumed that the caravan would be equally immaculate, parted with £500, but we were shocked at the interior state when we got there. Ants were nesting in the roof space, and dead ones would drop on one during the night! It was a shame as the site was perfect with a swimming pool, catering facilities in the lodge house and many showers. After a few years, we decided to offer the caravan to Gillian's parents on the back of their having to leave a villa near Almeria in Spain because of serious local pollution. They loved the caravan and would spend the whole winter there but finally moved to a tiny flat in Benidorm. We were happy to accept about £50 from someone who wanted the caravan to breed chickens and sell eggs. I began to take a greater interest in French football, both OGC Nice and AS Monaco being fairly close. We spent quite a few holidays in the "second home" flat of a good friend just outside Cannes. We were always very welcome as my wife was incredibly houseproud, and our friends would come down and find their flat prepared to an immaculate standard!

By 1978 we thought of buying a flat ourselves on the French Riviera and were shown around the area by several estate agents. We decided on Nice because we really loved cities more than rural areas and there was always something to do there all year round. The coastal areas seemed lovely in summer but rather deserted in the colder months. One attractive flat was situated on the Gairaut hill in North Nice with amazing views over the city with the sea in the distance. The good thing was that at the bottom of the drive was a city bus stop with regular and frequent service into the centre. At the time, the proposed block was only a hole in the ground, but the fact that one could pay in instalments was appealing. The agent proudly pointed out the Stade du Ray, the home of OGC Nice, in the foreground as an important selling point. I suggested that, in view of the prevalence of violence associated with football, it might not be the best selling point, but for me, of course, it indeed was. The flat was due to be completed in three years, but due to the hill on which it was being built collapsing and the developer going bankrupt, it wasn't finished for another two. We wondered whether the promised tennis court and swimming pool would ever be seen, but they were finished, although curiously, they were on someone else's land!

OGC Nice were largely in the top division although in 1981/82 they were in the 2nd division as they were to be from 1996 to 2001. AS Monaco also alternated at that time between the 1st and 2nd divisions, although much more often in the top league.

Chapter 40 - Season 1973/74 and the World Cup

We had signed Alan West from Burnley for £100,000 at that time. He was always very popular, and he stayed 8 years. He was the captain for some years and was an excellent passer of the ball. He has been the pastor of a Luton church and was for many years the Chaplain of the club. In late 2017 he was succeeded by Revd David Kesterton, vicar of All Saints Church on Shaftesbury Road, and indeed a Hatters season ticket holder himself.

1973 was marked by the appearance of a new orange and navy blue strip to replace Luton's traditional white and black. I have to say I much preferred the old one but the vote on it that the supporters were promised never materialised! One could write a whole book on the different strips after that, but I will spare the reader that. At least the new strip seemed to bring the Town luck as in 1974, in their new strip, they were promoted to the top division as runners up to Middlesbrough, albeit 15 points behind! One unusual record was struck when in the FA Cup 4th round at home to Bradford City, Luton went ahead after 15 seconds with a City own goal by Jim Fretwell, one of the fastest own goals ever! Amazingly as we went up, Manchester United went down in 21st place with only 32 points. A famous goal that might have been crucial in United's relegation was scored by Denis Law, who was by then a City player having been transferred from United! It, in fact, didn't influence the final league positions and United's relegation.

However, we only lasted in the top league for one season. In 1975, we were relegated back to Div 2 while, unsurprisingly, Manchester United were promoted back up to division 1 as champions. They have been in the top flight ever since.

In that same 1974 promotion season, our centre half John Faulkner was obviously concussed after a heavy collision with a team-mate but insisted on playing on for the last 30 minutes to ensure the 1-1 at WBA in the penultimate game. It was long before the head injury and concussion protocols were introduced, and there has always been speculation that head injuries and even heading itself might lead to dementia in footballers later in life. Remember also that in that era, the footballs were made of leather and were very heavy, especially when wet. John Faulkner played 209 games from 1972 to 1978 and was extremely dependable. Eric Morecambe apparently missed the last game of the promotion season with a heavy cold and is reputed to have said that he would have to celebrate with cough mixture instead of champagne.

The 74 World Cup in West Germany saw Italy lose out, finishing 3rd in their group behind Poland and Argentina. England did worse failing to qualify for the final stages after an amazingly one-sided match against Poland in which they had most of the play but were denied by the visiting goalkeeper Jan Tomaszewski, who Brian Clough had famously called a clown! Norman Hunter, replacing an ageing Bobby Moore, had erred to give Poland the lead, and although Allan Clarke equalised with a penalty, the winning goal that was needed if England were to qualify never came. In a group match, East Germany beat their neighbours, the West, 1-0 but both qualified for the next round. East Germany were eliminated, while the West team went on with wins over Yugoslavia, Sweden and Poland. In the final, Germany won 2-1 over the Netherlands, who had included Johan Cruyff, probably the world's best player of the era. The Dutch had opened the scoring in the second minute through a Neeskens penalty awarded by English referee Jack Taylor. The Germans then equalised through a Breitner penalty, but a characteristic Muller goal in the 43rd minute won it for the Germans. It had been the only World Cup or European Championships for which East Germany entered or qualified as a separate nation before unification in 1990. A feature of the German team for several years had been the telepathic understanding between Beckenbauer and Muller, friends and roommates. Muller won most of the individual awards available and was described as the original "fox in the box". Sadly Muller had problems in retirement with firstly alcoholism and, in his later years Alzheimer's.

Chapter 41 - Season 1974/75

The 74/75 season had, as usual, started with the FA Charity Shield, for which we got tickets. It featured league champions Leeds versus Cup winners, Liverpool. It was a fierce affair noted for the red cards given to both Billy Bremner and Kevin Keegan for fighting and many horrific tackles as well. The match ended in a 1-1 draw, but Liverpool won the penalty shoot-out 6-5. The managers were worthy of note, both Bob Paisley for Liverpool and Brian Clough for Leeds being new to the posts, succeeding Bill Shankly and Don Revie, respectively. Clough, of course, lasted only 44 days in that post before moving on to 2nd division Notts Forest and entering an unbelievably successful 18 years! In two years, he got Forest promoted and then league champions. He helped them to win two successive League Cups, one at our expense, of course, and two successive European Cups. He was a controversial character who would never have been considered seriously for the England managership, but it was always said that he was "the greatest manager that England never had". It was the week before the opening Division 1 matches which in Luton's case was home to Liverpool and which we lost 1-2, having taken the lead. In fact, it took us until the 10th match to record a win, and that was the only one in the first 21 games. So by Christmas, we were 6 points adrift and clearly heading for relegation. In 1974 Luton manager Harry Haslam had signed teenage twin brothers called Futcher, both from Chester, for a combined fee of £125,000. The one Paul was a classy central defender, the other Ron a centre forward who scored 40 goals in 120 league games for Luton. In only his second appearance, Ron scored a hat trick against Wolves and raised hopes that we might escape relegation, but it was not to be. Ron later went on to have a long spell in the North American League with Minnesota Kicks. In 1974 another landmark was that while Harry Haslam continued as manager, there was the signing of David Pleat as a coach, aided by Uruguayan Danny Bergara. They had a particular role in bringing on youngsters, and from then on, I have always been impressed with our youth system, which has produced so many great players, many of whom naturally feature in this book.

On another Saturday, there was unwelcome news that Chelsea fans, despite drawing 1-1 with us, took it on themselves to torch and burn out their train home. On another occasion in Paris, Chelsea fans prevented a black man from boarding the metro train, chanting, "We're racist, we're racist, and that's the way we like it." It was a period when, unfortunately, hooliganism was still rife, and the influence of racism added to the problems.

I remember one special match in that season when although we were heading down to Division 2, we beat a very strong Leeds team 2-1, whose next match was to play Barcelona in the semifinal of the European Cup. We followed it with another win over Arsenal, this time 2-0. Leeds got to the 1975 European Cup final, but they lost 2-0 to Bayern Munich. However, their supporters rioted in Paris, and the club was banned for 4 years, later reduced to two. I only went to some of the away games, my professional commitments restricting the possibilities but also, to be honest, I was fearful of the crowd violence that was unfortunately always likely to be there. Millwall had already shown what could happen when in April 1974, they had caused serious trouble at our Oak Road end, including three stabbings. In spite of it all going on around them, our players concentrated enough to draw 2-2. It highlighted the continuing dreadful reputation of Millwall supporters. Much of their origins were blamed on their location in Dockland and the consequent physical and potentially aggressive nature of their supporters. Their firm earned the title of The Millwall Bushwackers and became known as one of the most notorious hooligan gangs in England. As a result, the FA closed their ground, the Den, on five separate occasions and inflicted numerous fines on the club. In the 80s, they were known to have close links with the far-right National Front. One away match I did attend in 1975 was the penultimate match of the season at Birmingham City, where very surprisingly, we won 4-1 although facing relegation. Presumably, I wanted to savour our last away match in the top league before relegation was confirmed on the last day when fellow strugglers Spurs won 4-2 against Leeds, who were by now in that season's European Cup final. Our relegation meant that we faced the well-known phenomenon of a club finding themselves in a lower division having to pay players who were still on higher league contracts. Another character signed at the time was Pasquale Fuccillo, a local boy, the son of Italian immigrants who lived in Bedford. Bedford had a large Italian community who had come over in the late 1940 and especially in the 50s from the villages of Southern Italy, the Mezzogiorno, to work mostly in the brickworks. Fuccillo, always known as Lil, was eligible to play for both England and Italy but sadly didn't make it for either. However, he scored 24 goals in 60 appearances from midfield for Luton in spite of twice breaking his leg in the same place and was immensely popular. He was in the team that won the 2nd division in 1982 under David Pleat. He had a very short spell as manager after Ricky Hill was sacked. Another midfielder, local boy Andy King was also signed in 1974. Unfortunately, after two successful seasons, Andy had to be sold to Everton for a derisory £35,000, and similarly, Barry Butlin, our top scorer of the period, went to Nottingham Forest for £120,000. I realised then, if I hadn't known it before that, sadly, Luton was always going to be a selling club. In 1974/75, our first Division 1 match saw us at home to Liverpool. We took the lead but lost 2-1. In the summer, the Futcher twins had been signed and from December were regulars in the team. The fact that none of our players scored more than seven league goals in that season largely explains where the problem lay.

Who can forget Ricky Hill, part of Luton's most successful ever team, helping them to that League (Littlewoods) Cup victory over Arsenal in 1988? He, a local boy born in Cricklewood, was spotted by David Pleat and joined Luton in 1976 and made his debut against Bristol Rovers at 17 years of age. He went on to score 54 goals from midfield in 436 games. He deservedly won 3 England caps, although it should have been a lot more. His first cap was in 1982, a 2-2 draw with Denmark in Copenhagen, incidentally Bobby Robson's first game as England manager. His second was against West Germany in the same year, which ended in a 1-2 defeat and lastly, in 1986, a 4-0 win over Egypt. Finally, in 1989 he went abroad to spend one year at Le Havre in France before returning to join David Pleat at Leicester. In 1972 he set up a local black football club called Ebony FC.

We also had an Australian international centre forward, Adrian Alston, who scored a few goals but could not prevent us from being relegated along with Carlisle and Chelsea.

Chapter 42 - Seasons 1975/76 to 1978/79

In season 75/76, now down in Division 2, we managed to finish 7th. The penultimate match of the season was marked by the debut of Ricky Hill, a match against Bristol Rovers when Ricky scored his first goal for the club.

Eric Morecambe had resigned amid boardroom disagreements and was followed by three other directors leaving Denis Mortimer at the helm. Denis was very unpopular for seriously supporting the move to Milton Keynes. A serious cash crisis resulted in the sale of Peter Anderson to a Belgian club Royal Antwerp for a giveaway price of £55,000, about half of what we were hoping to get. Peter, who had come from Hendon, incidentally after further spells in the USA, finished up at Millwall and then finally back at Hendon. He made 181 league appearances for Luton and scored 34 goals. The next season 76/77, we managed to finish 6th, only four points behind a promotion place. I recall towards the end of the season a 5-0 win over Carlisle with 5 different players being on the scoresheet.

1976 had been a year of tumultuous events in Italy. The PCI (Partita Communista Italiana), led by Enrico Berlinguer, was on the ascendancy gaining over 30 percent of the votes in the general election and having more than 2 million members. Obviously, it had close links to Russia, and for a while, it was feared that Italy might topple into the orbit of the Soviet Union. Unfortunately, the unions organized many protests and strikes, with up to 40,000 workers marching through the city of Fiat, Turin. In spite of it, Fiat was on the ascendancy doing well in global sales.

What do I remember about 77/78? Early in the season was a memorable 3rd match in which we achieved a 7-1 win over Charlton with Jimmy Husband scoring four of the goals! It was towards the end of his Luton career, by which time he had scored 44 league goals. Later on, we scored four without reply against Sheffield United and also won 4-0 over Blackpool. The goals were well spread around, with no individual scoring more than Ron Futcher's ten and Jimmy Husband's seven. Unfortunately, it became necessary to sell swashbuckling and immensely popular fullback Steve Buckley to Derby after four years at Luton.

At Luton, the news was of the departure of manager Harry Haslam in 1978 after 6 years and his replacement by David Pleat. Of course, David went on to be one of the most successful and charismatic managers in the club's history in his two spells. In 1978 we finished 13th but amazingly only one point above the relegated clubs. Pleat brought in numerous new players, but an important one was undoubtedly striker Bob Hatton who came from Blackpool, and it was hoped would help to progress fellow forward Brian Stein, who had arrived during the previous season from Edgware Town. Another of the real stars of the era was winger David Moss who had joined from Swindon for £110,000 at the end of the 77/78 season and scored two goals on his debut in a 6-1 win over Oldham. I remember him vividly as a player who could regularly do really exciting things. In 221 league games in his seven-year spell and even as a winger, he managed to score 88 league goals as a Hatter, although 24 of them were from the penalty spot! It was a good goalscoring record for a winger. He was the regular corner kick and penalty kick taker and very reliable. Finally, he left in 1985 on a free transfer and returned to Swindon Town.

In the early eighties, I decided to promote myself to become a season ticket holder. The seat I acquired was right by the corner flag at the Oak Road end of the now all-seater Bobbers stand, and I remember the man from the ticket office saying that it was a great seat, so close to the corner flag that I could pinch David Moss's backside as he prepared to take corners!

It was true as there had never been much space between the pitch and the stands at Kenilworth Road, and this had been a handicap, especially for the long throw specialists who need a good run-up.

An early game in 78/79 was a 7-1 victory over Cardiff City, but again only heralded 18th place and a close call with relegation.

Chapter 43 - World Cups and England Managers

The year 1976 was the time for the qualifiers for the World Cup to be played in Argentina in 1978. A key game that year took England, managed by Don Revie since 1974, to Rome to play an Italian side with six Juventus players in their team. The referee was the Israeli Abraham Klein. He had not been chosen for the 1974 finals after the terrorist attack on the Israeli athletes at the 1972 Olympic Games made it possible that he could have been a target for a further terrorist attack.

England lost 2-0 to an own goal and a Bettega header and, in the end, failed to qualify on goal difference from the Italians. It meant that England had failed to qualify for the second World Cup running. The fact that Argentina, the home nation, won by 3-1 against the Netherlands didn't seem too important to me. Two things come to mind, the ticker tape and confetti welcome for the hosts and Mario Kempes scoring 2 of the three goals in the final and finishing up as the top goalscorer with 6 goals, followed by Dutchman Rob Rensenbrink with 5 goals.

Major international news had been the resignation of Don Revie as England manager in 1977. At the end of 1969, Revie was awarded an OBE. However, he was later found guilty of offering bribes to other managers and players and given a 10-year ban, which was later lifted. His reputation was in tatters, and he was never forgiven. He took up a lucrative post in the United Arab Emirates reputed to be worth £340,000 for a four-year contract, a salary that made him the highest-paid manager in world football.

Revie was succeeded by Ron Greenwood, who had been manager of West Ham for 13 years. He brought stability, respectability, and class, if not great, results between 1977 and 1982. He got England to the 1982 World Cup in Spain, but they failed to get past the second group phase, and he then resigned to be succeeded by Bobby Robson, who did eight years and took England as far as the World Cup semifinal in Italy in 1990. Having already received a CBE in 1990, he received a knighthood in 2002.

Season 78/79 for the Hatters started with three big home wins, 6-1, 3-0, and 7-1! However, our away form didn't match that, and we finished up in a dangerous 18th position. Brian Stein was the top scorer with fourteen goals, followed by David Moss with 13. In 79/80, David did even better with 24 goals to Bob Hatton's 18 but it only heralded a creditable 6th place. Goalkeeper Milija Aleksic of Yugoslav origin ("elastic" as he was nicknamed) was transferred to Spurs in December 1978 and played in the two matches of the 1981 final against Manchester City, the ones characterized by the fall and rise of Ricky Villa. He was replaced by Jake Findlay, who came from

Aston Villa, was very dependable, and stayed until 1985 when he was transferred to Swindon. Luton, however, finished 18th in 78/79, very narrowly avoiding relegation.

Chapter 44 - Referees

How could one write a football-related book without featuring a referee? I will cite two; the first is Roger Kirkpatrick, who refereed in the professional game in the 60s and 70s. What made him so memorable was firstly his appearance with a stocky build, almost bald head, and very prominent bushy sideburns. It earned him the nickname "Pickwick." Secondly, his ability on all possible occasions to run backwards, something he could amazingly do just as fast as most could run forwards. The crowd would anticipate his backward runs and loudly cheered each one! The other would have to be Italian Pierluigi Collina. He won the "Best Referee of the Year" title on six consecutive occasions and is considered to have been the best referee of all time. He had an economics degree from his home town Bologna University and refereed for 14years in Serie A and for 10 years was FIFA listed. His appearance was characteristic, with complete alopecia (baldness) adding to his stern and ferocious look. His nickname was inevitably Kojak! Over the years, he was selected for all the most important games, including the Olympics, World Cup, UEFA Cup, and Champions League finals. After retiring as an active referee, he has been Chairman of the FIFA referees committee.

Chapter 45 - David Pleat

David deserves to be singled out for his many contributions to Luton Town. He was a player for us from 1964 to 1967, making 70 league appearances and scoring 9 goals. He went on to play for three more clubs before he moved into coaching, initially in 1971 with Nuneaton Borough and later with Luton. He became manager at Luton in 1978. His first managerial spell ended when he was poached by Tottenham Hotspur in 1986 and took Mitchell Thomas, a local boy and one of our most talented fullbacks, with him. This alienated him from many supporters, but by the time he came back for a second spell in 1991, he had largely been forgiven. In fact, Thomas, at the age of 30, came back to Luton for a second and longer spell in 1994. Pleaty led Luton to promotion to the top league as Champions in season 81/82 and to the FA Cup semifinal against Everton in 1985. Most importantly, he was responsible for a very attacking and attractive style of football which has partly continued to this day and is what the fans now demand. It is certain the Luton team that was to go on and win the 1988 final under Ray Harford was largely Pleat's team. His short spell at Spurs was pretty successful, including a 3rd place, FA Cup final, and League Cup semifinal. Although no actual trophies were won again, there was much comment and coverage about the style and the attacking football Spurs played, helped by lone striker Clive Allen's 49 goals. In fact, Glenn Moore writing in the Independent, described the play as "some of the best attacking football of the last two decades."

Some dubious off-the-field behaviour involving alleged kerb-crawling, later on, forced Pleaty to leave Spurs, who at the time also had Terry Venables lined up to succeed him. He did return to Luton (via Leicester) but was less successful, the Hatters being relegated in his first season back and consequentially missing out on the newly created Premier League. He did get us to an FA Cup semifinal in 1994, where we lost 2-0 to Chelsea at Wembley. Luton from a league below were no match for Chelsea, but the highlight was the Chelsea fans giving Luton's Kerry Dixon, of course one of their star ex-players, a fantastic reception. In 1998, Pleaty returned once again to Spurs as Director of Football, his eye for a player making him a valuable asset. Since then, he has been very much a media man writing for newspapers, especially the Guardian and Daily Mail, summarising on radio and TV, and very much in demand as an after-dinner speaker.

Chapter 46 - Artificial (Plastic) Pitches

I was often taken to QPR at Loftus Road by their orthopod, another surgeon with whom I worked at Charing Cross. He got me access to the director's box and player areas. The QPR manager in 79/80 was Tommy Docherty "(the Doc"). He took over at a time when QPR had just been relegated to the Second Division and got the team to fifth place and to within four points of promotion back to the first division. I remember after a particularly bad home defeat, 4-0 to Ipswich, the Doc found us both in the dressing room and said, "the trouble with this club is there are too many f…..g doctors"! One thing I learnt about sports medicine from one of their goalkeepers with a dislocated finger was that if a player had just come off the field with an injury, they had very high adrenaline levels, and you could do almost anything to them, however painful it was. The next day most of them were like babies, and even the site of the smallest needle would cause them to go pale and sweaty and panic!

Any Luton supporter of a certain age will remember the frequently terrible state of our pitch, especially at the Oak Road end in those days. It was not helped by a slope towards it, so that that end was often a quagmire. It must be stressed that in that era, pitches at many grounds were often very muddy and barely fit for play.

So the idea of an artificial turf pitch was very attractive. However, the only thing that they had in common with real grass was their appearance! They had been pioneered in the 60s in the USA, first using Astroturf in the Houston Astrodome. Not everyone was impressed. A baseball star Dick Allen said, "If a horse won't eat it, I don't want to play on it."

I particularly remember some matches on the artificial pitches. The first was at Queens Park Rangers, where they had just installed the first Omni-Turf pitch in 1981. It was like a carpet laid on top of a thick layer of concrete with only sand to act as a cushion. The inaugural match was played on it against the Town on the 1st September 1981. Although Luton did not yet have their artificial pitch, their players seemed to cope very well. The ball certainly travelled fast on the surface, and Ricky Hill really stood out with his amazing ball control, deft touches and accurate distribution. He helped Luton to a 2-1 win, the goals coming from Aizlewood and Hill himself. Hill's silky skills were particularly suited to the plastic pitch, which later was installed by three other clubs, Luton, Oldham and Preston. Ricky Hill won three England caps, his first also being the first for manager Bobby Robson. He was only the fourth black player to play for England after Viv Anderson, Laurie Cunningham and Cyrille Regis.

Luton installed their artificial pitch in the summer of 1985 using Sporturf International from the En Tout Cas company. This was a multi-layered surface that consisted of base levels of broken stones and bitumen macadam with a novel drainage friendly texture. It was topped with sand and then the artificial surface itself. It cost £350,000, including installation. A match against Liverpool in 1986 had ended 4-1 to the Hatters, a match that is remembered for a Mike Newell hat-trick and many comments and groans from then Liverpool manager Kenny Dalglish about the pitch! Later another memorable match was also at home to Liverpool, which Luton won 3-0 in the FA Cup. Dalglish had again moaned and said afterwards, "on an artificial pitch, you get an artificial game". It was obvious that the ball bounced much higher on those pitches, encouraging better ball control and the skilful players who were able to keep the ball more on the ground. The bounce was often so high that goal kicks could bounce over the opposite crossbar. The physical effect on the players was a high incidence of friction burns, but whether there were more or less muscle and joint injuries remains debatable. Goalies always wore tracksuit bottoms to protect themselves from potential burns. Oldham, under Joe Royle's managership, profited from their artificial pitch by achieving promotion to the top division as champions, a 32 game unbeaten run, including a League Cup final and an FA Cup semi-final in 1990 against Manchester United. The latter was played at Maine Road Manchester, and the Oldham supporters sang loudly, "We can play on grass as well".

The artificial pitches were widely criticised on the basis that they gave a team with one an unfair advantage. There was plenty of evidence for that being true. Preston were the last club to profit and prospered for a while afterwards. In their first season, they won a promotion to Division Three. But the others, including Luton, suffered from a variety of relegations, boardroom issues and financial crises in that era. The QPR pitch was removed in 1988, the year that the FA banned them. The Luton and Oldham ones were removed in the summer of 1991 and the Preston one in 1994. The last match on a plastic pitch was a Third Division Play-Off semi-final second leg between Preston and Torquay. In the end, when Preston had qualified for Wembley after extra time, many of their supporters swarmed onto the pitch and ripped up sections of it! By 1995 the artificial pitches had all been removed from and banned from all football league grounds. Away from the football league, they were permitted in the lower leagues and in the FA Cup. Later on, there was a renewed interest in those types of pitches, especially with 3G technology, which then indeed did get FIFA and UEFA approval. In 2007 England played on one in the Luznicki Stadium, Moscow, in the qualifiers for Euro 2008. They lost 2-1, and after losing a thrilling game, 2-3 to Croatia at Wembley, failed to qualify for the tournament proper. The pitches are particularly popular in countries with extremely cold climates. Their use is still accompanied to this day by fear of more injuries and scepticism with psychological fears from visiting teams. However, they seem destined to stay longer than did the first generation.

I went to the 1979 Cup final between Arsenal and Manchester United. It had to have been one of the most exciting finishes ever with Arsenal 2-0 up through Brian Talbot and Frank Stapleton. In the 86th minute, United's Gordon McQueen scored their first goal. Then they equalised through Sammy McIlroy before Arsenal's Alan Sunderland scored the winner in the last minute. It was from a move started by Liam Brady and was to be one of Brady's last games for Arsenal before signing for Juventus. Brady had come to the Bianconeri's attention when he played for a victorious Arsenal against them in the Cup Winners Cup semi-final.

At Luton in July 1979, a significant arrival signed by David Pleat was physiotherapist John Sheridan. He stayed until 1986, when he followed David Pleat to Tottenham. In addition to his undoubted skills as a physio, he was characterised by a permanent limp acquired after a serious accident when he was 14. That limp made him very noticeable as he ran onto the field and aroused unusual attention and banter by fans, especially those of the opposing team!

Chapter 47 - Three Foreigners at Juventus

The 1980s were one the most successful periods in Juventus history and a time that I seemed to have been able to watch them on many occasions. So I have singled out three of the greatest foreigners to have played for them then. I am not including Charles or Sivori, who have been described earlier. Nor the many that came later, including Deschamps, Zidane, Nedved, Trezeguet, Ibrahimovic, Higuain and Ronaldo. The first was Liam Brady. Juventus had signed him from Arsenal in 1980 for a reported fee of £500,000, and in the two seasons he was there, he helped them to two top league championships. He will be remembered for his very cultured left foot, which he used to perfection from his attacking midfield position. He always seemed to have time on the ball and was a master at scoring free and penalty kicks. Unfortunately for him, Juventus signed the great Frenchman Michel Platini in 1982. It was obviously a great coup for the club, but it meant exceeding the permitted number of two foreigners per club allowed at that time in Italy. Contrast that with the latest statistics showing that nearly 60% of players in Serie A are foreigners! That does not include the "oriundi" players born abroad to Italian parents. So Liam had to be sacrificed and was transferred to Sampdoria of Genoa. Over his career, he won 72 caps for Ireland. Many overseas players overcame the rules ban by adopting Italian nationality, including Sivori and Camoranesi born Argentinians. Mostly they were of South American ancestry. Dare I say that while immensely skilful and successful, they both retained most of the worst features of Argentinian footballers! Brady being a proud Irishman, had never for a moment considered nationality change.

In 1982, both Platini and Boniek joined Juventus, and both could justify a chapter each but suffice it to say that apart from his amazing skills, Platini was renowned for rarely conforming to the required team dress of blazer and trousers when on club duty and always played with his shirt outside his shorts. There is plenty more to be said about Platini; sadly, not all good. Midfielder Zbigniew Boniek I will remember as one who lit up a cigarette whenever possible and certainly on the coaches to and from games. Smoking was not unusual among the players at that time, and most of them had a particular favourite brand, surprisingly mostly French such as Gauloises! He also was characterised by his moustache. Hirsute players were a rarity in those days and, of course, not a tattoo in sight! Zibi was known as a big match player, producing his best performances in the floodlight European evening matches. Indeed, his president Gianni Agnelli called him the "Bello di notte", a play on the film Belle de Jour. He had come to Juve after a seven-year spell in his native country at Widzew Lodz. He won 80 caps for Poland, scoring 24 goals, and scored 15 goals in 81games for Juve. He played for his country in three successive World Cups, those of 1978, 82 and 86. He was a very talented player, but at Juve, he was helped by having so many outstanding players around him. He was very much a playmaker as well as a goalscorer. The goal he is most remembered for was the winner in the 2-1 victory over Porto in the final of the Cup winners cup in 1984. Juve went on to win the super cup against Liverpool 2-0, with Zibi scoring both goals. He finished his playing career at Roma. He had a short spell as manager of Poland. Latterly he has headed the Polish football association and is a vice president of UEFA. It was probably the period of Platini when he was at his best, a time when he was generally considered to be the best player in the world. He was often seen as the club's poster boy and won the Ballon d'Or in 1983, 84 and 85. His passing ability was second to none, and his ability from free kicks and penalties was exemplary. He was rewarded twice by the French government with the Chevalier and later Officier of the Legion d'Honneur. A feat was to be the top scorer in Serie A in three consecutive seasons. As an international, he got 72 caps and scored 41 goals, an amazing record for a midfielder. To complete the full house, he captained France to victory in the 1984 European championships and 3rd place in the 1986 World Cup. Amazingly in spite of so many accolades, he was criticised by some coaches for lack of stamina and neglecting defensive duties! His role in the Heysel Stadium match in 1985 is described later. A long period in administration included the organising of the 1998 World Cup held in France, service on many EUFA committees and rise to the UEFA presidency in 2006. He didn't stand for the FIFA presidency in 2015 when Sepp Blatter finally resigned amid the corruption scandals. His administrative days were finally sullied by his ban from FIFA organised football for ethics violations and his possible role in the award to Qatar of the 2022 World Cup. His ban was to last from 2015 to 2023.

March 1980 saw the introduction of shirt sponsorship, and for the Hatters, the first to take it up was Dunstable based motor company Tricentrol. They did it for two years in a deal worth £50,000. Many companies have followed them, but I particularly remember Easyjet for as well as the orange livery on their planes and on our shirts, they also had advertising around the ground. They also paid Brentford to advertise on the roofs of their stands, so they were very visible from the planes on their final approach to Heathrow airport! Of course, the airline had quite a bit in common with the football club, especially the orange colour and its headquarters in Luton.

Chapter 48 - Kidnapping and Terrorism in Italy

Italy had suffered from a wave of kidnappings and terrorism in the late 1960s and 1970s. Especially the children and wives of the rich in the north were targeted. They were taken, and then large ransoms were demanded. Turin seemed to be particularly affected, presumably due to the relative economic success led by Fiat. The risks led to expensive cars being left in the garage while smaller, less significant ones were used to drive the famous! They often wore disguises or cover-ups to make themselves less obvious. A special driving style was adopted where the driver would slow right up if approaching a red light in the distance, so they didn't actually ever have to stop until they reached their destination! A number of the drivers would have a bulge in their hip pocket, suggesting a small pistol in case of need.

April 1969 was when a terrorist bomb wounded 6 people at the Fiat Pavilion at a Milan Fair. Later in the year, a bomb exploded in Milan's Piazza Fontana, killing 17 and wounding 88 more. Unfortunately, the Brigate Rosse (Red Brigades) group came into prominence at that time. They were a far-left armed organisation. They aimed to destabilise Italy by sabotage attacks on factories and also by bank robberies and kidnappings. Turin, with the Fiat plants and Juventus football club, was thought to be a prime target.

Those years, characterised by social and political turmoil, were known as the "Anni di Piombo" (the years of lead). Mafia linked terrorism was active in Sicily and the southern mainland perpetrated by the Cosa Nostra in Sicily, the Camorra in Campania, the 'Ndrangheta in Calabria, and the Sacra Corona Unita in Puglia. There were many more incidents, such as on the 2nd August 1980 when a bomb exploded in Bologna railway station, killing 85 people and injuring over 200 more. It was first attributed to the Red Brigades but was finally found to be perpetrated by a neo-fascist group called Nuclei Armati Rivoluzionari (Armed Revolutionary Nuclei). The Red Brigades infamously were also responsible for the killing of Aldo Moro's bodyguards in central Rome and the murder of the former prime minister himself. Nearly two months after the kidnapping, his body was found finally in the boot of a Renault 4. Terrorism in Italy is still commemorated with a concert in the main square of Bologna, the Piazza Maggiore, every year on the date of that railway station massacre.

Chapter 49 - Ajax 1981

An interesting excursion in September 1981 was to watch Ajax play Spurs in the Cup Winners Cup. In 1934, Ajax had moved from the Het Houten stadium to the De Meer Stadium in east Amsterdam, both designed by architect and Ajax board member Jordanus (Daan) Roodenburgh. The new stadium could accommodate 29,500 people, and Ajax continued to play there until 1996. Big European and national fixtures were more often played at the Olympic Stadium, which could accommodate about twice that number of spectators. In 1996 they moved to the newly built Amsterdam Arena, which later in 2018 was renamed the Johan Cruyff Arena. It was designed by another Dutch architect Rob Schuurman. It had a retractable roof which as so often had a negative influence on the growth of the pitch due to the lack of sunlight and fresh air.

A friend and colleague, a gynaecologist, and I decided to go, lured by the fun of a trip to Amsterdam, such an exciting city, as well as by the football. Much was expected from these two teams with reputations for exciting football, and it was Tottenham who showed their prowess with outstanding performance and a thoroughly deserved 3-1 victory. The Spurs played their best football in the first half as they established a two-goal lead. They took the lead after twenty minutes through Mark Falco, who was causing the home defence numerous problems. After 34 minutes, he earned Spurs a corner, and from Tony Galvin's kick, he added Spurs' second. Midway through the second half, Ossie Ardiles fed Ricky Villa with a free run on goal to score the third. Ajax immediately responded to pull one goal back, and while they tried to reduce the deficit, goalie Ray Clemence was at his very best, making great saves on a couple of occasions. Spurs saw out the match for an excellent win. The friend I went with seemed to always know the best bars and clubs wherever we were and so a very good, really unforgettable evening was had.

The result in this first leg made the return match something of a formality, which Spurs went on to win 3 – 0 with all the goals coming in the second half, scored by Tony Galvin, Marc Falco and Ossie Ardiles.

Chapter 50 - Season 1981/82

My gynae friend also lured me to Frankfurt to see Eintracht play Spurs in the second leg quarter-final of the Cup Winners Cup in March 1982. That first leg ended 2-1 to Eintracht with an away goal by Glenn Hoddle, while a 2-0 victory to Spurs in the home leg ensured Spurs passage to the semis, where they sadly lost to Barcelona. Again I got the distinct feeling that the possibilities in the city after the match were more exciting for my friend than the match itself!

81/82 was a most memorable season for Luton as we got promotion to the top flight as champions and thus began the finest era in our history. The goals came especially from Brian Stein, Steve White and David Moss. Mal Donaghy had arrived from Larne in Northern Ireland in 1978 and also scored nine goals in his ever-present 42 appearances that season. He came for the bargain price of £20,000 and was a real stalwart of the defence until ten years later, Manchester United swooped for him with an irresistible offer of £650,000. That was a hefty fee at the time for a 31-year-old defender. At only 5ft 9in, he was rather short for a central defender but still managed to score 21 goals. He made 408 league appearances while at Luton, as well as gaining 91 caps for Northern Ireland. He was, of course, a member of our team that won promotion to the top league in 1982 as well as the famous Littlewoods Cup victory of 1988. He also helped Luton to their highest ever top league position, 7th in 86/87.

A big transfer had taken place in 1981 with Brian (Nobby) Horton coming to Luton from Brighton and being made captain. At the same time, Tony Grealish went in the opposite direction to Brighton, where he was the captain in the 1983 FA Cup final against Manchester United, who, after a 2-2 draw, won comfortably 4-0 in the replay. Our ace marksman of the era was Brian Stein, with 21 goals, while Steve White had also managed 18. Brian later played alongside Paul Walsh and Mick Harford at different times. Stein was another of my many favourites. He did not have the build of a typical English centre forward but made up for it with strength and immense skill both as a provider and particularly as a goal scorer. He would often receive the ball with his back to the opposing goal making it difficult for defenders to rob him of the ball. He would then spin round in either direction and unerringly hit the back of the net. He played altogether over 400 games for us and scored 130 league goals. In spite of his South African birth, he was eligible for England and played alongside Paul Walsh to earn his one cap against France in Paris in February 1984. Unfortunately, we lost 2-0 to unsurprisingly two second half Michel Platini goals. He was part of a famous football family. His younger brother Mark also played for Luton, while Edwin, his older brother, played for Barnet. Surprisingly Brian left Luton after the Cup win in 1988 to try his luck with Caen and then Annecy, both in France. His time there was marked by the fact that on 31st May 1989, he scored one of the very few hat tricks by an English player in a major European league. In fact, I think he was the last till Jadon Sancho repeated the feat for Borussia Dortmund against SC Paderborn in 2020. I think on balance; I would have to put Brian Stein at the top of the Town goal scorers' talents!

Paul Walsh was a diminutive but very skilful striker. Signed from Charlton for £400,000, he was sold two years later to Liverpool for £700,000 before playing for a few more top-flight clubs, especially Tottenham Hotspur and Manchester City. He earned five England caps, and after retiring at the age of 34 after a cruciate ligament rupture, he has found his niche as a successful TV pundit. He is also in demand as an after-dinner speaker.

There were a few memorable games that I got to see, including early in the 81/82 season when we beat our closest rivals Watford 4-1 at home, possibly our biggest victory over them. Watford conceded two penalties from which Moss scored, and Brian Stein scored the other two. Being six days after my birthday, I treated it as a belated and very welcome birthday present. In April, I went to an away match at Cambridge, where I must say to my surprise, there was quite a bit of fighting on the normally tranquil meadows before the match. The result was 1-1. Then there was a home match in which we beat Shrewsbury 4-1 to clinch promotion, and finally, happily for me, a fine 2-1 win at Chelsea. So we ended the season with 14 unbeaten games having had a run earlier in the season of 12 unbeaten and all season only losing four games. It was wonderful to finish as champions, eight points ahead of 2nd placed Watford.

The season 81/82 had also been noted for it being the season when 3 instead of 2 points were awarded for a win. It was supposed to encourage more attacking play, but I never believed that to be the case. Sadly, it was a season when Aston Villa fans rioted in Brussels, and UEFA issued their severest warning yet, threatening to ban English clubs from Europe.

Chapter 51 - 1982 World Cup in Spain

Italy won the 1982 World Cup in Spain with a team containing six Juventus players, Zoff, Cabrini, Gentile, Scirea, Tardelli and Rossi. As I have noted, Bettega sadly missed the triumph due to a knee injury. Paolo Rossi was only cleared to play after a ban due to his involvement in the Totonero betting scandal was miraculously reduced from three years to two. In the finals, Italy qualified in 2nd place in Group 1 behind Poland, in spite of only drawing their three matches against Poland, Peru and the Cameroons. Meanwhile, England topped their group. There was then a second group phase, in which West Germany knocked out England and the hosts Spain, while Italy knocked out both Argentina and Brazil. They beat Argentina 2-1, the striking feature being Diego Maradona man marked by Claudio Gentile by means fair but mostly foul. In fact, Gentile committed 23 fouls on Maradona alone but remained on the field to the end, showing how different refereeing standards were in those days! If nothing else, he enhanced his reputation as one of the most ruthless but effective defenders of all time. The next tie against Brazil was one of the greatest and most memorable World Cup matches ever. A Rossi hat trick for the Azzurri with Brazil only scoring two gained the victory by one goal. In the semi-final, Italy beat Poland 2-0 with two more Paolo Rossi goals, while West Germany beat France 5-4 in a penalty shoot-out after drawing 3-3. The final played in Real Madrid's Santiago Bernabeu stadium went to Italy 3-1 with goals from Rossi, then Marco Tardelli with his famous celebration, and finally Alessandro Altobelli of Inter Milan. So Rossi finished as the golden boot with 6 goals, one ahead of Karl-Heinz Rummenigge. The Italian manager was Enzo Bearzot in the middle of an 11-year spell as National coach. The victory was the first Italy victory since 1938, and in this final, the President Sandro Pertini was regularly seen on the television screen getting as excited as the most enthusiastic fan. 5 red cards were given in the tournament, not surprisingly 2 to Argentina, including 1 to Maradona, but very surprisingly one to our own Mal Donaghy for shoving a Spanish player Camacho. As far as I can discover, Mal was only sent off once playing for Luton in his 408 league appearances.

Chapter 52 - Season 1982/83

That season was noted for a September result when a Paul Walsh hat trick gave us a 5-3 win over Notts County, and later in the month, it was Brian Stein's turn to score a hat trick in a 5-0 win over Brighton. Brian Horton was back for Luton against his old team and was inspired, but for some reason, Brighton chose not to play future Hatter Steve Foster. An away game at Liverpool ended in a 3-3 draw, Stein 2 and Moss scoring the goals, but the notable feature was that the Hatters had to play three different players in goal. They started with regular keeper Jake Findlay, but when he was injured, Kirk Stevens, a full back, took his place, and he was also later replaced by Mal Donaghy. There was apparently no goalkeeper on the substitute's bench. Each goalie conceded one goal, without which, of course, the Hatters would have had a memorable victory. A 1-0 win over Watford at Christmas was particularly welcome, easing our problems a bit at the foot of the table. Luther Blissett had missed a sitter justifying his "Luther Missit" tag. Paul Walsh got two more hat tricks, away to West Ham and at home to Swansea, before the season ended in last gasp survival. We hung on for 18th place, saved by the famous last game Raddy Antic goal at Maine Road described in Chapter 61.

Chapter 53 - Season 1983/84

83/84 season ended with us in 16th place and safe, but only 3 points above the relegation places. We had been as high as 5th in early December. We scored 4 goals three times, but our results against Manchester United, losing 2-0 away and 5-0 at home, as well as a 6-0 loss at Anfield, summed up our inability to cope with the best. Even United only finished in 4th place, 6 points behind champions Liverpool. Brian Stein and Paul Walsh were our leading scorers again, but only with 11 league goals for Walsh and 9 for Stein. There had been boardroom issues with chairman Denis Mortimer threatening to sell our England stars, Walsh, Stein and Hill. There was a consortium of about 40 local businessmen who wanted to buy the club and move it to Milton Keynes. The club was losing about £5000 a week and was only kept afloat by the generosity of the existing directors. Mortimer resigned in 1984, and in spite of his undoubted support for the relocation to Milton Keynes, on the plus side were the facts that he really saved the club from the many issues in the 70s and was responsible for the appointment of David Pleat as manager in 1978.

Mortimer was replaced by David Evans, who, with his fellow directors, put in enough money to provide David Pleat with a substantial transfer pot. Six players were brought in. They included Steve Foster, Mick Harford, David Preece and Peter Nicholas.

Chapter 54 - David Evans

This is the moment to describe one of the more charismatic and controversial figures in Luton's history, David Evans. He was a keen but not very talented sportsman who was appointed to the board in 1977 and became chairman from 1984 with Luton in the top division. He stepped down as chairman in 1989 and resigned from the board in 1990. He came from a modest background of which he was very proud but had made a lot of money with his industrial cleaning company. He is remembered especially for welcoming the plastic pitch and introducing mandatory membership cards for the home supporters, and banning away supporters. This was in response, especially to the riots by the so-called Millwall supporters at a 6th round FA Cup tie at Kenilworth Road in March 1985. Somehow amid the mayhem and resultant stoppages, Luton still managed to win 1-0 with a Brian Stein goal in the 31st minute. Evans was blunt about Luton's financial woes and was in favour of a move to Milton Keynes, thinking that there were too many obstacles to a move within Luton. He was in charge of Luton when they won the Littlewoods Cup, undoubtedly the greatest day in their history. He was also very involved in cricket with the Lord Taverners and the MCC. In 1987 he had managed to get elected as the Conservative MP for Welwyn and Hatfield, and being both blunt, controversial and right-wing in his views was definitely one of Mrs Thatcher's favourites. He was defeated, however, in the 1997 election by Labour's Melanie Johnson.

Most of the talk was still about relocation, and a lot of money was spent on many feasibility studies. Milton Keynes couldn't decide whether it wanted a football club there or not. It is history how they finished up with the old Wimbledon renamed the Milton Keynes Dons. Helped by supporter power, Wimbledon was re-formed as AFC Wimbledon and admitted to the Combined Counties League Premier Division for the 2002/3 season. I remember seeing them playing at Dunstable Town in 2004 and was amazed by the size of their support. It was the one, and only time I went to watch football in Dunstable, but I found Creasey Park to be a cosy and friendly ground! AFC's rise was meteoric, reaching the League's league 2 by 2008. That meant 5 promotions in 9 seasons to get up to the football league's 4th tier and 6 promotions in 13 seasons to get into League 1. I can't forget their famous Conference playoff victory over the Hatters at Manchester City's Etihad stadium in 2011, getting them into the football league. After five seasons, they were promoted to League 1, and since then, they have been in League 1. By contrast, MK Dons had spent every season in league 1 or 2 except 2015/16, when they spent one season in the championship but finished that season in 23rd place.

Chapter 55 - Argentinians

I can't go on without some discussion about Argentina and its role as a soccer superpower. One of the great derbies in world soccer is between two famous Buenos Aires teams River Plate and Boca Juniors. River Plate tends to have the support of the more affluent classes, whereas Boca Juniors has the support of the population at large. Argentinian footballers have regularly made their way to Europe, starting with Alfredo di Stefano to Real Madrid. It was common for the immigrant footballer to become eligible to play for their country of residence rather than birth, hence Di Stefano playing for Spain. I want to highlight Spurs' two Argentinian imports: Osvaldo (Ossie) Ardiles and Ricardo (Ricky) Villa. There is much similarity between their stays in England, so they can largely be taken together! However, a striking difference was in their appearance. Ossie was always immaculately turned out and clean-shaven, whereas Ricky sported a large beard which made him look rather untidy and fierce. Ossie had signed from Huracan in 1978, whereas Ricky came from Racing Club de Avellaneda, both teams in the greater Buenos Aires region. Ossie had been part of the Argentina winning team in their home 1978 World Cup. That was a tournament for which England, for the second time running, had failed to qualify. In fact, it nearly didn't happen as Argentina had undergone a military coup and installed a dictator. The result was that several countries wondered whether they should participate, but in the end, they all did. Johan Cruyff did pull out, although many years later, he denied it was because of the politics. Diego Maradona, although already a professional at 17 years of age, was considered by the manager to be too young to cope with the undoubted pressures of a home tournament. His place was taken by Mario Kempes, who turned out to be their best player and top goalscorer in the tournament.

In their second round of group matches, Argentina needed to beat Peru by four goals and indeed did by six! There has always been suspicion that the result had been decided off the field even before the match started. There were many other accusations about activities favouring the Argentinians. They went on to beat the Netherlands 3-1 after extra time in the final in Buenos Aires. The Dutch had many famous players at the time, including Ruud Krol, the captain, Johan Neeskens, Rob Rensenbrick and Johnny Rep. Unusually Ossie, considered one of the gentleman footballers, was booked in that game! The atmosphere has been extraordinary at all the Argentine matches with streamers, ticker tape, flares and other attractions throughout. While Ricky only stayed at Spurs till 1983, Ossie went on till 1988. Ossie scored 16 goals, and Ricky 18 for Spurs but one of Ricky's was particularly memorable. Ricky had been substituted in the FA Cup Final of 1981 against Manchester City in the 68th minute with the score at 1-1 after contributing rather little but was picked for the replay. In it, he scored the first goal, but later on, he went on a mazy dribble past several defenders to score the third and winning goal. The goal was elected Wembley Goal of the Century in 2001. From villain to hero in just four days! Ossie became famous for his part in the Spurs song created by Chas and Dave, "Spurs are on their way to Wembley", when he famously pronounced Tottenham as "Tottingham".

Ossie had a difficult choice to make when Argentina invaded the Falkland Islands in April 1982 to be confronted by the British forces. He felt he couldn't continue to play in England and went on loan to Paris Saint Germain for the season, where he made 14 appearances. As a result, he missed the 82 FA Cup final and replay and Spurs victory. He did play a part in the 1984 UEFA Cup final second leg, which Spurs won on penalties against Anderlecht of Belgium 4-3 after an aggregate score in normal time of 2-2 over the two legs. Both Argentinian players were inducted into the Spurs hall of fame in 2008. The Falklands war was, of course, won by the British with the Argentinian surrender on 14th June 1982. Curiously much later in 2014, both Ossie and Ricky were involved in a road traffic accident in, of all places, the Falkland Islands. They were there to film a documentary, and Ossie suffered a head injury that required several stitches. Luckily he made a full recovery.

Argentinian footballers are now all over the world, with currently 10 in the Premier League. The most renowned were possibly Carlos Teves and Sergio Aguero at Manchester City. But at present, there are over 30 in Italy, Paolo Dybala and till recently Gonzalo Higuain at Juventus, for example. Also, one can cite many Argentinian managers in Europe, such as Bielsa at Leeds, Simione at Atletico Madrid and Pochettino at Paris Saint Germain. Maybe it is not surprising as Argentina has benefited from Italian immigration on a large scale resulting in over 50% of the population having some degree of Italian heritage. There are several players born in Argentina who have played for the Italian national team. Some have indeed been part of World Cup final victories for the Azzurri. One might cite Raimundo Orsi in 1934 and Mauro Camoranesi in 2006. Orsi is particularly interesting as he managed to play 13 times for Argentina and 25 times for Italy! He played for Juventus at a time when they won 5 successive Serie A titles between 1930-31 and 1934-35.

Chapter 56 - VIP at Villa Park!

On 2nd March 1983, Juventus were drawn to play against Aston Villa in the quarter-finals of the European Cup, the first leg being at Villa Park. I arranged with Giampiero to go and agreed to meet him to collect my ticket at a hotel close to the Birmingham International Centre. He offered me a seat in the courtesy car laid on for him to go to the ground, which I was happy to accept. At the stadium, I was ushered into an executive lounge where by chance David Pleat and assistant Luton manager David Coates were having a drink. Of course, I introduced myself as a Luton supporter and bought them both another drink. I learnt from Pleaty that he had just signed Paul Elliott, a defender and Paul Walsh, a striker, both from Charlton Athletic. Elliott was a classy defender who left Luton for Aston Villa in 1985 but sadly, in 1992, suffered a serious knee injury in a tackle by Dean Saunders, after which he never played again. He filed a lawsuit against Saunders which he lost. He went on to become a pundit both in the UK and in Italy (having played there for two years with Pisa) and was famous for being one of the first black footballers to play in Italy. He was a popular contributor to Football Italia, a UK television programme showing Italian football which ran from 1992 to 2002. The charismatic presenter was mostly James Richardson. Later, Paul did a lot of work with young players and with anti-racism earning an MBE and later CBE for services to equality and diversity in football.

The Villa match itself was memorable in many ways. The Juventus team at the time was managed by Giovanni Trapattoni and was full of household names made famous by Italy's World Cup win in Spain in 1982. They included Zoff, Cabrini, Gentile, Scirea, Tardelli, and Rossi. Juve at the time included those two outstanding foreign players, Michel Platini, the Frenchman and Zbigniew Boniek, the Pole.

I took my seat in the director's box and was sitting next to an Italian lady who turned out to be the wife of the Juventus doctor and herself a qualified anaesthetist, so we had plenty in common! The game started with a first minute headed goal by Paolo Rossi. Although Gordon Cowans equalised for Villa, the game was won for Juve with a Boniek piledriver, eight minutes from the end. It was not just a win for the Bianconeri, but the first time Juventus had ever won a competitive match in England. That really excited Boniperti, who had always continued to express huge admiration for English football. After the match, I went back to the Juventus team's hotel to say goodbye and express my thanks for a memorable evening. In those days away teams often stayed overnight rather than flying straight back after the match. To my amazement, I was asked to join them for dinner, which I nervously did, surrounded as I was by all those superstar footballers!

Everyone was very happy and boisterous in view of the famous win! I have no memory of the menu, being, as you can imagine, rather overwhelmed by it all and struggling with my rather limited Italian. Juventus won the second leg in Turin 3-1 with two goals from Platini and one from Tardelli. In the semifinal, they played and beat Widzew Lodz, Boniek's previous Polish club. Sadly, they lost in the final that year 1-0 to Hamburg's Hamburger Sport-Verein, in Athens. They then bade farewell to goalie Dino Zoff as a player after 476 league appearances in 11 seasons for the club and 112 international caps. During his time, he won 6 Serie A titles, 2 Coppa Italias and 1 UEFA Cup. He went on to manage Juve amongst other clubs winning a Coppa Italia and a UEFA Cup in 1990. He also managed the National team in 1998, leading them to a losing final in the Euros in 2000, beaten by France. A few days later, he resigned following strong criticism from AC Milan owner and politician Berlusconi. He returned to club management with Lazio.

Chapter 57 - Season 1983/84

In 83/84, we finished 16th, and the season was sadly noted for a 6-0 defeat at Liverpool and a 5-0 defeat at Old Trafford, as well as many other heavy losses. A goal difference of minus 13 sums it up, but at least we retained our top league status. Paul Walsh with 11, Brian Stein with 9 and Trevor Aylott with 8 were the top but rather meagre league scorers. Goalie Les Sealey came from Coventry City and was ever-present in that season and stayed until 1990 when he left for Manchester United. He is remembered for missing the 1988 League final through injury but played, albeit not very well, in the 1989 one giving away that penalty converted by Nigel Clough in the 3-1 defeat to Notts Forest.

For me, another treat was to go to Manchester United versus Juventus in April 1984 for a European Cup Winners' Cup semifinal. I again met Giampiero at the team hotel, and again we drove together to the match in a courtesy car. Giampiero was very nervous when we got stuck in traffic, coming as he did from a country with spates of kidnapping and the extensive activities of the Red Brigades. On a lighter note, the driver kept calling Boniperti "Botticelli"! Sitting in the director's box at Old Trafford was special, surrounded as I was by so many VIPs. I have always considered Old Trafford to be our finest football stadium, with the Stretford end being even more passionate if less tuneful than the Anfield Kop. The match ended 1-1 with the Juve goal scored by an emerging Paolo Rossi but equalised by Alan Davies. The return leg ended 2-1 to Juve with another 90th-minute goal for Rossi following an early one for Boniek. Norman Whiteside had equalised in between the two Juve goals. Juve went on to win the final in Basel with a 2-1 win over Porto, all the goals coming in the first half from Vignola and Boniek for Juve and Antonio Sousa for Porto. Good news followed with the announcement that Italy had been awarded the 1990 World Cup. I started planning right away!

Chapter 58 - Season 1984/85

84/85 was characterised by a steady 13th place finish, a run in the Milk (League) Cup to the 4th round, and a long FA Cup run to the semifinals. Some money was miraculously found to buy four players. Steve Foster came from Aston Villa, David Preece from Walsall and Peter Nicholas from Crystal Palace. Steve Foster went on to captain the side in the heady years of 88/89, and Preece, a diminutive midfielder, stayed for 11 years, making nearly 400 appearances. Such was his popularity and esteem that after dying of throat cancer at the tender age of 44, a new family stand having been built in the gap between the Main and Kenilworth Road stands was named after him and opened by his widow. Peter Nicholas played for us from 1985 to 1987, making over 100 Luton appearances and earning in all 73 Welsh caps. It was the season that Mick Harford came to Luton from Birmingham, and his very successful two spells as a player and two as a manager have undoubtedly put him at the top of any list of Luton greats. Harford had only played for the second half of the season but was still the top scorer with 15 league and 1 Cup goals, followed by Brian Stein and Emeka Nwajiobi with nine each. Mal Donaghy and Brian Stein were also ever present in both league and Cup. Nwajiobi was Nigerian born but played for Luton, his only league club, from 1983 to 1988, scoring a total of 20 goals. He did earn four caps for Nigeria. Sadly, his career was then ended by a severe injury, but luckily he had acquired a degree in pharmacy before becoming a professional footballer, so he had a ready-made career to renew. He played in the team on that infamous day when the Millwall supporters rioted.

A historic match was at home to Manchester United, who we had not beaten since 1937 in spite of trying on about 30 occasions! So there was little optimism. However, a Mick Harford penalty scored in the 68th minute was followed by a Norman Whiteside equaliser and a dramatic trademark Harford bullet header gave us victory in the 89th minute. That unexpected victory was understandably marked by very dramatic and prolonged celebrations. We did beat them again 2-1 in 1987 with goals from Mick Harford and Brian Stein, but we haven't had a victory over them since then. By coincidence, we drew Watford in the FA Cup again, this time in the 5th round. The home match was a goalless draw, the first replay ended 2-2, and we won the second replay 1-0. So after beating Millwall in that infamous match 1-0, Luton got to the semifinal of the FA Cup for only the second time in their history and were drawn against Everton, the Cup holders to be played at Villa Park. Again bad planning meant that I was away at a meeting in Stockholm! I remember vividly playing truant from the lectures to try and get the commentary of the match on the BBC World Service. I always travelled with an expensive Sony radio to be able to get the football news first and any other news second! To get any reception at all on this occasion, I had to stand on our hotel room's balcony and hold the radio as far as I dared over the edge. Even that was only partially successful, which was very frustrating. However, I heard enough to know that Ricky Hill had scored for Luton with a powerful shot from the edge of the penalty area in the 38th minute. They held on till 5 minutes from the end when Kevin Sheedy equalised with a deflected free-kick. Extra time was tight, but sadly again, 5 minutes from the end, Derek Mountfield, the Everton centre half, scored the winner for the Toffees with a header from a free-kick. So near yet so far again! Incidentally, Everton lost the final to Manchester United to a Norman Whiteside goal in the 110th minute.

It was the year when another disaster struck football, in this case, the Bradford City Valley Parade stadium fire, when 56 people lost their lives, and there were over 250 injuries. The stadium was very old, had wooden terracing, and there was a build-up of litter under the main stand. The day was supposed to be a day of celebration as it was the last game of the season, and Bradford had just won the 3rd division title. Although there was no fencing so spectators could, in theory, get out easily, the turnstiles had been locked, so many who tried to get out through them were trapped inside. Surprisingly in spite of the fact that it was established that a cigarette had started the fire, it took until 2007 for smoking to be banned in football grounds.

Chapter 59 - Hooliganism

Hooliganism was rife from the 1960s onwards, although it can be traced back to the 14th century! Not only in relation to football but elsewhere, such as the Notting Hill carnival and in seaside resorts. Perhaps the first reported football episode was at a friendly match between Preston North End and Aston Villa in 1885. On 6th November 1965, Millwall beat west London club Brentford 2–1 away at Griffin Park, and during the game, a hand grenade was thrown onto the pitch from the Millwall end. Brentford's goalkeeper Chick Brodie picked it up, inspected it and threw it into his goal! It was later retrieved by police and found to be a harmless dummy. There was fighting inside and outside the ground during the game between both sets of supporters, with one Millwall fan sustaining a broken jaw. The Sun newspaper ran the sensationalist grenade-related headline "Soccer Marches to War"! Millwall's ground was repeatedly closed three times in 1920, 1934 and 1950 after crowd disturbances, and of course, they were the perpetrators of the 1985 riot at Luton. By 1965 at least 25 football related episodes had been reported each year. While it is by no means confined to England, it has been dubbed the "English disease"! Hooligan firms were attached to too many clubs to list. Racism played a part as more and more black players featured in the teams. They were frequently targeted by monkey chants and the throwing of bananas. Homophobic abuse appeared as well on many occasions. It was a time when very few gay footballers had "come out". There was also sectarian violence, as exemplified by Celtic and Rangers in Glasgow. The hooligans were often associated with far-right groups such as the National Front and the British National Party. The need to segregate supporters seemed to have been overlooked by the police and the clubs themselves. The 1966 Chester report found that the incidence of football violence had doubled in the sixties compared with the previous twenty-five years. In 1969 Sir John Lang's report suggested that more seating might lower the incidence of violence. The 1972 European Cup Winners Cup final between Rangers and Dynamo Moscow in Barcelona was noted for the Rangers fans invading the pitch and engaging in violent conflict with anyone who came in their path. It was, of course, broadcast across Europe, alerting the continent of the dangers that also lay ahead for them. The 73/74 season was marked by violence at many grounds by so-called supporters who by then were mostly formed into gangs. The Spurs supporters rioted in Rotterdam when they lost the 1974 UEFA Cup final to the host Feyenoord. It was believed that the violence was a factor in the retirement of Spurs iconic manager Bill Nicholson who had led his team to that historic double in 1960/61. The problems of hooliganism attracted more and more publicity which probably aggravated the issues. The Daily Mirror even published a league table of hooligan notoriety.

74/75 had been marked by the Leeds supporters rioting in Paris and causing much damage before, during and after defeat to Bayern Munich in the European Cup Winners Cup final, and the club received a four-year ban from Europe, subsequently reduced to two. A 17-year-old fan was stabbed to death at Blackpool. Then came trouble in St Etienne with Manchester United, who were forced to play the second leg more than 200 miles from Old Trafford!

The national team continued to be infected by the disease, and there was trouble both in the ground and in the city when they played Luxembourg in a qualifier in 1983 for the 1984 European Championships, which was marred by serious crowd trouble both outside and inside the ground. 50 English supporters were arrested as, in spite of a 4-0 victory, England were knocked out of those European Championships by results elsewhere. The disturbances were a repeat of those in 1977 when England fans had also run riot. This time the overstretched Luxembourg forces had to be helped by those from neighbouring Germany. The Luxembourg Minister of sport said that his country would never again host an England team.

On 13th March 1985, it came to Luton in a big way. The occasion was a 6th round FA Cup tie against Millwall. The prize for the winner was to be a coveted place in the semifinal. This was one of many crowd violence scenes in England that I was unfortunate enough to witness first-hand. Before the match, there had been serious trouble in the town with major disturbances and considerable damage to property. In fact, the Arndale shopping centre was forced to close early. During the match, there was further major crowd disturbance and violence, including a pitch invasion by so-called Millwall fans. There seemed to be serious overcrowding with the away support double the number that normally Millwall got for their home games! Whoever they were, they were acting in part under the influence of excessive alcohol. It seemed that only some were true Millwall supporters, the rest miscellaneous collections of those who enjoyed fighting and violence. There were actually three pitch invasions, one before the match kicked off, another while the match was in progress, in which play was stopped for about 25 minutes, and George Graham, the Millwall manager at the time, pleaded with the away supporters to stay in their stand with limited success, and a third after the final whistle. Seats were ripped out and thrown onto the pitch, causing several injuries. In view of my profession and training, I felt it was my duty to go on to the pitch and try and offer any help and especially first aid to anyone in need. I particularly remember one of my "patients" was a policeman, one of the 31 injured. Typically, the trouble coincided with the match being televised, so the whole nation was able to witness it. In spite of the mayhem, Brian Stein managed to score the only but winning goal. Les Sealey, in Luton's goal in the second half, had to defend the goal at the Millwall "supporters" end and had to suffer a constant bombardment from a variety of missiles. I have never before or since seen a goalie position himself so far out of his goal and indeed mostly outside his penalty area. After the game, the mayhem then continued in the surrounding streets causing further widespread damage and destruction as well as many more injuries. All the trouble makers had been at the Kenilworth Road end, where the visiting supporters were packed in. It's amazing to think that today crowd control and behaviour largely is in the hands of matchday stewards, with the police being readily available but much less visible inside the grounds. The police have tried various measures to contain crowd disturbances. They included "bubble matches" where all away supporters had to travel together on designated transport, usually club coaches, from the specific pick up points. Another was kettling, a tactic involving the formation of large cordons of police who then move to contain a crowd in a limited area. Inevitably a Football Association enquiry was held. They held that Millwall had failed to take all necessary precautions in their plans for the match, but the result was a small fine which was cast out on appeal. In the end, the only punishment for Millwall was a very tarnished reputation and that they were aligned with everything bad in football and society at large. One result was that David Evans, then Luton chairman, introduced the ban on away supporters from the start of the 86/87 season, introduced identity cards and wanted to put fences up again. Even home supporters had to carry membership cards, a prelude to identity checking when purchasing tickets. Measures were put in place to prevent away supporters from obtaining tickets for home areas. Luton were thrown out of the next season's Football League Cup when they refused to allow Cardiff City supporters in for one of the early ties. The ban on away supporters lasted for 4 years until the 1990/91 season. Improvements at grounds that did come out of it were the installation of monitored CCTV and the tighter segregation of fans, often with a controlled space between the rival fans. Incidentally, Ken Bates, the equally controversial Chelsea chairman, threatened to put up electric fences at their ground. In fact, I think he did install one but never got permission from the authorities to switch it on! I liked to think that would be my last close call with major football violence. How wrong I was. To prove that it has still not gone away were the scenes at the very recent UEFA final between England and Italy at Wembley where there were riots at the entrance to the stadium as about 2000 so-called supporters broke through disabled entrances. The violence continued after the match in both Leicester Square and Trafalgar Square. 86 people were arrested that day.

Chapter 60 - European Championships 1980

In 1980 England had reached the finals of the European championships, their first appearance in a major tournament for 10 years. It was to be held in Italy, and I really wanted to go and easily persuaded my good friend Richard to come with me. Because of the reputation of the English and other fans, I was a bit apprehensive, but my love of football and Italy soon overcame that. The first England match was in Turin at the Comunale stadium, where at that time, both Juventus and Torino played their home matches. The atmosphere was tense, although the crowd was not very large. England scored first in the 26th minute through Ray "Butch" Wilkins, but three minutes later, the Belgians equalised, setting off scenes that were very frightening. The Italian police chose to use tear gas to control the trouble at the England end, and the game was held up for more than five minutes. The match ended 1-1. It confirmed to me that we were now exporting our problems to the continent of Europe and was not just a domestic issue. The second England match was against the hosts in a full Turin stadium, but amazingly in spite of Italy winning with a Marco Tardelli 79th minute goal, there seemed to have been only minor disturbances. Perhaps it was because, obviously, the England supporters were heavily outnumbered. The Italian squad had a host of household names, including goalkeeper Dino Zoff (then 38 years of age), central defenders Franco Baresi and Gaetano Scirea, full-backs Antonio Cabrini and Claudio Gentile, midfielders Romeo Benetti and Franco Causio, and forwards Roberto Bettega and Alessandro Altobelli. Of course, they all gelled two years later in time for the 1982 World Cup, which Italy famously won in Madrid against West Germany. To my mind, Franco Baresi and Gaetano Scirea were two of the great sweepers (liberi in Italian) of all time. Antonio Cabrini and Claudio Gentile were two of the hardest but most skilful fullbacks I ever saw! The only notable additions to the Italy squad from 1980 to 1982 were defender Guiseppe Bergomi only 18 years old, and striker Paolo Rossi. Tardelli's goal in Turin against England in 1980 was significant but nothing compared with his goal against West Germany in the final of 1982, which triggered off that famous run across the pitch, screaming loudly. That must be one of the most shown celebrations of scoring a goal in football history. So England's next and final match was against Spain in the famous San Paolo stadium in Naples. The stadium is often called Fuorigrotta (outside the cave in English) after the area in which it is situated. It was a vast stadium with great views from all parts. It was the third-largest in Italy at the time, behind Milan's San Siro and Rome's Stadio Olimpico. I remember us parking right by the stadium, which could have been a serious risk in view of the reputation that the Neapolitan fans had. I don't remember much about the game except that England won 2-1 with goals from Trevor Brooking (a bit of a rarity, he only scored five international goals in total in his 47 appearances) and Tony Woodcock. Again all was pretty peaceful. It clearly helped if the England team was winning! However, the results were not good enough for England to advance any further. Italy got to the third-place play-off where they drew 1-1 against Czechoslovakia but lost the penalty shoot-out 8-9. No extra time was played at that time. The final in Rome was won by West Germany, who beat Belgium 2-1, Horst Hrubesch scoring the two goals, the second with a typically powerful header.

Our car was happily found to be intact, and we set off for the hotel we had chosen from some old guidebook we had used. It was on the Bay of Naples, which is, of course, one of the most famous and scenic areas of Italy. When we alighted at our hotel, we discovered that it had been converted into an old people care home! At 43, we thought we were a bit too young for that and so drove on to a hotel about which I cannot remember any detail. However, I do remember well visiting Sorrento, Amalfi and Positano amongst other interesting places in the bay of Naples, such as Pompei with its great history and Mount Vesuvius with its famous volcano.

Chapter 61 - Raddy Antic

In 1980 Luton had signed a Yugoslav midfield player called Radomir (Raddy) Antic and by then, 32 years of age. He had played one match for Yugoslavia and will always be remembered very fondly. In 1982 we had had that momentous season achieving promotion to Division 1, but in the following year, we were threatened with relegation. The last match of the season in 1983 was away to Manchester City, who had to win or draw to stay up whereas we had to win. As you would expect, it was a very tense match with a minimum of open play. Suddenly, with Luton on the way down, Brian Stein, barely fit in his first match back after a broken foot, crossed the ball. The City goalie, Alex Williams, punched the ball out to Raddy Antic, who had come on as a substitute. Antic controlled the ball and scored one of Luton's most memorable goals four minutes from the end to ensure their survival. The shot went through a crowd of players and took a helpful deflection! It was celebrated more widely than any promotion, championship or Cup, especially by manager David Pleat. Who could forget his wild leaping celebratory run across the pitch, hopping and waving his arms wildly in celebration? He was wearing a light brown suit and beige slip-on shoes. In fact, the shoes were auctioned later at a Luton commemorative dinner and fetched £4,000. Raddy stayed one more season and left in 1984, soon to retire and take up coaching. He always cited Pleaty as the major influence on his coaching methods. That he finished up with 12 different coaching posts suggests that he wasn't totally successful. However, he was the only one ever to have coached both famous Madrid clubs (Real and Atletico) as well as Barcelona. He did win the double for Atletico in 1996. He also later coached the Serbian national team, by then an independent nation, for two years, leading them to the 2010 World Cup finals, where they, unfortunately, finished bottom of their group behind Germany, Ghana, and Australia. In fact, they had beaten Germany 1-0 but lost to Australia 2-1 and to Ghana 1-0.

Chapter 62 - Mick Harford

There can be no doubt in my mind that Mick Harford was and still is the really outstanding figure in the history of Luton Town. He was born in Sunderland and will always be remembered as a typical English centre forward, tall at 6'3", robust but equally good with feet and head. He was signed by manager David Pleat in 1984 from Birmingham for £250,000 and stayed till 1990. His most prolific season was 85/86 when he scored 22 goals out of a total of 186 league goals for all his different clubs. In 1988 he earned two England caps against Israel and Denmark but failed to get on the score sheet. Then he was transferred to Derby for £450,000, a nice profit for the Hatters. But after only a year there, the Rams were relegated from the 1st division. In that season, 1991, he scored a famous headed own goal for Luton past Peter Shilton to help Luton stay up. He has mostly denied that it was a deliberate act, but it didn't harm the already relegated Rams but saved the Town! In 1991-92 he was back at Luton for a second time costing £325,000. He scored another 12 goals but was then poached by Chelsea, who paid £300,000 and kept him for a year. His sale increased the unhappiness with then-chairman David Kohler. Then after very short spells at his home town club Sunderland and at Coventry in 1994, he joined Wimbledon as a player. At 35, his value had dropped to £50,000! It was the last club he played for, but where he scored a further 9 league goals in 61 appearances before making his move into coaching. Harford developed his further skills and then came with his old Wimbledon manager Joe Kinnear to Luton following our relegation to the third division in 2001. In his role as first-team coach, Harford helped mastermind the successful season of 2001–02, which saw Luton promoted to the second division. Following the 2002–03 season, the club was sold to a new consortium, and Harford and Kinnear were then promptly sacked. Harford was to be offered his job back but refused to work under the new board. However, the new owners were forced out by supporter power, and Mick was back initially as a sidekick to the new manager and fellow ex-Town striker Mike Newell. In 2003/04, they led the Town to 10th place. Harford was also responsible for player recruitment; a role he is still undertaking to this day! He then joined Joe Kinnear at Nottingham Forest, where he was manager for a short time. Mick then had a series of short term coaching and managerial posts at a variety of different clubs. However, in January 2008, he returned to Luton at probably the lowest point in the club's history. I refer to the 30-point deduction. It is very difficult to imagine any club needing 10 wins before their results started to count! Of course, it was beyond them, and they were duly relegated, as happened again in the following season. Amazingly Mick had managed to get them to the final of the Johnstone's Paint Trophy at Wembley in 2009 as a league 2 side where they beat league 1 Scunthorpe 3-2 after extra time. A crumb of comfort for big Mick and everyone connected with the club. They were, therefore, in free fall right down to the Conference. Who could have thought that a club could fall so quickly? The first season in the Conference (09/10) did not start that well, and Mick left by mutual consent! In fact, we got to the play-offs at the end of that season, where we lost to York. Mick didn't reappear till 2016 when he was appointed as a chief recruitment officer, in other words, chief scout. Comfortable in his important role, the club were rocked by manager Nathan Jones leaving for Stoke City with Luton riding high in Division 2. Guess who was asked to step in but big Mick, and he guided the club to promotion to Division 1. At the start of the 19/20 season, Graeme Jones, who had been assistant to Roberto Martinez with the Belgium national team and had been waiting in the wings, took over. Sadly, we lost fullbacks, Jack Stacey to Bournemouth and James Justin to Leicester, and we found it hard going. Then the coronavirus struck, and all football was suspended on 13th March 2020. In the next month, it was announced that Graeme Jones and three of his assistants had also left by mutual consent. There was only one obvious person to take over, the faithful Mick Harford! And then, in May, Nathan Jones, who had not been very successful at Stoke, was surprisingly re-appointed to try and save Luton, at that time six points from safety from relegation and with the worst goal difference of any of the threatened clubs. Who was to act as assistant manager? Of course, Mick Harford! and he is still with us in that role. So technically, one would say that Mick had two spells as a player for us and then three different spells as a manager! The affection in which he is held was manifested by the support he received when he recently announced that he was suffering from prostate cancer.

Chapter 63 - The Heysel Stadium

The worst tragedy that I witnessed first-hand was the Heysel stadium disaster. On 29th May 1985, I set off for Brussels with a good friend and fellow anaesthetist to attend the European Cup Final between Juventus and Liverpool. Liverpool were the defending European Champions Cup holders, having beaten another Italian team Roma in the previous season's final by a penalty shoot-out. The reader will understand my already considerable attachment to Juventus, and as you can imagine, I was thrilled to be going and eagerly looking forward to it. I had laid the plans. The tickets were to be picked up at the hotel where the Juventus team was staying, and a colleague and good friend in Brussels had very kindly offered us accommodation for the night. On arrival in Brussels, we said a quick hello to Giampiero, who duly passed over the precious tickets. We then headed to our host's house, which was in Overijse, a rather posh suburb very close to Brussels, to say hello and drop off our overnight bags. Then on to the stadium. During the walk from the station to the ground, we were very aware of a very subdued atmosphere around us punctuated by frequent sounds of police sirens and ambulances. It was obvious something serious had or was happening. When we got into the ground, we could see the devastation and horrific scenes with bodies being taken out of the stand behind one of the goals and initially just laid out on the pitch. Even with our background, we were shocked and really upset by what we saw. It was apparent that the casualties were Italians, and soon we discovered the ghastly truth that the Liverpool supporters from the bay next to them had thrown a lot of masonries found in the derelict stadium and then charged the Italian fans and in the pushing and shoving a retaining wall had collapsed into an access bay causing the, mostly retreating, Italians, to be crushed. The Liverpool fans, as might have been predicted, were mostly drunk. The Juventus fans at the other end invaded the pitch and started retaliation of their own. Getting to our seats, I realised we were sitting next to a very nice Italian who I had met on previous occasions in Turin. While we had only come from London on this occasion, he had come from Toronto, where he lived as he often did for big Juventus matches. He immediately advised us not to speak any English, as you can imagine the state many Italians were in. The mayhem went on for a long time. While this was going on, the public services tried to restore some sort of order. At one point, the two captains, Phil Neal and Gaetano Scirea appealed to the crowd for calm, and if it was achieved, they said they would play. Obviously, the decision ultimately rested with the UEFA officials and being fearful of letting out both sets of fans in the state they were obviously in allowed the game to go ahead. Most of those in the dressing rooms claimed that they did not know the extent of the disaster or that there were to be 39 deaths as well as about 600 injured. Anyway, after a delay of about 1 hour and 40 minutes, the teams came out, and the match started.

The Juventus team had many of the players who had won the 1982 World Cup for Italy as well as Frenchman Michel Platini, perhaps the finest player of his generation and Zbigniew Boniek, the Pole. As you would imagine, the match was played in a very strange and subdued atmosphere. The players didn't seem to have much appetite for the game, and the fans were relatively quiet as well. It was heading to the inevitable goalless draw, which would have necessitated another 30 minutes and possibly a penalty shoot-out. I don't believe the referee Swiss Andre Daina thought that was desirable and looked for a way to end it. In the 58th minute, Boniek was tripped clearly just outside the area, but Daina awarded a penalty which Platini duly dispatched. So the match ended 1-0 to Juventus, and at the end, Platini and some of his teammates celebrated the win like any other and were later severely reprimanded by Boniperti. Like others, Michel Platini claimed that he had not been aware of the extent of the disaster. So we nervously were to leave the stadium, but my Italian friend offered to take us back to the Juventus hotel in one of the executive coaches, which seemed to be the safest option, and we were very grateful. Obviously, I didn't seek out Giampiero, knowing how distraught he must have been and how busy with all the necessary press conferences and meetings. There was a problem that we couldn't communicate with our Belgian friends to tell them that we were alright but that we would be very late back to them for which we were very sorry! All the telephone lines were kept for emergency calls only, so there was no way we could even let our wives know that we were actually quite safe. It turned out that mine had been contacted by several friends who had been watching the television to see if she had any news of her husband. Of course, all she knew was that we were with Italians, and it was they who were almost exclusively among the casualties. So the next step was to find our way back to our hosts' house, and we took a taxi that was waiting outside the hotel. I should point out that my friend was a typical and obvious Englishman dressed accordingly in a cloth cap and gaberdine RAF blue raincoat. When we got in the taxi, the driver asked where we were from and was obviously familiar with what had happened. My French saved us as he said: "Oh, thank goodness if you had been English, I would not have taken you," and I gesticulated to my friend not to say anything, or our cover would have been blown! So safely back to our Belgian home, and luckily by then, communications had been restored, and we were able to explain everything to our hosts and our wives. Juventus had won their first-ever European Cup, but what a hollow victory it had turned out to be. The tragedy resulted in all English clubs being banned from Europe till 90/91, with Liverpool getting an extra year's ban. Fourteen of the Liverpool fans were convicted of manslaughter and given three-year prison sentences. While the Liverpool fans were clearly to blame, it became apparent that the dreadful state of repair of the stadium had been known for some time and that the top man from each club, Peter Robinson, CEO and Giampiero Boniperti, President, had previously urged the authorities, in this case, UEFA, to move it to a safer stadium. UEFA had sadly refused the request.

Finally, I can only sum it all up by saying that what should have been the most wonderful day turned out to be the most terrible day of my life. The next day we sat in the Grand Place, Brussel's fine central square, where the atmosphere was still subdued. At least we could drink excellent local beer and eat that well known Belgian favourite mussels and chips before heading home.

Everyone asks how is it that whenever there is real drama in or around a football stadium, I always seem to be there! I can only guess that was the price I paid for seeing so many matches in so many different countries.

Chapter 64 - I've Found a New Friend

In 1985/86, I was examining candidates for the anaesthetists' fellowships, the passport to higher specialist training and a necessity to be eligible to apply for consultant posts. As you can imagine, the candidates were as varied as the examiners. That year I was paired with Group Captain Colin McLaren, a well-known RAF anaesthetist whose specialty was the air rescue and repatriation of casualties from all over the world. Without military background myself, I did not expect us to have much in common. Amazingly on the first morning, a Monday, I opened my briefcase and lying on the top was the pink La Gazzetta Dello Sport that I had bought on my way to the Examination halls in Queen's Square as I often did on Monday to catch up with the weekends Serie A matches. I also hoped that it might help improve my Italian. He immediately recognised a fellow football fan and thus started a very warm friendship that continued until his sad demise in 2020 at the age of 92! Luckily our wives got on very well as well, which helped to cement and maintain the relationship. Colin had been a football referee up to league standard and was an ardent Manchester United supporter to the end. Manchester was the town of his birth, and much later, he went into football administration, serving on the Wiltshire FA council close to his home near Wootton Bassett. In the end, he was elected an honorary vice-president of that Council and, of course, as a result, was also often to be found at Swindon Town matches. Naturally, he will frequently feature in my future football life.

In October 1985, we hit 7 goals past Peter Shilton's Southampton, then managed by ex-Hatter Chris Nicholl. Brian Stein scored a birthday hat trick! It was Luton's biggest win for almost 10 years. Ten years later, an FA Cup tie at Southampton ended 6-0 to the home side, almost cancelling out the 1985 score and giving them real revenge.

In 1986 we installed a whole row of 25 executive boxes on the opposite side to the Main stand and where the Bobbers stand had been. They have always looked a bit strange to me and did not fit in well with the appearance, and they reduced the atmosphere in the ground. While bringing in much-needed finance, they further reduced the gate capacity. The much-loved stand they replaced had been called the Bobbers Stand from a time when the admission was a bob, short for one shilling or 5 pence in today's money! There has always been a supporters' membership club, the Bobbers Club, beneath the stand and with its own entrance on Oak Road. The Oak Road end was made all-seater. The same year the Kenilworth Road Terrace was given a long-overdue roof, and very controversially, a membership scheme was introduced after the various major crowd issues. The ban on away supporters resulted in our exclusion from the 86/87 season's Littlewoods Cup.

It is difficult to forget a titanic 3 game FA Cup struggle against Arsenal in February and March 1986. The first game at Luton ended 2-2 with a Ricky Hill masterclass and the replay at Arsenal 0-0. Unusually the venue for the 2nd replay was decided by the toss of a coin which Luton won to the dismay of Arsenal manager Don Howe. So two days later, that second replay at Luton gave the town a comfortable 3-0 win with 2 goals by Mark Stein, who had replaced the injured Brian Stein and an own goal by David O'Leary. So they had earned a 6th round home match against Everton, which they lost but also only after a replay. It was a coincidence to be playing Everton again just a year after our previous semifinal loss to them. It was the period when Gary Lineker was playing for Everton, who he described as the best club side he had played in, and before his £2.8 million transfer to Barcelona. Barcelona were impressed, no doubt, by Lineker's performance in the 1986 World Cup in Mexico, where he won the Golden Boot with 6 goals in spite of England going out in the quarters to those 2 Maradona goals.

On 16th May, David Pleat resigned as manager, having been lured by Spurs, who had just been turned down by Alex Ferguson.

Chapter 65 - Sion and Aberdeen

In autumn 1986, we went on holiday to Haute Nendaz, a ski resort in the Valais Canton of Switzerland. I found out that there was a 16th final second leg Cup Winners Cup match between Sion and Aberdeen at that time managed by Alec Ferguson. Aberdeen had won the first leg at home 2-1, so it was all to play for. The Sion ground was about 10 miles from Haute Nendaz down a difficult mountain road, but a football fanatic is not put off by such minor hazards. I got into my seat in the cosy 11,800 capacity stadium with fantastic views of the Alps and found myself sitting next to a reporter from the Scottish Daily Express who filled me in with all the background. He told me that it was to be Ferguson's last year at Aberdeen. He pointed out that the stars were Scottish international central defender Alex McLeish who went on to win 77 international caps, and Jim Leighton, the goalkeeper who would also go on to win 91 caps. Jim sadly was credited with his own goal after only 5 minutes. Aberdeen's cause was not helped by the expulsion of Jim Bett on 38 minutes, by which time they were already 2-0 down. My newfound friend went into raptures about a short red head called Gordon Strachan, who had been the star of Aberdeen until he was transferred to Manchester United in 1984. The match ended Sion 3 Aberdeen 0, which, as the Dons had only won the first leg 2-1, was not enough to prevent exit from the competition. It was a bit of an anticlimax because the Dons had beaten the same opponents only four years before in the preliminary round of the same competition by an aggregate score of 11-1. As I had the mountain road back to negotiate, I declined the kind offer of my neighbour to share a wee dram with him. After all, it seemed very unlikely that he would stop at one!

Chapter 66 - Season 1986/87

It was a record season as under John Moore's management, we finished in 7th place, our highest ever league position. The same season in October, Luton had one of their best wins, 4-1 against Liverpool, thanks to great team performance and a Mike Newell hat trick. Mike had signed from Wigan in 1986 but only stayed with us for nearly two seasons. In the same season, we repeated the feat with an FA Cup 3rd round 2nd replay 3-0 home result against Liverpool with the goals shared between Brian Stein, Harford and Newell. The first match had ended 0-0 on a snow-covered plastic pitch in full view of the TV cameras. The replay was postponed because Luton declined to make the journey in very snowy conditions. Again it caused a storm of anger from Dalglish, aggravated when the Town held them to another 0-0 draw after extra time. Newell left for Leicester early in the next season, the Foxes at that time being managed by David Pleat, who had previously signed him for Luton. Mike was to reappear as manager in 2003 and lasted four pretty controversial years.

In 1986 Liverpool beat Everton 3-1 in the FA Cup final, Ian Rush scoring two goals. After the match, Boniperti came to our house with his charming wife and proudly showed us Ian Rush's shirt, which signified that Juventus were signing him. The fee was 3.2 million pounds, a record at the time. After one season in which he remained with Liverpool on loan, he finally moved to Turin. He was replacing the irreplaceable Michel Platini, who was to retire in June 1987, a hard task for anyone. Indeed he was not a great success in Italy, scoring only 8 league and 6 sundry other goals in the one season compared with 30 in his previous season at Liverpool. He was considered to be homesick much of the time, but the truth was he could not often get the better of the much tighter Italian defences. On one of my visits to a Juventus game in Rush's season, Giampiero took me into the dressing room before the game to talk to Ian and to see if the encouragement of a Brit would cheer him up and perhaps even help him to play better! Needless to say, I did my feeble best but without any obvious effect. When you haven't ever spoken to someone before, it is very difficult to assess whether their state of mind is different from their norm or not. The famous quote attributed to him but later denied was that "It's like living in a foreign country". He had his newlywed wife Tracy to support him, but it didn't seem to help his football! He later admitted that he had had difficulty integrating himself into the dressing room and adapting to the Italian style of play. In the end, Juventus only finished 6th, unacceptably low for them, and Rush returned to Liverpool for another record fee of £2.7 million. He was preceded by British players who had joined Juventus by the largely forgotten William Jordan, who lasted one season in 48/49, and John Charles and Liam Brady, both very successful. After them, the only British players to join Juve have been David Platt for a short spell in the 90s and, most recently, Aaron Ramsey on a four-year deal from 2019.

Chapter 67 - 1986 World Cup in Mexico

This one was held in Mexico. It had originally been given to Colombia four years before, but they were unable to host it for mostly economic and security reasons. Unusually the Italy squad only had two bianconeri, Cabrini and Scirea, who were both nearing the end of their careers. Although the Azzurri got through to the last sixteen, they lost there to France 0-2, one of the goals inevitably being scored by Platini. England got through to the quarter-finals, where they lost to Argentina in one of the more controversial matches. To English supporters, Diego Maradona's "Hand of God" goal and his amazing dribble and second goal both in the game against England will all be very familiar and unforgettable. Somehow they sum up Maradona's personality and skills perfectly! It has been considered by many that the Argentinian victory over England was seen as revenge for the Falklands Islands defeat! France and Belgium were the losing semifinalists, and Argentina went on to win the Cup with a 3-2 final victory over West Germany. Some consolation for England was that Gary Lineker was the leading goalscorer with 6 goals, one ahead of Maradona, Brazilian Careca and Spaniard Butragueno.

Chapter 68 - Juventus 1986/87

In November 1986, there was another exceptional week in my football calendar. We went to the flat in Nice with 2 special Juventus matches on the horizon! The first was on Wednesday the 5th November and was a European Cup second round second leg match between Juve and Real Madrid. Gillian came with me, and we drove on the old roads from Nice through Sospel, across the Col de Tende, through the ski resort Limone Piemonte, on to Cuneo and across the plains to Turin. Very scenic but almost too much for an 8-year-old Fiat 126! It helped to break up the journey at a good restaurant in Savigliano! As satellite navigation was not yet available to us at that time, the journey into Turin city centre was rather difficult, but we made it to our hotel. We thought it safest to garage our precious little car, and when we checked it in, the garage attendant took one look at the English number plates and congratulated us on driving it from England! We didn't bother to tell him how it had come to Nice from England on the French train auto couchette some years before and had stayed there ever since. The match was played in front of a full house of 62,000 at the Stadio Comunale. The stadium was a real football stadium with a great atmosphere, only to be replaced four years later for the 1990 World Cup by the unpopular Stadio Delle Alpi, which was much larger but horrible by comparison. The match was tense. Juve had lost the first leg 1-0, but that was quickly cancelled out by a Cabrini goal in the 9th minute. No more goals even after extra time meant a penalty shoot-out in which Real prevailed 3-1, Juventus missing 3 of their 4. We got safely back to Nice the next day.

So the next highlight was to be Juve Napoli on the following Sunday. Napoli were traditional fierce rivals of Juventus, but the obvious attraction for me was to see Diego Maradona in the flesh. Any football fan would want to see him, especially in my case to follow seeing Pele and Eusebio in earlier days, and Johan Cruyff, Michel Platini, Lionel Messi and Cristiano Ronaldo later on. Maradona had joined Napoli from Barcelona in 1984 in a record 12 million euro deal. I had invited Colin and his wife to join us in Nice. On the day of the match, we left the girls to do their thing and set off for Turin. We rented a car this time, leaving the 126 to the girls! A better car encouraged us to take the motorways from Nice to Genoa (the A10 around 194 km) then the motorway A26 direct to Turin (another 175 km). Of course, that viaduct section of motorway above the Genoa port area, the Ponte Morandi, famously and tragically collapsed in 2018, leaving 43 people dead. It has been rebuilt to designs by the famous Italian architect Renzo Piano and re-opened in August 2020. Piano is perhaps best known for the Pompidou Centre in Paris, the Lingotto in Turin, a conversion from the FIAT factory, and the Shard in London. About 30km outside Turin, the fog appeared and started to thicken. The Po valley is known for its fog, although I thought it was rare for matches to be postponed or abandoned. You can imagine the panic in our minds. Imagine going all that way to find the match postponed. Luckily by the time we got into Turin, it had more or less cleared. We had first-class VIP seats as we had had for the Real Madrid match. The preliminaries were marked by the appearance on the pitch of the famous Argentinian Omar Sivori, by now 51 and forever a hero with the Juventus fans from his days as part of il trio magico composed of himself, Boniperti and John Charles. The match, as expected, was dominated by Maradona. One remembers his "bull-like" physique to go with his short stature, only 5 foot 5 inches, and his position as a classic number 10. His low centre of gravity helped him to be very flexible and dribble past several players on a run. He was clearly a dead ball specialist and scored many of his goals from free kicks or penalties. That season Napoli went on to win the double, so the excitement was at its height, and Maradona was a clear icon. His later issues off the field are well documented, especially his cocaine and alcohol addictions. He also got involved with politics forging close relationships with the President of Cuba, Fidel Castro, Che Guevara, the well-known Argentinian Marxist revolutionary and Hugo Chavez, president of Venezuela. Maradona got into big trouble with the Italian tax authorities owing at least 37 million euros, mostly interest on previously unpaid tax. In spite of this, he was appointed manager of his country in 2008 and lasted until 2010. We saw him again at the South Africa World Cup in 2010, and he seemed to be a very sad, very overweight figure. Napoli were dominant, winning 3-1 in spite of a Michael Laudrup goal in the 50th minute, giving Juve the lead. I was really pleased to see Laudrup, who went on to play for both Barcelona and Real Madrid. He also amassed 104 caps for the Danish national team. He really was a very elegant footballer and probably one of the best of his era. Napoli at the time had Ciro Ferrara in defence, who went on to play for Juventus in 1984 and for another 10 years. Maradona didn't score, but he did almost everything else and was really impressive. The Napoli goals were scored by Ferrario, Giordano and Volpecina, names unfamiliar to me! I remember Diego's habit of placing his hands firmly clasped behind his back when facing referees, presumably to make sure he couldn't assault them. We remember on leaving the stadium seeing the jubilant Napoli supporters dancing on car roofs, luckily not including ours! That season they went on to win the double, so their excitement was at its height, and Maradona was a clear icon. Juventus had to settle for 2nd place and entry into next season's UEFA Cup. Napoli won the title again in 89/90, but Napoli have not won it since then, and indeed, apart from Sampdoria in 1991and Lazio in 2000, no one has won it outside of Juventus, Inter with 19 titles and AC Milan with 18 since 2001. Juve, by contrast, have now amassed 36 wins!

On the return journey, we used the two-lane Turin Savona motorway A6, which turned out to be about the same distance as going via Genoa. Both were full of trucks which were driven as though they were overgrown Ferraris! That motorway had also been financed by the Agnellis to facilitate the Torinesi getting to the Ligurian coast for their relaxation. It seemed that Finale Ligure was the most fashionable destination. Most of the income from the motorway tolls went to the owners - an Agnelli owned management company.

We went straight to Giampiero's house to offer thanks and commiserations. Colin was particularly impressed by the high-security front gates! Giampiero was his usual gracious self and did not threaten to ban us from future matches, which he might well have done after our presiding over two crucial home matches, which both ended in defeat! Even the hugest black Pyrenean mountain dog you have ever seen, unsurprisingly called Blackie, had greeted us warmly! Napoli went on to win the Scudetto for the first time that year. Juventus had to settle for 2nd place and entry into next season's UEFA Cup.

Chapter 69 - Season 1987/88

1987/88 was undoubtedly to be one of the most memorable seasons in our history. At the end of 86/87, John Moore resigned as manager after one season. Although he took Luton to their highest ever position (7th in the top league), John decided that management was not the job for him. Ray Harford, who had been his coach, took over the manager's job in 1987. John Moore remained with the club in a coaching capacity, especially looking after the youth players helped by Marvin Johnson, who, after 15 years and 373 league and 67 Cup appearances as a player, helped with the coaching for a further seven. Marvin was one of the very rare one-club men and was immensely popular with fellow players but especially the fans who nicknamed him "marvellous"! There was frequently the chant from the Luton Supporters, "Marvin for England," whenever he was in possession of the ball. He was the captain in season 95/96. His coaching career was extensive, and he should be remembered as the one who brought on Curtis Davies, Leon Barnett and Kevin Foley, all of whom made it to the Premier League. Indeed Curtis and Leon fetched around £2.5 to £3 million each when sold in 2005 and 2007 both to West Bromwich Albion, who were oscillating between the second and top division as they are now. Danny Wilson had been signed from Brighton, but Mike Newell was sold to Leicester. We finished 9th in the league, but then there were the amazing Cup exploits. In the FA Cup, we got to the semifinal at White Hart Lane, where we lost 2-1 to Wimbledon, Dennis Wise scoring the winner after John Fashanu's penalty had equalised Mick Harford's goal. They were to be the eventual winners, surprisingly beating Liverpool 1-0 in the final thanks to a Lawrie Sanchez headed goal from a Dennis Wise free-kick and the save of a John Aldridge penalty by the Dons captain Dave Beasant. No one who saw it will forget the Princess of Wales's expression as she presented the winner's medal to Dennis Wise, adorned with a Wimbledon cap worn at a jaunty angle. Wimbledon were known as the crazy gang and renowned for their very physical and colourful style of play. There was always a crunching tackle waiting to happen!

In the Simod Cup, we got to the Final, having won at Everton and at home to Stoke and Swindon en route to Wembley, where on the 27th March, in front of over 61,000 people, we surprisingly lost 4-1 to Reading, who were a division below us. Their star was a very speedy winger/wing-back Michael Gilkes, born in England but eligible to play for Barbados, with whom he earned 5 caps. In the 14th minute, Mick Harford had scored with a goal that he later admitted he had handled into the net. Michael Gilkes then equalised in the 20th minute, and five minutes later, Reading's Stuart Beavon scored with a penalty past Les Sealey. Another two Reading goals from Mick Tait and Neil Smillie guaranteed a comfortable victory for the Royals.

In the League (Littlewoods) Cup, we progressed to the semifinal with wins over Wigan, played over 2 legs, Coventry, Ipswich, and Bradford City. So in the semifinals, we came up against Oxford United over two legs, with both matches played in very wet and muddy conditions. Colin came with me to both legs. Earlier in the season, we had beaten Oxford 5-2 away and 7-4 at home in the league, so you could say we were the favourites. Interestingly in the away first leg of the semifinal, Les Sealey, having been beaten by one penalty taken by Dean Saunders, saved another. The match ended 1-1 with a splendid Brian Stein left-foot strike. The second leg at home was switched to the Sunday afternoon to accommodate live TV coverage. It saw a powerful header from Brian Stein and a free-kick into the top corner by Ashley Grimes give the town a comfortable 2-0 win and a 3-1 aggregate to earn a place in the final. Only a David Evans climbdown over the away supporters ban had allowed Luton into the competition, having been banned the year before. A nasty head injury to Steve Foster should have made him leave the field, but he battled on to the end. It typified the man, fearless and strong, famous for his trademark headband and very aware of the significance of the match! It was around 1987 that playoffs were introduced for the four teams in the league who finished below the automatically promoted. They played a mini tournament of two-leg semifinals and a final at a neutral ground, mostly Wembley. We were involved in several later on, but I don't think we ever won one! Compare that with Blackpool, who have been involved with 17 playoff match wins, 8 finals appearances and 6 final victories meaning promotions! They and Huddersfield are the only 2 clubs to have won promotion from all three divisions via the playoffs!

Chapter 70 - Littlewoods Cup victory

So we were to face the mighty Arsenal in the final on Sunday 24th April 1988. They were the holders, having won the 1987 competition 2-1 in the final against Liverpool. It was their fourth League Cup final. We were in our first. So for me, the key issue was how many tickets I would be able to get as suddenly I had a host of friends and relatives who wanted to support me! I think I recall that the club offered four tickets to each season ticket holder, and later a further allocation became available. However, to get them, I had to make the journey from northwest London to Luton and join a long, slow-moving queue right along the length of Kenilworth Road. In the end, I somehow acquired an amazing 15 tickets, of course, not all at once. I felt after that the struggle to get to Kenilworth Road midweek and the queues for tickets, the time had come to promote myself to the cheapest of the executive areas called the Century Club, hoping that would eliminate the need in the future for going to Luton in person and the long queues. So the next challenge was to arrange to get us all to Wembley and to make it a memorable event, whatever the score was going to be. I knew Wembley well, having been born there, and my grandparents had lived there for as long as I could remember. There were two Chinese restaurants in Wembley Park Drive, so lunch at one of them seemed to be a good idea. The first was not interested at all, saying forcibly that they never opened on match days for fear of violence. The second also said that they didn't ever open on Sundays. However, when I told them I was proposing a party of 15, they suddenly thought they might make an exception! A great idea helped by the fact that in the mews behind were two reserved parking spaces which we were given permission to use! So after a good lunch that everyone enjoyed, we made our way down Wembley Way and found our various seats, all happily in the Luton section. Boaters were the usual headgear on special Luton occasions, and we had acquired a number to which my wife had added appropriate black and white ribbons. Hat making was a major industry in Luton, going back over 200 years and flourishing until the mid-20th century, after which it slowly declined. The town of Luton had become the global centre of hat-making, well known for its excellence in design and production. It is difficult to imagine that in past years it was unusual to see anyone without a hat. There are still a small number of hat factories in the Town. The crest of the club indeed incorporated a sheath of straw as well as the straw hat. The nickname the Hatters was indeed derived from the name plaiters.

The guest of honour at the match was Lady Grantchester, the granddaughter of Sir John Moores, who had built the Littlewoods football pools empire. In 1999 she was listed as the richest woman in the UK, with a family fortune of over a billion pounds. Philip Carter was also in the Royal box, being not only chairman of Everton but the president of the football league at the time.

There was interesting and worrying team news with both sides having selection problems. Darron McDonough, with injured ligaments in his knee in training and Les Sealey with a shoulder injury, were out of the Luton team, and Ricky Hill and David Preece were just back from injuries. Mal Donaghy also had an ankle injury. The goalkeeping jersey went to Andy Dibble for only his eleventh appearance of the season. Brian Stein was wearing a lightweight plaster cast on his arm to protect a healing fracture. Kingsley Black, a 19-year-old local boy, was preferred to Mark Stein. Significantly as it turned out, Arsenal had to play Gus Caesar in place of the injured David O'Leary in defence. The match itself was dramatic. Among the 95,732 supporters, over 35,000 were from Luton. It was the last season of standing behind both goals at Wembley. In the 13th minute, Preece sent a dangerous free-kick into the penalty area, which Steve Forster slipped on for Brian Stein to score. After 60 minutes, there were two substitutes Mark Stein coming on for Mick Harford, who had suffered an injury, while for Arsenal, Martin Hayes replaced Perry Groves. The arrival of Mark Stein was notable as he had absconded from the Luton team hotel the day before the match on hearing that he would only be on the substitutes' bench and was only persuaded to return to the squad just before the match. The Gunners substitution paid off as in the 72nd minute, Hayes scored after a scramble in the Town penalty area to equalise. Arsenal were obviously on top now, and three minutes later, Alan Smith scored to give them the lead. The 80th minute was the truly significant moment of the match. The skilful and speedy Rocastle was fouled in the box, and Nigel Winterburn stepped up to take the penalty, the first one he had taken for the Gunners. There can be little doubt that if he had scored to make it 3-1, an Arsenal victory would surely have followed. However, miraculously Andy Dibble, who had already made a string of great saves, correctly dived to his left to divert it for a corner, keeping it at 2-1. He was rightly selected as the man of the match. Two minutes later, a calamitous error by Gus Caesar allowed Mark Stein to cross for Danny Wilson to equalise with a header. It looked for all the world that the game was going to extra time. Ashley Grimes had come on for David Preece, and in the 90th minute, an extraordinary cross from the right close to the corner with his left foot (he only had a left foot!) was slid into the net by Brian Stein to earn the Hatters an unexpected but deserved victory. This meant the first victory in a major competition for us. Ricky Hill playing his first game since recovering from a broken leg, was the usual cultured midfielder, and of course, Brain Stein's two goals were crucial.

Naturally, we waited for the presentation of the Cup and the lap of honour. Particular praise went to manager Ray Harford for his team selection and for the tactics he employed.

So we all went back down Wembley Way in a celebratory mood, and I remember chatting briefly to Roberto Perrone, a BBC 3 counties radio presenter who I assumed was looking for people to interview. I obviously didn't qualify. We headed back to our house with several of our friends, and I remember it for the first and only time in my life, we cracked open a magnum of champagne! Even my parents, by then in their late 60s, came by to join in the celebrations. In the town, the celebrations went on and on, and the next day there was an open-top bus parade through about 20,000 supporters to a civic reception at the Town Hall. There was a dinner at the Savoy Hotel arranged for that evening. David Evans famously said in his after victory speech: "This is the greatest night in the club's history". I remember him continuing, "There are lots of things I would like to say, but I don't have the vocabulary (with an accent on u rather than a!) to say them"! For a small but family club that always seemed to pull together, it was a wonderful achievement. In fact, 87/88 was undoubtedly the greatest season in Luton Town's history with the Littlewoods Cup success, an FA Cup semifinal, a Simod Cup Final and 9th place in the league.

Chapter 71 - 1988 European Championships

1988 was the year of the Euros in West Germany. It was noted that in group 2, England did not manage to win a single game and indeed suffered a 1-0 loss to the Republic of Ireland, Ray Houghton scoring the goal. Their other results were 1-3 defeats by the Netherlands (a Van Basten hat trick) and also a 3-1 loss to the Soviet Union. Obviously, we were eliminated. In the semifinals, the Netherlands beat West Germany 2-1, and the Soviet Union beat Italy 2-0. The final was won 2-0 by the Netherlands. The Dutch first goal was scored by Gullit, and the second was an amazing volley by Van Basten, which is still regularly shown and admired. Gullit was a flamboyant personality and a wonderfully skilled footballer. Van Basten was just a class striker who was always a joy to watch and won three richly deserved Ballon d'Or amid a host of other individual awards. Unusually he spent his whole 14-year playing career with two clubs, Ajax and AC Milan, scoring a total of 282 goals in 379 matches.

So in 88/89, Luton had qualified for the season's UEFA Cup, but with the post-Heysel and Hillsborough ban in force, English clubs were denied entry. For us loyal Luton supporters, it was really a shame, even a disaster, that we were not able to partake in the competition but having personally witnessed Heysel, maybe it was a lucky escape. Of course, it didn't seem like that at the time, and I have always felt resentful that I was deprived of the one chance to see Luton play in a major European competition.

Chapter 72 - 1989 Another Cup Final

The 88/89 season was noted for another home win for Luton over Liverpool (1-0), but the away game was lost 5-0! The season was again dominated by the Littlewoods Cup campaign. This seemed to detract from the league form, where we finished as low as 16th and only two points above the relegation places. We got to the semifinal of the League Cup beating Burnley after a replay, then Leeds and Manchester City both by a two-goal margin and lastly Southampton again after a replay. The semifinal over two legs was against West Ham, the first leg away gloriously won 3-0, and the second leg won 2-0. I went to both games with Colin, and we were a bit shocked by the hostile atmosphere around and in the Boleyn ground. However, the margin of victory we hoped would make the second leg a formality which indeed it did. So we reached the final, having already played 8 matches in the competition. By then, Harford had scored 3 goals and Roy Wegerle 4 goals, and so the prospective final against Nottingham Forest brought back memories of that FA Cup Final of 1959. My preparations for it seemed to be a mirror image of the previous year with many tickets obtained and lunch on the day of the match in the same Chinese restaurant, again specially opened for us! Surprisingly the gate was only 76,000, so it was no wonder that I could get all those tickets. The Luton team showed some changes from the previous year's final. Brian Stein had left for France and had been replaced by Roy Wegerle, who had come from Chelsea. Roy was an interesting striker who earned 41 caps for the USA from 1992, although he had been born and raised in South Africa. He had gained US citizenship through his American wife. Dave Beaumont, a Scot who had come from Dundee in February, was in central defence alongside captain Steve Foster, as Mal Donaghy had by then left for Manchester United. Les Sealey, who had come after 7 years at Coventry, was back in goal. He, too, would later play for Manchester United in two different spells. Notts Forest had a lot of stars in their team, including captain Stuart Pearce alongside Des Walker, Nigel Clough, Lee Chapman, Neil Webb, Steve Hodge and Gary Parker, who had, in fact, played for Luton three years before. Gary was chosen as the man of the match, emphasising what we were missing! Their manager, of course, was Nigel's charismatic father, Brian. The first half was fairly even, maybe we shaded it, and Mick Harford did score with a trademark header in the 35th minute. I remember one of our group who was an ex Charlton player saying to me at half time I hate to tell you, but although you are winning, Forest will certainly go on to win. How did he come out with such an accurate forecast, but I suppose as an ex-professional, he had a better eye for the trends and tactics than we lesser, totally biased mortals? So the second half was marked by a Nigel Clough penalty in the 54th minute when Les Sealey had brought down Steve Hodge. Les, of course, was mostly a very successful goalkeeper who played in that spell for Luton from 1983 to 1990, but he, unfortunately, had a poor game in that final, including conceding that penalty from which Nigel Clough scored. Les never played for Luton again and tragically died after a heart attack at the age of 43 while working as goalkeeping coach at West Ham. That first Forest goal was followed by a Neil Webb goal in the 68th minute and another Nigel Clough goal in the 76th minute to give Forest, in the end, a comfortable win. It was Brian Clough's first trophy in 9 years and allied to son Nigel's 2 goals. It was an amazing family affair. Still, it was no mean feat for Luton to get to a second successive Littlewoods Cup final. Maybe I should quietly mention that our period of greatest success did correspond to the era of our plastic pitch!

Football obviously went to my head as in 1989 I achieved the nearly impossible feat of attending 3 matches in one day. All I remember is that it started with an 1130 kickoff at St Andrews, Birmingham, then a 3 o'clock kickoff at Northampton and finishing with a 7.30 pm start at Luton. It is a shame that the details have got lost with time, but that may not be so surprising. While I have found an amazing amount of football history from the literature and the Internet, those details will never surface again.

Chapter 73 - Season 1989/90

In the season 1989/90, to avoid the threat of liquidation, we sold the freehold of our ground to the Luton Borough Council for £325,000 pounds, and there was an agreement with the Council for us to pay a peppercorn rent for seven years. This was extended several times, the latest until 2028. Sadly Roy Wegerle was sold to Queens Park Rangers for £1m, a record for us at the time! We spent most of that money, £850,000, on Danish international striker Lars Elstrup who stayed for 2 years before returning to Denmark. An amazing match in that season was a 6-3 defeat at Southampton where the goals always seemed to flow! We struggled but ultimately succeeded in avoiding relegation thanks to three successive wins in the last 3 matches. The first was at home against defending champions Arsenal, which we won 2-0. The next was a home 1-0 win over Crystal Palace, leaving the away cliffhanger at Derby, which we won 3-2. Tim Breaker scored a rare goal and Kingsley Black two, the second one in the 90th minute! In that season, Kingsley was the top scorer with 11 goals. Amazingly it was only our second away win of the season! It still took Sheffield Wednesday to lose at home to Notts Forest, which they kindly did. The result condemned Sheffield Wednesday, at the time managed by Ron Atkinson, to relegation, and we finished in 17th place. We finished just above Wednesday by one goal, and with Charlton and Millwall cut well adrift. Ray Harford was sacked in January 1990 and replaced by former player Jim Ryan who only lasted one year before joining the coaching staff under Alex Ferguson at another of his former clubs Manchester United. He was replaced at Luton by former manager David Pleat who had been dismissed by Leicester in 1991.

We were clearly in financial difficulties, and it was rumoured that Alan Sugar was interested in buying the club and making it a nursery club for Tottenham. FA rules prohibited one person from owning more than one club, so it never got off the ground.

Chapter 74 - Turbulent Times

In May 1990, David Kohler and Peter Nelkin, both property developers, bought joint ownership of Luton Town from David Evans. Nelkin was appointed chairman and Kohler managing director. One of their first actions was to lift the very unpopular ban on visiting supporters. Luton's Kenilworth Road ground had been for "members only" since 1986. It was estimated that the club had lost about £1.5 million through the absence of away fans. At the time in the 90/91 season, they were losing around £10,000 a week and realistically, they would have needed gates of at least 15,000 in our dear old stadium to break even. Only two of the old directors, Henry Richardson and Mike Watson-Challis, remained on the board. Mike Watson-Challis was a 74-year-old Guernsey-based businessman who had made his money as director of Blue Arrow Employment and Recruitment Agency. He was also a keen fan who owned land close to Junction 10 of the M1 (the Luton turn off), which he saw as suitable for a new stadium. The next twist was the donation of that land to the club. It turned out that Mike's wife Sheila was the force behind the throne and was reputed to have given Mike the controlling interest in Luton Town as a birthday present! That land was much later to play a pivotal part in the most recent plans for a new stadium at Power Court in the centre of Luton. The funds for that hoped for stadium build would come from the developments on that land near Junction 10 that Mike and Sheila had originally owned but now belonged to the club. Mike had originally been on the board since 1987 but had resigned in 1991, not being on the same wavelength as Kohler and Nelkin. In the 90/91 season, Nelkin left unwilling to tolerate the protests and abuse from the fans and was replaced as chairman by Roger Smith for his second spell. Kohler stayed on as the chief executive. David Pleat, by then, had replaced Jim Ryan as manager and was well aware of the problems that lay ahead with a very small squad, few experienced players, and all amid a financial crisis. He was not helped by the forced sales of our very successful Dane, Lars Elstrup, for only £200,000 in 1991 and several other first-team players. Kohler was blamed by the fans, and there were regular chants and placards with "Kohler out" the theme. However, the fact remained that the Town were losing a staggering £850,000 a year. In 1992 Kohler had nearly sold the club to boxing promoter Frank Warren. Some would say that we had been punching above our weight for some years. It was generally acknowledged that the club could only stay in existence by selling players. Notable sales included Breaker and Dowie to West Ham. Two new directors, long-standing Luton fan Cliff Bassett, who was wealthy having founded Universal Salvage Auctions and who also owned a large area of land near Junction 12 of the M1, and businessman Chris Green joined the board in the 93/94 season.

Green also put lots of money into the club to help it survive. In 1999 Kohler finally stepped down as chairman and walked away with about a million pounds.

The idea for a stadium on Bassett's land came to nothing, so Bassett, a low key but immensely capable owner, sold the club on to Mike Watson-Challis and his wife Sheila in June 2000. The supporters, in desperation, formed "the fans of Luton action group" (FLAG), which was quite successful in raising money for the club. By 1992 Kohler had moved up to become chairman. His aim was to build a new stadium, "the Kohlerdome". Kohler had grand ideas about building a new larger 20,000 all-seater stadium on that land at Junction 10 of the M1 and close to Stockwood Park. It was to be indoors and modelled on the Pontiac Silverdome in Michigan, one of the stadia used for the preliminary rounds of the 1994 World Cup in the USA. It was to be covered and would have a movable grass pitch, both features that would increase its use for a whole variety of events and consequently increase the potential revenue. In 1996 planning permission for the Kohlerdome was granted subject to M1 widening, which was then refused in 1997 by the then Labour government. As the widening wasn't going to take place, there would not be a stadium on that site.

Kohler then transferred his attention to Milton Keynes with a view to building his Kohlerdome there. Initially, there was great support for the concept by the MK committees, but it came to nothing. By that time, we were in receivership and playing in the third level Division 2, and we continued to lose some of our best players. So we did raise money by selling John Hartson to Arsenal for 2.5 million pounds, and more surprisingly, Matthew Upson to the same club for a down payment of 1 million with maybe another million more to come. That for a central defender who had played just 2 minutes of league football for the first team coming on as a substitute in a league match against Rotherham. It was obviously money well spent as he went on to play 386 league games for a variety of clubs and to earn 21 caps for England. Young striker Tony Thorpe was sold to Fulham for a modest fee but later returned to Luton for three further spells! In the end, the club was refused planning permission for the Kohlerdome. Kohler remained very unpopular with the fans, and he had been attacked in his car, his house in Radlett vandalised, and a petrol bomb and matches posted through his letterbox in 1999. That led Kohler to want to resign as soon as he could sell his 60 per cent holding of the shares of the club. Meanwhile, Cliff Bassett was the main creditor but was owed £2 million pounds which he wanted to get back, so they had to call in the receivers who put the club into administration. The receivers immediately sanctioned the sale of two more players, Graham Alexander, popular as the first choice right-back and one who took and rarely missed penalty kicks and a young and very promising local boy Sean Evers. In return, the receivers sanctioned the signing of Sean Dyche and Tony Thorpe on loan. At the end of 1999, somehow, the players were able to keep us in a comfortable 12th position in Division Two, but again we entered administrative receivership. Bassett was a reluctant chairman and kept a rather low profile. He had left the board when the ban on away supporters was in place but had returned. It was obvious that the priorities were still a new stadium and increased funding. Mike Watson Challis had previously been on the board from 1984 to 1991, but in 2000 he bought the club back from Cliff Bassett. He is reputed to have paid around £3.5 million in a deal that included all the playing staff. Watson-Challis was very supportive of his managers at the time, who included Ricky Hill, Lil Fuccillo and Joe Kinnear, supported by Mick Harford. Kinnear had recovered from a heart attack and had had about 18 months out of the game.

Watson-Challis refashioned the board, which came to include John Mitchell, an ex Fulham player who had tried unsuccessfully to buy the club in 1993. Rob Stringer of Sony music, financial expert Eric Hood who worked for him, and for the first time a supporters representative, Yvonne Fletcher, were also on the board. I knew Yvonne from supporters club meetings and away trips on the club coaches. If I remember correctly, Yvonne retained her seat in the enclosure close to the players' tunnel, where she spent the first half with her friends. Only for the second half would she take her allocated seat in the director's box. She resigned from the board in 2003, saying that she could not function when there was such chaos and hidden agendas. On the financial side, the club was still needing about £4.5 million a year from Watson-Challis to cover existing deficits aggravated by low attendances. After three years as chairman and reportedly 20 million pounds poorer, Watson-Challis decided to resign and become an honorary vice president. Cliff Bassett was appointed director of football, a strange decision as, although a very successful businessman, he knew little about players or tactics and had few contacts within the game. Later Graham Kelly, the former FA chief executive, also joined. There seemed to be real progress in the quest for a new ground. It was hoped that the new stadium would be geared to daily activities rather than just used once a fortnight. A date for the completion of the new stadium was put at the start of the 2005/6 season!! David Kohler remained unpopular because of his further sale of Mick Harford and others. At the end of the season, the club was relegated, missing out on the new premier league, which had started in season 1992/3. It was sadly the beginning of the slippery downhill slope, which led right down to the Conference and non-league football in 2009.

Mayhem at the club was evident in the very early pre-season of 03/04, May to be exact. It was the year that Watson - Challis sold the club to a mysterious consortium for just £4, claiming that the deal struck was the best one for the club. The consortium remained anonymous, but a smarmy, smiling frontman arrived at Kenilworth Road by the name of John Gurney. Gurney had survived a charge of conspiring to import vast amounts of cocaine in 1999. He claimed to be backed by international investors whose identity was never revealed. He had previously been involved with Bedford rugby club, which he saw fall into serious financial problems. In the meantime, he set about dramatic change. He planned to change the club's name to London Luton FC to match the airport. He suggested a merger with the Milton Keynes bound Wimbledon was not out of the question.

Gurney planned to build a 70,000-seat stadium on stilts next to Junction 10 of the M1 and with a Formula One motor circuit involved. He would also share the new ground with NFL and NBA franchises. Within three days of his arrival, Gurney had sacked Joe Kinnear and his assistant Mick Harford by post. A fans phone poll was supposed to have been held then with eight names reduced to three, Kinnear, Newell and Cotterill. The result turned out to be quite irrelevant as although Kinnear was the elected one, Gurney had already offered the job to ex-player Mike Newell, who was out of work having just left Hartlepool! Understandingly it was not the easiest time for Mike to take over!

Joe Kinnear described Gurney as "a man with champagne ideas but Coca Cola pockets". So many grandiose but unlikely proposals led to a group called the Luton Town Supporters Trust being set up from about 3000 dedicated supporters to safeguard the club's future and to provide a unified voice to protest and wrestle control of the club from Gurney. Fans and sponsors were recommended by the Trust to boycott season tickets and sponsorships. It was suggested that a sum of £300,000 might be raised for the Trust to rectify the fact that the players and staff had not been paid while Gurney was there. The club, by then, was at serious risk of being declared bankrupt with the Football League withholding TV and league sponsorship money. Once again, an administrator was called in. The Trust went on to engineer a deal that put the club into administrative receivership, and that saw the end of the short but horrific Gurney era. The Trust acquired shares in the club's major creditor, Hatters Holdings. They were an off-shore company owed millions of pounds by the club.

It had been hoped to oust Gurney as It was unbelievable that such a group fronted by Gurney could have acquired control of the Town and the relief when he left was tangible. BBC2 showed a documentary called "Trouble at the Top", which is well worth viewing. His reign had lasted a mere 55 days but had seemed very much longer. Five years after he left Luton, Gurney was declared bankrupt, excluding him from any future involvement in a football club.

Chapter 75 - Forza Italia

Sadly 1989 was the year of a major and tragic car crash. In September, Gaetano Scirea was a recently retired outstanding Juventus central defender, a sweeper or libero in Italian. He was on a scouting mission in Poland to see one of Juventus's next Europa League opponents, Gornik Zabrje. He was in a car that turned out to have 4 gas canisters in the boot, which exploded when their car was involved in a head-on collision with a lorry. He and two others were killed instantly. The first leg of the match in Poland was marked by a minute's silence in memory of Gaetano. The tie was incidentally won by Juventus 5-2 on aggregate. A couple of years later, I was invited to the Juventus Stadium (Stadio Comunale at that time) and found myself sitting in the Tribuna d'onore ("director's box") next to Gaetano's widow Mariella Cavanna Scirea. She seemed to be a very charming and attractive lady who, in 1994, was also to become a politician, part of the Forza Italia party led by Silvio Berlusconi. He was not only the owner of AC Milan but the prime minister of Italy in four governments between 1994 and 2011. The south stand of the Juventus Stadium is named the Curva Scirea in Gaetano's memory and hosts the Juve ultras, called Draghi (dragons). Mariella fell out with the Draghi over what she saw as racist anti-Neapolitan chants and frequent anti-Semitic insults. If they did not desist, she suggested that Gaetano's name be removed from that stand. The controversy subsequently subsided. On a happier note, Berlusconi encouraged Boniperti to also become a member of the European Parliament as a representative for his party. Boni served for 5 years from 1994 to 1999, and I remember him showing me a beautiful watch which Silvio had given him with a personal message on the back!

Chapter 76 - Spectating in Style

Four of us, dear Colin, together with a friend of his who was a veterinary surgeon, a physician and myself, decided to treat ourselves to Wembley Olympic Gallery memberships. This gave us entry to all soccer matches played at Wembley as well as to the excellent seats, car parking, a meal in one of the lounges and often a VIP guest and entertainer. It was great to know that there would be no problem getting tickets for any of the big soccer games at Wembley. There were some matches too mundane for my friends to want to attend, so, for example, I took my wife to the 1989/90 FA Vase final between Yeading and Bridlington. There wasn't much to remember about the goalless draw, not the first or last time that my wife's attendance was associated with an absence of goals. Luckily the replay (as there was in those days) was played at Elland Road Leeds, too far for us to consider going, but it is recorded that Yeading won 1-0. In 2007 Yeading merged with Hayes to become Hayes and Yeading United and had two other landmark occasions. The first in 2016/17 as Southern league challenge Cup winners and the second scoring more than 100 goals to win the Southcentral division of the Isthmian league in 2018/19! My only other connection with that club had been to go to the frequent programme fairs that they held there in those days. On one occasion, I found the programme of the famous 1953 England versus the Rest of the World game in which Boniperti had scored his two goals. I was able to offer it to Boni on my next visit to Turin, and he was very pleased to read nice things about himself in it!

Chapter 77 - 1990 World Cup in Italy

I decided a year before that I would like to go to Italia 90, the World Cup to be played in Italy. I had a very charming patient who I had got to know quite well as I had anaesthetised her on several occasions for both gynaecological and obstetric matters. It had always been my philosophy to keep relationships with patients at a totally professional level, but she had mentioned to me on several occasions that they had a villa in Tuscany with six bedrooms and a swimming pool that we would always be welcome to use! Maybe this was the occasion to lay aside my principles, and so I approached her. "You know the villa you are always offering to me? Well, would I be able to use it from June 8th to July 8th next year"? She was surprised that I had such precise dates so far ahead but acquiesced immediately even when I also said I would want to bring different groups of friends to fill this grand villa of which she had shown me photographs. Of course, I offered to pay rent, but she absolutely declined that offer. So we circulated lots of our relatives and friends and as you can imagine the take up was quite substantial! They included football fans and others. I had to make clear to the fans that they would have to get their own tickets!

On the day my wife and I (with our elder daughter who was convalescing after a potentially very serious motorcycle crash) flew to Pisa airport where we were met by the lady who looked after the villa, and she drove us there finally up a very long, narrow and winding road. At intervals was the sign Attenzione Viperi ("beware of the snakes"), which was a bit ominous. We did regularly see them coiled up, sunning themselves on the road or nearby. We didn't get close enough to identify them, but they seemed quite big! The master bedroom was palatial but also inhabited by a couple of large geckos on the wall, which almost made my wife head straight back to England. On the next morning, we met the gardener who also looked after the swimming pool and the cook Simonetta, who, over the month, introduced us to many lovely Tuscan dishes. We were living in a style to which we were certainly not accustomed. We needed a car to get to the matches, and we were recommended to use the local garage, which rented us a fairly old Ford Escort. More about the car later, but it was certainly a contrast to my car at home, which was a very spacious and comfortable silver Citroen CX, nicknamed by one of my friends "the silver suppository".

I had got the tickets for the more accessible group matches through normal channels, and the first match for us was Yugoslavia versus Colombia in Bologna up the motorway from Florence. The two-lane motorway was unbelievably busy with, it seemed, everyone, including a huge number of very heavy lorries going much too fast. Changing lanes was virtually impossible! However, we got there safely and had time to visit the beautiful town of Bologna, including the extensive food market and, of particular interest to me, a very old anatomy theatre. Bologna has the oldest university in the world, founded in 1088. In view of that very prestigious university, Bologna is often known as la Dotta - the learned, but also La Grassa - the fat one for its exceptional cuisine and La Rossa the red from its predominantly left-wing politics. It was approaching lunchtime, and I followed my usual habit of visiting a butcher and asking them to recommend a restaurant. After all, they supply them with meat, so they should know! Incidentally, in small villages or towns in predominantly catholic countries, a good tip is to visit the church at 1155 and follow the priest! As they are unmarried, they usually eat lunch out, so they always know the best good value eating places. One anomaly we discovered was that Spaghetti bolognese does not exist in Bologna at all, so don't ask for it there! The meat-based sauce that the Bolognese eat is called ragù and is rarely served with spaghetti, more often with tagliatelle, thin flat ribbon strips of homemade egg pasta!

The car was safely parked in the centre of the city, and as we had had a glass (or two) of some good local red wine, we decided to take public transport to the ground. The stadium was built in the 1920s and didn't look as though it had changed much since, although apparently, it had been fully renovated for this World Cup. In 1983 the ground was renamed the Stadio Renato Dall'Ara in honour of a former president of the Bologna club. It is characterised by a strange tower-like structure behind the halfway line called the "Torre di Maratona".

The only name familiar to me in the Yugoslav team was Dragan Stojkovic, a midfielder who scored 15 goals in 84 appearances for the national team. At the club level, he played for Red Star Belgrade and Marseille, and finally seven years at Nagoya Grampus Eight in the Japanese J League, where he played 184 matches and scored 57 goals. Maybe Grampus Eight will be best known to British fans for being the club where Gary Lineker finished his playing career from 1992 to 1994 and for being managed by Arsene Wenger in 1995-96 after he left Monaco and before he came to Arsenal. There were more familiar names on the bench, including Darko Pancev, who came on in the second half, and Alen Boksic and Davor Suker. In the Colombia team was Carlos Valderrama, never to be forgotten for his copious afro blond hairstyle. He played for three years at Montpellier; otherwise, he spent virtually his whole career with Colombian clubs. He won 111 caps and scored 11 goals in his international career. The other well-known character was goalkeeper Rene Higuita one of the first keeper sweepers. He was known as El Loco (the madman) for his high-risk playing style. He regularly dribbled for large distances from his goal but, even more famously, was, as far as I know, the first and maybe the last to use the face down scorpion kick to clear shots even when standing on his own goal line. He regularly took free kicks close to the opposition goal and penalty kicks with a very high success rate. He managed to score an amazing 41 goals in 380 appearances for 12 different clubs, as well as 3 international goals in 68 games. I say amazing, but he is only in 5th place of goalscoring goalkeepers, a long way behind Brazilian Rogerio Ceni, who played for Sao Paolo and managed to score a phenomenal 131 goals between 1990 and 2015. Higuita had a very chequered time off the pitch, including a few months in prison for his role in a ransom paid in relation to a kidnapping. Andres Escobar, a full-back, was in the team but very sadly achieved notoriety when he conceded an own goal in the next 1994 World Cup, leading to the USA eliminating Colombia. 5 days later, he was shot in a car park in Medellin at 3.30 am and bled to death. The assassin was heard shouting goal after each shot. In the UK, football pundit Alan Hansen a day later was heard to say that "the Colombian defender warrants shooting for a mistake like that", necessitating a public apology from the BBC.

In the match, Davor Jozic, a Yugoslav defender who at the time was playing for Cesena in Italy, scored the only goal, although Higuita made a splendid penalty save late on. The exit from the stadium and 21 bus back to the town centre was uneventful, as was the drive back to the villa.

All the England Group games were played in Cagliari on the island of Sardinia, which was very inconvenient for us residing as we were in Tuscany, and as soon as the draw had been made, we knew it would be impractical, and we would not be able to go to any of them. It was always postulated that the England team were banished to the island in view of their reputation for attracting a hooligan following. Maybe I could have found a patient with a property in Sardinia, but we were really happy where we were, and of course, there was widespread television coverage. Both England and Italy qualified for the first of the knockout rounds, both topping their groups. Italy had maximum points, England had two draws; 1-1 against Ireland and 0-0 against the Dutch and a single win, 1-0 over Egypt. Germany looked ominous with 5 points and 10 goals, compared with England with their meagre 2 goals! In the first knockout round, Italy were drawn against Uruguay to be played in Rome, and we managed to get two tickets courtesy of Giampiero. My wife decided to abdicate in favour of my good friend Richard's son, who must have been about 20 at the time. I know the journey there was uneventful, and we found somewhere convenient to park the car. We went to the hotel Quirinale on Via Nazionale, where the Italian football hierarchy was staying and briefly saw Giampiero to pick up the tickets. The hotel was close to the Tiber River. An interesting sight was of several Italians crouched on the pavement around a small TV set framed with large pieces of cardboard to keep the sun off the screen. They were watching the Republic of

Ireland, managed of course by charismatic Jack Charlton, playing Romania. We should have stayed to watch it as it ended 0-0 and then a 5-4 penalty shoot-out win for the Irish with David O'Leary scoring the deciding 9th penalty. The Stadio Olimpico was on the other bank of the Tiber, so for the first and only time in my life, I went to watch a football match by boat. What fun! The stadium grounds were full of elegant marble statues, very Italian. We got into the stadium in good time for the 9 pm kick-off, and I found myself sitting next to Boniperti's elder son. I had met him on several occasions in Turin and indeed had been at his wedding the year before, and it was nice to be able to hear all the news of the family. As we took our seats, the ground was invaded by clouds of very small black flies which got everywhere, reminding me of a short working spell spent in the north of Newfoundland one June! It must have been about ten minutes before they moved on, and we could start to really enjoy the game. The atmosphere was terrific, as you would expect with Italy playing and over 73,000 in the ground. The Italy team was full of names I knew, whereas, in the Uruguay team, the only one I had really heard of was Enzo Francescoli. He had helped Marseille to the French league title that year, but soon after the World Cup, he moved to Italy and played for Cagliari and later Torino. He finished his career in Argentina with River Plate. The Italy team unusually had very few Juventus players, only the then relatively unknown Salvatore (Toto) Schillaci and Roberto Baggio, the latter now a Juventus player having left Fiorentina for Juve controversially around that time. There were another three in the squad, goalkeeper Stefano Tacconi, second choice to Walter Zenga and midfielders Luigi di Agostini and Giancarlo Marrochi. Schillaci had 3 seasons with Juve from 1989 to 1992 before being transferred to Inter Milan. The Italian team was managed by Azeglio Vicini, who was known for introducing a more attacking style to the previously rather defensive play for which Italy has been renowned. The first half was pretty even, but in the 65th minute, Schillaci scored with a screamer from just outside the D and then Aldo Serena, who had come on as a substitute, scored with a trademark header to seal the win for Italy in the 83rd minute. The whole atmosphere at the end was euphoric, but we were able to get out and return to our car uneventfully. We set off on the over 200-mile journey back to the villa. I drove the first part to Orvieto, a hill town a little bit off our route, but where we were able to sit in the square and admire the beautiful floodlit 14th-century cathedral. I was always one who tried to mix football with a bit of culture! I let Thomas do the second part of the driving, and all was well until we were on the last lap between Florence and our villa near Massarosa. He had been going as fast as he dared, and the old banger rebelled and died. It was about two in the morning, and we had to phone his father to come and rescue us. It was in the early days of mobile phones, but luckily, we had one. I am not sure what we would have done without it! Anyway, Richard, with another of our guests who luckily had a rented car, turned up about half an hour later and got us back to the villa safely but tired and sheepish. The next morning, of course, we had to contact the garage and tell them where their vehicle had broken down and been abandoned. They went to rescue it to find it started perfectly and suggested it had just overheated the night before. They weren't too pleased either, but anyway, we then treated the old banger with greater respect, and it didn't give us any more trouble.

The next match I went to was the following day again in Bologna, where England, managed by Bobby Robson, were playing Belgium in the first knockout round. The kick-off was also 9 pm, and I wondered about the wisdom of going after the fatigue and dramas of the previous day and especially the issues with the car! Of course, I gave in, and we just went there and back without any other excursions. I had wondered about leaving early to make an easy exit. Then I realised that there could be extra time and a penalty shoot-out, and so I stayed on. The match was goalless at 90 minutes, and extra time loomed. Of course, in the 119th minute, a Paul Gascoigne free-kick was put into the net on the volley spectacularly by David Platt to get us into the next round when we would play Cameroon. Platt was being noticed by Italian clubs, and it was no surprise when he joined Bari in 91/92 and then Juventus in 92/93. Finally, he played for Sampdoria of Genoa before returning to England to play for Arsenal and, lastly, Notts Forest. There were some other interesting results, especially Argentina knocking out Brazil 1-0, Germany beating the Netherlands 2-1, and Yugoslavia beating Spain 2-1 after extra time. So on to the quarter-finals and particularly the England match against Cameroon in Naples. It really was too far for any of us to want to go there, but that was a pity as it was a very exciting match. David Platt continued his goalscoring streak with the first goal in the 28th minute. The well-known Roger Milla, now 38 years of age, came on at half-time and inspired 2 Cameroonian goals to give them the lead. The first was a penalty scored by Kindé in the 61st minute and the next by Ekeké in the 65th. But finally, Gary Lineker scored 2 penalties in the 83rd and 105th minute to give us the victory. Another interesting match was Argentina beating Yugoslavia in a penalty shoot-out after the match had ended 0-0. The shoot-out was memorable for 5 of the first ten penalties being missed, including one by Diego Maradona. Italy beat the Republic of Ireland 1-0, the ever-improving Toto Schillaci getting the goal. Germany narrowly beat Czechoslovakia 1-0, which meant guess who was waiting for us in the semi-finals? No less an opponent than Germany, managed by Franz Beckenbauer, and it was to be played in the Juventus newly built Delle Alpi stadium in Turin!

Chapter 78 - A Rare Semi-Final for England

By then, a new quartet had come to stay with us, and one of them was desperate to join me on the trip to Turin for the crucial semi-final match against Germany. All the stadia for 1990 were either new or had been rebuilt, and Juventus had been involved in the building of their new stadium, the Stadio Delle Alpi, so named after the nearby mountain range that forms a backdrop to the city. It did belong to the Turin council rather than the club, and the council insisted that it included an athletics track, although in the years it existed, I don't think it ever did host an athletics event! It really detracted from the atmosphere with the spectators that much further from the pitch. In that World Cup, it hosted 5 games in all, including Brazil's three Group C matches which included a 2-1 win over Sweden, a 1-0 win over Costa Rica and also 1-0 against Scotland. In the round of 16, the notable result was a 1-0 win for Argentina over Brazil, also played in Turin. In 2002, Juventus later purchased the stadium from the council for 25,000 euros. However, it was never popular, but it remained in use until 2009 when it was pulled down and replaced on the same site by the Juventus Stadium, which opened in 2011. I remember that Boni was part of the celebrations to mark the opening of the Juventus stadium when he famously said in Italian, of course, "Vincere non è importante è l'unica cosa che conta", or "Winning is not important. It is the only thing that matters." So the urgent need was to get two tickets, and as on so many occasions, my good friend Giampiero obliged. The tickets would be for collection at the stadium on the day! We left Tuscany in the morning and drove all the way to Turin. We stopped on the way for a good lunch in Asti, a town in Piemonte best known for its sparkling, rather sweet wine Asti Spumante. Piemonte includes Turin and is a province well known for its excellent food and wine. As I was the driver, I had to be very careful with the wine but really appreciated the excellent food, which included the excellent specialty dish Brasato (braised) beef cooked with local Barolo wine and served with polenta (cornmeal)! I have always loved the Grissini (breadsticks), a Piemonte specialty that is always on the table in that part of Italy. We drove on to Turin, got there nice and early and found a good parking space close to the stadium. One is always a bit apprehensive going to a big match far away and not in possession of the tickets, and this was no exception. We had been given definite instructions and went to the office we had been told would have the tickets. Nobody seemed to know anything about it at all, and we were sent on to several different places until finally they were located. I was spoilt by the fact that some of the tickets that came via Boniperti were complimentary but, unfortunately, not these. I don't recall the price but remember I was shocked by it! To this day, I still wonder if 2 complimentary tickets weren't lying about somewhere! At least we were in very good time for the 8 pm kick-off. Germany were clear favourites, having had much better performances and results up to then. They were managed by the exceptional Franz Beckenbauer. Also, it was their eighth semi-final in the last nine tournaments compared with none by England. As was the dreadful habit, the England fans loudly booed the German anthem. The match itself was pretty tense, with England probably shading normal time and Germany extra time. Germany finally opened the scoring through Brehme in the 59th minute. The goal was due to a deflection off Paul Parker that looped over a back-pedalling Peter Shilton. It was to be Shilton's penultimate and 124th match for England, and I remember thinking that he really looked his 40 years of age with slow movements and some indecisions. In the 81st minute, Gary Lineker scored a goal with an accurate cross-shot to bring the team's level. It was Lineker's tenth World Cup goal, four in this tournament to add to his six in 1986. So we came to the end of normal time, and for the third game in a row, England were going into extra time. On 99 minutes, Gascoigne got himself booked for what the referee saw as a bad tackle, and as it was his second yellow card of the tournament, it meant that he would miss the final if we got there. Everyone remembers those tears as he came off. We also remember Gary Lineker passing a message to the bench that they should keep an eye on Paul, who was obviously very disturbed. We came close to winning it when Waddle hit the post after 105 minutes. And then we thought England had scored, but Platt's headed goal in the 111th minute was disallowed for offside. What drama and stress for we supporters, added to in the 118th minute when Germany hit the bar. Full time ended with players of both sides embracing and confirming that the match had been played in great spirit. The first six penalties were all scored, but at 3-3, Stuart Pearce hit a weakish shot straight at Illgner, who having dived away, still managed to save it with his feet. Then Thon scored, meaning Waddle had to score to keep us in the competition. Very sadly, he hit it inches over the bar giving victory and a place in the final to Germany and for us a rather meaningless 3rd place match against Italy, who had lost to Argentina in their semi-final the day before. So a sad walk out of the stadium and a rather quiet and long 193 mile drive back to the villa.

I don't think either of the two final matches deserves much comment, but for the record, England lost 2-1 to Italy in the Stadio San Nicola in Bari in a game that at least saw three goals in a 15-minute second-half spell. In the 71st minute, Shilton erred very badly, failing to deal with a back pass allowing Roberto Baggio to score. It was particularly sad as it was to be his final international. In the 81st minute, David Platt scored a headed equalising goal from an accurate cross by Tony Dorigo to bring the team's level. But Schillaci was then fouled by Paul Parker just inside the penalty area 5 minutes later. Toto got up to convert the kick to win the hosts the third place and win him the tournament's Adidas Golden Ball and their Golden Boot for his six-goal tally. England had the consolation prize of the Fair Play award, having not received any red cards and the lowest average number of yellows per match.

The same evening the amazing 3 tenors concert was held in the historic Terme (Baths) di Caracalla in Rome. The Baths were built in AD 212, during the reign of emperors Septimius Severus and his son Caracalla, but inaugurated by Marcus Aurelius Antoninus in AD 216. I can't describe how much I would love to have been there and heard it live, but it seemed more difficult to get tickets for the 8000 seat venue than the final itself! It was the first time Jose Carreras, Placido Domingo and Luciano Pavarotti had performed together, and the famous Zubin Mehta conducted two orchestras, Maggio Musicale Fiorentino and Teatro dell'Opera di Roma. It was a huge success, watched by around 800,000 television viewers. The recording became the best selling classical album of all time and made huge profits for Decca Records. They came together again during three further World Cups in Los Angeles in 1994, Paris in 1998 and Yokohama in 2002. The next year they did their last concert as a trio.

The final between West Germany and Argentina was full of cynicism and doubtful behaviour, especially by the Argentinians. Just when it was heading for the extra time, the referee awarded Germany a penalty which Brehme converted. That gave them their third title to add to three-second places, making them at that time the most successful football nation in history. So it was soon time to pack up the villa, thank our helpers in a customary manner and head back to London. As you can imagine, although it was 30 odd years ago, I remember it all very clearly and wondered if I might ever have an opportunity to do something similar in the future.

Chapter 79 - Season 1990/91

In this next season, we had a new shirt sponsor, Vauxhall, who were Luton based at the time and finished in 18th place, just enough to keep our place in the top flight for another season. By January 1990, Mick Harford had been sold to Derby County for £450,000, which understandably really upset the fans. In the last match of the season at home to Derby, Mick scored one of the most controversial own goals when he glanced a header past Peter Shilton and into his own net. Was it deliberate to help his old club or an accident? Most are convinced that he knew exactly what he was doing, but he has sometimes denied it! It didn't matter terribly to Derby, who were already relegated by quite a large margin, but Luton had to win to stay up. Anyway, Luton won 2-0, and it was Sunderland who joined Derby in relegation. Of course, only two teams were relegated at that time. It was the third season in a row that we had avoided relegation only in the last match. Lars Elstrup had scored the second to give us a 2-0 victory and safety in 18th position! Lars had come to England in 1989 from Odense and signed for a record fee for the Hatters of £850,000. He stayed for two seasons and scored 18 goals. In the 90/91 season, I managed to get to more matches than usual, including several away fixtures, maybe still with the euphoria of England's gallant failure in the World Cup. It seemed only a matter of time before we lost our 1st division status. It was to be the last season on the plastic pitch. So as predicted, it had been a tough season for the Town. Jim Ryan, who had been a very popular and successful player after signing from Manchester United, remained the manager for what was to be his one and an only full season at the helm before being replaced by the returning David Pleat. Quite a contrast from Ryan's Luton playing career, which had lasted for six years from 1970 to 1976 and included 184 league appearances and 21 goals. Afterwards, he finished his playing career in the United States. Popular manager Jim Ryan's reward for saving the club from relegation was dismissal! So as predicted, it had been a tough season for the Town. Apart from the league matches, we won one round of the FA Cup before losing to West Ham after a replay, lost to Bradford City after a replay in the now named Rumbelows (league) Cup, but survived two rounds of the Zenith Data Systems Cup (Full Members Cup). In addition, we played in a strange indoor 6 and a side tournament sponsored by Guinness, which I believe we won, beating Liverpool 4-0 in the final! Maybe because it was played on an artificial grass surface! The season was marked by the 18 goals scored by Lars, aided by Kingsley Black with 10 goals and Iain Dowie with 7. Kingsley had, of course, come into prominence in the famous Littlewoods Cup final win over Arsenal in 1988 when he was only included due to an injury to Darron McDonough. Local boy Black had come in at the age of nineteen, and he showed unbelievable promise and went on to have a great career winning 30 Northern Ireland caps. In 1991, he was transferred to Nottingham Forest for £1.5 million (a record at the time) after five years with us. Brian Clough, then manager of Forest, had obviously kept an eye on him after he played for us in the 1988/89 League Cup final and also league matches against Forest. Midseason Tim Breaker left for £600,000 to West Ham after 250 games in 8 seasons. Another memorable feature was the penalties taken by defender John Dreyer. He rarely missed or had them saved in spite of a one-step run-up! It was a very unhappy season with some heavy defeats and no victories by more than two goals. Brian Stein had come back from France but was a shadow of his former self scoring only three goals in 39 matches. New sponsors were Universal Salvage Auctions, and that was accompanied by horrible shirts in blue, orange and white. On the playing side, defender Trevor Peake came from Coventry and made 202 appearances in 7 years, and Scott Oakes and Des Linton also came in. Phil Gray came from Spurs for £275,000 and scored 22 goals in 59 appearances. Later he was sold to Sunderland for £800,000 but returned in 1997.

I had a near neighbour who was then in his sixties and had for years been an enthusiastic Spurs season ticket holder as well as a very keen member of the MCC. He had 5 sisters, and amazingly neither he nor any of them ever married. So there was little to stop him from pursuing his sporting interests. When we played at White Hart Lane the week before Christmas, it seemed obvious to go together. It was an amazing match in which, at one point, Spurs went down to nine men, two players having been sent off. Spurs had both Gary Lineker and Paul Gascoigne in their team, so maybe they didn't need all eleven players! Soon the deficit in players was reduced to one when Ceri Hughes, our combative Welsh midfielder, also got sent off, and in spite of the numerical advantage, Luton couldn't make up the score and lost 2-1. Sadly Ceri suffered a very severe injury soon after and missed the rest of the season. However, he played for eight years for Luton and earned 9 caps for Wales in spite of many injury breaks. Unfortunately, Iain Dowie, who had come from non-league football at Hendon, was sold to West Ham for £480,000. He later earned 59 caps for Northern Ireland and scored 12 goals. He became a media man, often being involved in televised games for Sky TV and also was involved in property surveying. One of the matches of the season was a 3-1 win over Liverpool, who were suffering managerial change with the resignation of Kenny Dalglish and the temporary appointment of Ronnie Moran. It was played on Luton's hated plastic pitch. Iain Dowie scored two goals and afterwards predicted correctly that Arsenal would take the title. In 1991 part of the Kenilworth Road end became all-seater which it was hoped would reduce trouble but certainly changed the atmosphere for some time. It further reduced the already small ground capacity.

In 1990 another football landmark was the appointment of Slovakian Josef Venglos as manager of Aston Villa. He was the first manager from outside Great Britain and Ireland to manage a top league English team. He was not totally successful, lasting only the one season when Villa finished in 17th place. Amazingly at present, there are about 14 foreign managers as compared to about 6 British ones in the premier league. Unfortunately, I see the "Italian influence" in many of them, by which I mean to score a goal and try and defend successfully for the rest of the game!

Chapter 80 - Season 1991/92

This was the season when Luton finally lost their top league status. No time is good to be relegated, but it was a particularly bad time as it meant that we would not be part of the newly created Premier League with all its advantages and money. Mick Harford had returned to the Town and scored 12 goals before joining Chelsea in August 1992. David Pleat also came back, but he could not prevent relegation. The Oak Road end always had an amazing entrance path on Oak Road leading across the back gardens of several houses before actually reaching the stadium. It was given over to away fans in that year, although in time and if space permitted, a section was allocated at the main stand end to home supporters with then an empty section separating them from the visiting fans. The 91/92 season was a struggle all through, although moments of excitement were a 1-0 win over champions Arsenal followed by a 2-0 win over Chelsea.

Towards the end of that season, I remember inviting one of my trainees, who was also interested in football, to lunch at my parents' house prior to watching Luton play Manchester United. He was apparently impressed by the contents, which included a wide variety of antiques, and asked my father which would be his favourite works of art. In true dealer mode, he replied, "Anything on which there is a profit!"

The match ended 1-1 thanks to a Mick Harford goal towards the end of a season in which soon after, we were finally relegated from the top division. The last match of the season was in Nottingham against already relegated Notts County. We were in 20th place and needed to win to survive. I went up to Meadow Lane with a good friend and fellow supporter, and we were amazingly among 5000 Luton supporters! It was a very long and sad day as we were finally relegated after a 2-1 defeat with a Julian James goal being insufficient. My good friend emigrated to Guernsey, so he only rarely came to matches after that. It meant participating in the new second-tier, now strangely called Division 1 for 92/93. We have never returned to the top flight since. The plastic pitch had finally been removed, the ban on away supporters lifted, and a new stand built. A new stand was constructed on the angle between the main and Kenilworth Road stands. It was a family stand seating 711 fans and was opened in 1991. It was later formally named and called the David Preece Stand and opened by David's widow in 2008, one year after David's death.

The early 90s were the seasons when the best players in Europe seemed to be in Italy. The three Dutchmen Ruud Gullit, Frank Rijkaard and Marco Van Basten were at AC Milan and three Germans Andreas Brehme, Lothar Matthaus and Jurgen Klinsmann were with Inter Milan. I can add Argentinian Gabriel Batistuta at Fiorentina. Juventus had Toto Schillaci, Dino Zoff and Roberto Baggio, amongst other great Italians.

Paul Gascoigne has to be mentioned as he was one of the great mavericks but had wonderful skill as an attacking midfielder. He would light up any game with his ability to improvise and do the unexpected. He made his name with Newcastle and Spurs and with England, for whom he made 57 appearances and scored 10 goals. He had wonderful skills but not the temperament to match. His overenthusiastic foul tackle in the 15th minute of the 1991 FA Cup final against Nottingham Forest resulted in his having to leave the field with a cruciate ligament injury. He was injury-prone, with not all of them being suffered on the football pitch. He went to Lazio in Rome in 1992 for a fee of 5.5 million pounds, a signing on fee of £2 million and a contract worth about £22,000 a week! However, he was disappointing and was never able to settle up to all sorts of pranks and mischief, often fuelled by alcohol. He had weight problems which were never really resolved. After a 1-1 draw against Juventus, for which Gazza had been dropped by Lazio coach Dino Zoff, he was asked for his opinion as to why he was not playing, and he responded with a loud belch into the reporter's microphone. That cost him a £9000 fine, but he still managed to endear himself to the fans and the media. In his last year at Lazio, he managed to break his leg, tackling Alessandro Nesta in training. He was later transferred in 1995 to Glasgow Rangers and then on to Middlesbrough and two years later Everton. We saw him once at the Nice airport although he was trying to avoid the paparazzi, he made it more difficult by wearing a suit in an extraordinary bright colour!

That year we went with three friends to Verona to see the famous open-air opera in the wonderful roman amphitheatre. I remember vividly hearing a relatively unknown 26-year-old singer called Cecilia Bartoli, who, of course, later would become one of the world's greatest coloratura mezzo-sopranos. After lunch on one of the days, we found ourselves drinking coffee in our hotel's bar. Amongst the other guests were the Sampdoria football team, newly managed at the time by Sven-Goran Eriksson, preparing to play the Hellas Verona team in a pre-season friendly. Hellas were famous because, as amongst very unlikely successes, they had won the championship for the only time in their history in 1985. I immediately recognised Des Walker, who had just signed from Nottingham Forest, and Roberto Mancini, the well-known Italian international. Sampdoria had been runner up the season before losing to Barcelona at Wembley and, before that, had won their one and an only Italian league title in 1990/91. However, Walker did not have a successful season in Italy, leaving after a year to join Sheffield Wednesday. He had been played in a lot of the matches at full-back rather than his normal central defender position, which had not helped. Of course, Mancini was and is one of the most famous Italian footballers playing from 1982 to 1997 for Samp scoring 132 goals, as well as for a host of other clubs. He later managed many more, including Inter to three consecutive Serie A titles, a club record. Then Manchester City to one league title and one FA cup final victory, as well as in later years he is still managing the Italian national team. We went over to have a chat with them both. It seemed Roberto was giving Des a lesson in how to make and drink espresso coffee! They were both very friendly, although Des was rather shy, suffering, of course, from a lack of Italian. We never did discover how the match went, but as a friendly, it probably doesn't matter very much. I saw that Sampdoria Barcelona 1992 European Cup final played at Wembley. It was the last final before the cup was re-formatted as the Champions League. Barcelona were managed by Johan Cruyff. Not for the first time. I am not sure how I got the tickets, but anyway, it was a dour affair with some excellent goalkeeping from Zubizarreta for Barca and Pagliuca for Samp. Stars for the Samp team included Lombardo, Mancini and Vialli, and for the Barca team, Ronald Koeman, Michael Laudrup and the Bulgarian Stoichkov. It was only settled by a 112th-minute long-range free-kick goal by Ronald Koeman. Ronald had played for Barcelona for six years before finishing his playing career with Feyenoord back in Holland. As a Dutch international, he earned 78 caps scoring 14 goals. He is renowned as the highest-scoring defender of all time, with 239 goals. He must be one of the best-known football figures around, taking into account his playing and managerial record. He managed in six different countries, including his native Netherlands. He had recently succeeded the less known Quique Setien as Barca manager. Quique was dismissed after an 8-2 Champions League quarter-final defeat to Bayern Munich in 2020. Koeman only lasted one year at Barca, during which time they won the Copa del Rey with a 4-0 win over Bilbao. The next season the results were poor by Barca's standards, and he was dismissed.

Italy had a TV highlights programme called Novantesimo Minuto which translates as the Ninetieth minute. It started in 1970. It appeared just an hour after the final whistles and initially had the highlights of all the Serie A games. Of course, in those days, all the games were played on the same day and kicked off at the same time. There was no other coverage of games in Italy except Italian internationals and European cup ties involving Italian clubs.

Very cleverly, in 1992, TV Channel 4 started a programme in the UK called Gazzetta Football Italia, cashing in on the undoubted interest in football and Italy that the 1990 World Cup had generated. The compere was to be Paul Gascoigne, who was at the time with Lazio, one of the

Rome teams, but he really did not fit the bill. The honour went to one James Richardson, who will always be remembered for eating large ice creams on scenic terraces in Italy surrounded by a pile of Italian sports papers. James was the son of a dealer in Russian icons, and James could be seen as an icon of football punditry! The format was a magazine programme on Saturday morning and a live match from Serie A on Sunday afternoon. Richardson was perfect for the job speaking several languages and having real skill and humour as a presenter and interviewer. The show went on till 2002, but James is still to be seen and heard regularly in the media. Even today, there is an equivalent program called Golazzo. As far as I know, Italy is unique in having three daily sports papers. They are the pink La Gazzetta Dello Sport based in Milan, Tuttosport from Turin and Il Corriere Dello Sport from Rome! Another feature of Italian football soon to be copied in other countries was detailed crowd choreography, so the fans made all sorts of wonderful decorations with flags, scarves and other things on the stands. The spectators commonly managed, in spite of heavy security, to smuggle in flares, smoke bombs and a whole host of potential missiles.

The 1992 football season was known for two big changes in England. Firstly goalkeepers were no longer allowed to pick the ball up from a pass from a teammate's foot. The idea was to speed up the game by reducing time-wasting tactics and encouraging goalies to become more skilled with their feet. So the concept of the sweeper-keeper was introduced. For me, it has been one of the rather few really successful changes to the rules.

The other and the far more confusing thing was the renaming in 1992 of the 1st division as the Premier League. This was done to better take advantage of lucrative sponsorship and TV rights which it certainly did. The richer clubs profited, but those promoted from the division below usually really struggled. In 1995 the premier league was reduced from 22 to 20 teams, increasing the share of the already massive cake for each club left. Inevitably the players' salaries rose astronomically, and their newfound riches, as well as the usual spare time, led to a spate of problems. It would be impossible to name all the players who ran into trouble with alcohol, drugs or gambling, but of course, George Best, Tony Adams and Paul Merson were among the most well-known. While Tony and Paul were among those who recovered, George sadly did not and, in spite of a liver transplant, died at the relatively young age of 59. Tony Adams has been very successful with his Sporting Chance clinic, a charitable foundation for those sportsmen suffering from these afflictions. In 1999 he received an MBE for his services to professional football. In the end, Paul Merson seems to have made an amazing recovery, now appearing regularly as a pundit on Sky Sports. Among the notorious gamblers was Keith Gillespie, who played for Newcastle at the time they were managed by Kevin Keegan, and they really challenged Manchester United for the title. In the Newcastle side were two charismatic foreign players, Faustino Asprilla from Colombia and David Ginola, a Frenchman. Gillespie is reputed to have lost more than seven million pounds and, indeed, in 2010, was declared bankrupt. In spite of this major problem, he earned 86 caps for Northern Ireland. John Hartson, the ex Luton youngster, is another with a recovered serious gambling addiction which is due to the launch of a new foundation named the JH gambling and addiction workshop to help those struggling with those addictions. I have always seen gambling addiction as a hidden addiction not noticed necessarily and probably more damaging to the person and their families as a result.

Chapter 81 - Season 1992/93

The year 1992 was the year of the European Championships in Sweden. Only eight teams were included in the finals. It was the first Europeans in which a unified Germany had competed, as did the Commonwealth of Independent States, representing the newly dissolved Soviet Union. Yugoslavia had topped their group and had therefore qualified for the finals, but due to international sanctions resulting from the ongoing wars and the breakup of that country, they were excluded by UEFA just ten days prior to the competition. Their place went to Denmark, who had finished second in their qualifying group behind Yugoslavia. Their preparation was unusual, with many of the Danish players having to return from their holidays by the seaside! Both Laudrup brothers (Michael and Brian) had quit the national team in 1990 after disagreements with newly appointed manager Richard Møller Nielsen. He had got the job in 1990 only after the German Horst Wohlers had been chosen as manager but could not leave his post with Bayer Uerdingen 05. Brian Laudrup, then playing for Bayern Munich, did re-join the squad for those Euros. The team relied heavily on goalkeeper Peter Schmeichel whose greatest claim to fame was saving Van Basten's penalty in the semifinal shoot out, the only one not to be scored in that match by either side! The Denmark squad contained 12 players out of the 20 who played for Danish clubs. The squad were not expected to do very well, but in Group 1, the Danes advanced with Sweden ahead of England and France. From Group 2, the Netherlands and Germany qualified, giving us the four semifinalists. In that round, Denmark beat the 1998 winners, the Netherlands who lost 5-4 on penalties after a 2-2 draw. The other semi saw Germany beat the hosts Sweden 3-2. The surprise finalists Denmark went on to beat reigning World Cup winners Germany 2-0 to win their first international trophy. Lars Elstrup was in that squad, having by then left Luton to return to Odense, and he scored the winner against France in a group match, coming on as a substitute for Brian Laudrup. He also converted one of the winning penalties in that semifinal shoot-out. He was an unused substitute in the final when Denmark won to prove that underdogs can sometimes win. In total, Lars earned 34 international caps and scored 13 goals for his country. Much credit must go to controversial manager Richard Møller Nielsen who in 1995 received the Silver Medal of Merit from the Danish state. It was the last tournament with only eight teams and the last with only two points awarded for a group stage win. A strange feature of the finals was the absence of any British referee while Italy and Switzerland each had two!

In 1992/3, Luton finished in 20th place in the newly named Division 1, just avoiding relegation. A rare win was 2-0 over Watford, but 19 goals from Northern Ireland's Phil Gray, who had been an apprentice at Tottenham, was the decisive factor in our survival. Steve Claridge was signed from Cambridge in August but only scored 2 league goals in 16 games before returning to Cambridge in November. In all, Steve made over 30 career moves, perhaps an all-time record! Steve did a lot of media work and was another of the well-known big gamblers. Mention should also be made of Kerry Dixon, who was born in Luton in 1961 and started his career at Dunstable Town before going on to first Reading and then Chelsea, where he scored 147 league goals and earned 8 England caps. He came to Luton in 1993 from Southampton on a free transfer and stayed until 1995, having made 88 appearances and scored 20 goals.

A sad event in that season was a car crash in which Luton youngster Darren Salton was in a car driven by Paul Telfer, a fellow Scots player who went on to earn one full cap. In the other car was a lady who very sadly died. They were returning from the golf course. Darren Salton was a young Scots central defender, and he suffered serious injuries necessitating several days on a life support machine and a period in a coma. Although he made an amazing recovery, his leg injuries prevented him from ever playing at the top level again. Before the accident, he had earned 7 under 21 caps for Scotland and was considered a future star player.

It was the year of the centenary of Liverpool FC, and Giampiero was invited to the commemorative ceremony. In fact, he was the only foreign football president to be so honoured. It was a special moment for him when he was introduced to Queen Elizabeth, and he found her to be very knowledgeable about football and especially the events at Heysel. A photo of their warm handshake sits proudly in his office. It is not like me to boast, but I can beat that, having been presented to the Queen three times. The first time was during her visit to the old Charing Cross Hospital in the Strand, then much later when she came to open the new Charing Cross Hospital in Fulham in 1973 and lastly at the opening of the Royal College of Anaesthetists in Russell Square in 1993. She seemed to have an amazing memory recounting several events from her previous visits.

In 1993, the death of Gaetano Scirea had a profound effect on Boniperti. He felt personally responsible for Gaetano's death and wanted to resign from his executive position. Indeed he was replaced for a while by Luca di Montezemolo famous for being the manager of the Ferrari formula one team that won the world championship with driver Niki Lauda in 1975 and 1977. In 1982 Montezemolo also masterminded Italy's hopeful America's Cup team Azzurra, the first Italian yacht club to enter the event. He headed the organising committee for the Italia 90 World Cup. Giampiero was very unhappy at the way football was going, especially the excessive expenditure on players, both transfer fees and salaries. His ideas were totally different to those of the new breed of owners and chairmen of the clubs. He was a new type of football club president chosen for his reputation rather than his wealth. In the first-ever all Italian UEFA Cup final in 1990, Juve beat Fiorentina 3-1 on aggregate. It was noteworthy for being 23-year-old Roberto Baggio's last match for Fiorentina before his transfer to Juventus. That transfer, a record at the time of about £8 million pounds, caused riots in the streets of Florence and increased the already intense rivalry, even hatred, between the two clubs. I don't remember the details, but I remember that Franco Zeffirelli, the most famous Italian producer of opera, films and TV of the time, got involved in the rivalry between Fiorentina and Juventus while siding with Fiorentina. Franco was also a senator in the European Parliament from 1994 until 2001 for the Forza Italia party at the same time as Boni. Baggio won the Ballon d'Or in 1993, playing in a Juve side that included Gianluca Vialli, Antonio Conte and Jurgen Kohler. In 1989, I accompanied my parents to Florence for an art dealer's conference of an organisation called CINOA (Confederation Internationale des Negociants en Oevres d'Art), of which my father was then the president. With my amazing luck and frequently a victim of coincidences, Juve were playing in Florence that Sunday, and I was able to go. The violence in the streets around the ground was widespread and very frightening, even though I had seen plenty of it back home. The away Juve supporters, especially the Draghi, marched together in large numbers towards the ground in a very threatening and frightening manner. The stand I was in was open and standing, although we mostly sat on the stone terracing. I cannot remember the result but only that I got safely back to reunite with the family and was able to add a further club to the grounds I had visited but would not be keen to go again. Boniperti's tenure ended in the summer of 1994, but he has continued as Honorary President and remains an icon. His final and very significant act had been to sign Alessandro Del Piero from Padova. Roberto Baggio fell out with manager Marcello Lippi and left Juventus for AC Milan in 1995.

Chapter 82 - Season 1993/94

In 1993 Phil Gray had left for Sunderland for a fee of £775,000. One of the comebacks of the season was giving Stoke a two-goal lead and then scoring six, including a Kerry Dixon hat trick. The main goalscorers were Kerry Dixon (20), Scott Oakes (13), Paul Telfer (8) and John Hartson (7), and for the second season running, we finished in 20th place. The last ten games produced only one win, three draws and six defeats. John Hartson, as a youngster, had issues stealing a credit card from the family who were lodging him, and the £50 withdrawn was to finance a growing gambling addiction. In all, for the Hatters, he managed 63 appearances and 13 goals. In total, he made a total of 400 league appearances for eight clubs scoring 167 league goals. His longest spell was with Celtic. He also appeared in 51 matches and scored 14 goals for Wales. His gambling became a major problem, but in spite of that and a serious testicular cancer issue, he had a very successful career, including much media work after retirement as a player. The good news was the return of Mitchell Thomas from West Ham, who in his second spell made 186 league appearances. We had a great run to the semifinal in the FA Cup, beating Southend in the 3rd round and Newcastle, managed by Kevin Keegan, after a replay in the 4th round. A very young Tony Thorpe scored the equaliser in that away draw, and then we won the replay 2-0 with goals from two other very young players, John Hartson and Scott Oakes. After beating Cardiff 2-1 in Wales, the quarter-final brought us together with old foe West Ham, and after a goalless away match, we won the replay 3-2 thanks to a Scott Oakes hat trick. The semifinal played at Wembley, unfortunately, resulted in a 2-0 defeat by Chelsea, managed at the time by Glenn Hoddle. Of course, Chelsea were a league above us at the time, but they went on to lose the final 4-0 to Man United.

In the same season, Juventus changed coaches, Marcello Lippi replacing Luigi Maifredi. From 1976 Juventus had gone on to always have Italian managers with the one exception of Didier Deschamps in 2006/07. The team was strengthened by the arrivals of Ciro Ferrara, Didier Deschamps and Paulo Sousa. The forwards were considered strong enough with Vialli, Ravanelli, Roberto Baggio and Del Piero already there. At the same time, there were boardroom changes with Agnelli appointing the trio of Roberto Bettega (yes, the ex-footballer) vice president, Antonio Giraudo CEO until 2006 and Luciano Moggi Sporting Director. Boniperti left in April of that year but received the title of honorary president. Giraudo was to be responsible for the building of the Stadio Delle Alpi in time for the 1990 World Cup, the floating of the club on the stock market and a lucrative sponsorship deal with the oil company Tamoil. The club was stripped of its 2005 and 2006 titles and relegated to Serie B with a 9 point penalty but managed to win promotion back to

Serie A at the first attempt. Moggi also expressed unwelcome negative views about gay footballers. As a result, he resigned in 2006 and gave up all involvement in football administration except for some media work.

Chapter 83 - Man Utd in Barcelona

On the 2nd November 1994, Colin and I embarked on a day trip to Barcelona to see his beloved Manchester United in the Champions League group stage. We got to Luton airport very early and, not for the first time, were struck by the amount of beer being consumed! Being a couple of squares, we settled for all day breakfast and a coffee. The aircrew had quite a job keeping the fans in their seats, not surprising with all that beer on board. On arrival at Barcelona's El Prat airport, we were welcomed by an enormous police presence who proceeded to escort us to coaches, which took us straight to the ground. It was about 3 hours before kick-off, but again the police kept us confined, and there was no way we could even get to a shop to buy a scarf or even a programme, if there were any. It always amazed me how few clubs that I visited abroad sold programmes. Obviously, they were losing a considerable sum of potential revenue! Not surprisingly, we were taken straight to our section, which was in the third (top) tier but still gave us a fantastic view. With all that time to spare, one had time for many thoughts. One of mine was of the Spanish patient I had had who was a dentist and a Barcelona season ticket holder. He lived and worked some distance from Barcelona and said that he was never able to get to midweek matches because of his work, and I would be welcome to use his ticket for any of those matches. Sadly I never got round to taking him up on the offer. The match itself was not so enjoyable with United losing 4-0! Eric Cantona was absent because he was suspended, and there was at that a limit on the number of foreign players allowed in a team. As a result, Peter Schmeichel was replaced in goal by Gary Walsh. The Barca team included Pep Guardiola, who, of course, went on to be one of the most successful managers of all time and Ronald Koeman, who also had a distinguished career not only as a player but also as a manager. The four goals were shared between Hristo Stoichkov with two and Romario and Ferrer with one each. As a genuine football fan, I could appreciate the speed with which Barca attacked and passed the ball to each other. That style has continued for many years and has contributed in a big way to their continued success. Not surprisingly, we were kept locked in our area for a good hour after the final whistle, and then we were escorted straight back to the airport. The police stayed with us until we were through the check-in and security and were no longer their responsibility. As usual, like for any team that has lost, the return journey was pretty quiet.

Chapter 84 - Season 1994/95

In 94/95, the Kenilworth Road end of the stadium was converted finally to an all-seater. All victories over Watford are worthy of comment, and a 4-2 win at Vicarage Road, particularly so! Luton used unusually a three at the back formation, and Paul Telfer scored twice and Scott Oakes and Kerry Dixon one each. On 27th December, we had a belated Christmas present with a 3-0 win over Sunderland. Trevor Peake played his second game in two days at the age of 37! In the League Cup, we lost a penalty shoot-out in a replay against Fulham, both matches having ended 1-1. One of my mistakes in that season was to drive down to Southampton for a FA cup 4th round replay on a very wet evening in February. We had drawn 1-1 in the home match. Southampton had Alan Ball as manager. Their team included Bruce Grobbelaar, newly arrived from Liverpool, in their goal, and Matt Le Tissier, a rare one-club man, who scored two of the six goals that the hosts scored without reply, one of which was a penalty. His 33rd successful kick out of 34 penalty kicks up to then. Le Tissier overall produced a masterclass, and we, being 4-0 down after 40 minutes and 6-0 after 67 minutes, were obviously never in the game. It seemed a very long drive home, particularly as there was heavy rain. That season we did not have any notable goalscorers, Dwight Marshall topping the list with thirteen. I remember Gary Waddock, a red-haired defensive midfielder who always gave 100% and earned 21 caps for the Republic of Ireland. He stayed for almost 5 years before retiring from playing in 1998 and going into management. Last heard of; he was on the Cambridge United coaching staff. We finished the season in 16th place, safely above the relegation zone.

It was a period in Italy which was also marked by serious football violence. In early 1995 a fan had been fatally stabbed outside the Genoa stadium. The better news was that Juventus won their 23rd Scudetto, although the capocannoniere (top goal scorer) with 26 goals was Fiorentina's Argentinian striker Gabriel Batistuta. He may be remembered for scoring hat tricks in two successive World Cups.

Chapter 85 - Eric Cantona

Cantona had started in French football at Auxerre but, after several short stays at a number of other French clubs, came to England to Leeds United. In 1986 he had received a three-month suspension for aiming a dangerous kung-fu tackle on Nantes player Michel Der Zakarian, resulting in a three-month suspension. This was later reduced to two months as his club Auxerre threatened to make the player unavailable for selection in the national team. In 1991/92, he had helped Leeds United to the title and then to victory in the 1992 Charity Shield in which he scored a hat-trick in a very exciting 4-3 win over Liverpool. He then moved to Manchester United for the 1992-93 season and also immediately helped them to the title. On the 25th January 1995, Manchester United were the visitors to Crystal Palace on a cold and wet night. Once again, Colin persuaded me to go with him, and we were to witness one of the most bizarre events that we ever saw at a football match. In the 49th minute Eric Cantona, always controversial, was shown a red card by referee Alan Wilkie for a bad foul on Richard Shaw, the Palace defender who had frustrated him up to then by marking him very closely. He took the long walk back to the dressing rooms, which were in the corner of the pitch. As he was walking along the touchline escorted by United kit man Norman Davies it was reputed that a Palace supporter Matthew Simmons shouted some abuse at him using the words "F**k off back to France, you French bastard". Cantona responded with the kung fu kick that he had exhibited before and some punches. The result was a long ban during which he had to suffer an eight-month suspension, a £20,000 fine, and do 120 hours of community service. At a later press conference, he came out with the famous quote, "when the seagulls follow the trawler, it's because they think sardines will be thrown into the sea!" He was banned by United until the end of the season. He was also stripped of the captaincy for a year by French national team manager Henri Michel for insulting him on TV, calling him a bag of shit. In view of his history, maybe we shouldn't have been so surprised by the events at Crystal Palace. As far as that match was concerned, United took the lead in the 57th minute, but defender Gareth Southgate equalised, and the match ended in a 1-1 draw. Eric returned to playing on the 1st October 1995 at home to Liverpool and helped United to a 2-2 draw, making the first for Nicky Butt and then scoring a penalty himself. His goals helped United to overhaul a 12 point deficit to overtake Newcastle, managed then by Kevin Keegan, on the way to the title and in the same season, they also won the FA Cup final against Liverpool. Undoubtedly Alex Ferguson was the driving force in persuading a reluctant Eric to return from France and prove that he was the same genius of a player. In 1988 he was dropped for a year by manager Henri Michel for insulting him on TV.

Characteristically Eric would play with the collar of his number 7 shirt turned up. He was responsible for a unique goal celebration when after scoring against Sunderland with a sublime chip over the goalkeeper, he stood absolutely still and motionless before turning around and raising both arms! Eric was part of the Manchester United team that won four premier league titles in 5 years and, amazingly, three league and Cup doubles. Eric played a total of 45 matches for France, in which he scored 20 goals. For a tall man, he had outstanding technical skills with his feet and goalscoring ability with both head and feet. He was always provocative and aggressive, and he retired early in 1997 at the age of 31. He went on to have a very successful new career in acting and was in demand by advertisers, especially Nike. His first major film role was in playing Paul de Foix opposite Cate Blanchett in Elizabeth. His second wife, Rachida Brakni, directed the stage play Face au Paradis (In front of Paradise), in which Eric made his stage debut in 2010. Most recently, he appeared in a video for the Liam Gallagher song "Once". He has put considerable energy into the Fondation Abbé Pierre, which works to provide housing for the underprivileged.

He was one of the first to be admitted to the English Football Hall of Fame in 2002 and, in 2021, to the Premier League Hall of Fame as well. Pele included him in his FIFA 100 list of the greatest living players. Amazingly nearly 25 years later, the Old Trafford crowd still sing his name during matches.

Chapter 86 - A Semifinal with Man United

During the season 94/95, Manchester United got to an FA Cup semifinal against Crystal Palace to be played at Villa Park on a Sunday, April 9th, and Colin was keen to go. Luckily I didn't have to miss a Luton game as we had played and beaten Notts County 2-0 the day before. To be fair, Colin came with me to that Luton match as well, and at least I was able to show him a winning performance from our Division one team, who were to finish in 16th place that season! The contrast between the two stadia, Kenilworth Road and Villa Park, was, of course, massive! We drove up and planned to get there early so as to find parking and a suitable eatery nearby. Not unusually, the street parking spots were policed by the local youths with their "can I look after your car, mister". I cannot imagine what the consequences of refusing would have been, but once the money was safely in their possession, they moved speedily on to the next arrivals. The next problem was in that particular area of Aston all the restaurants were unsurprisingly of Asian origin, a food that Colin really didn't like! I think, in the end, we found a small cafe with a bit of chicken that had not been curried on the menu. We ate it watched closely by several of the children of the proprietor, which was a bit off-putting, to say the least! Anyway, we survived it and took our places in the stands in good time to witness an exciting game that went to a 1-1 draw and on to extra time. Palace had scored early in the first half through our friend Iain Dowie, but full-back Denis Irwin had equalised for United with a wonderful free-kick. Armstrong put Palace ahead again in extra time, but a Gary Pallister headed goal from a Gary Neville long throw in meant that the game ended 2-2, and a replay was necessary the following Wednesday evening again at Villa Park. Being hard-working people, we couldn't make that - a pity as United won 2-0 with goals from the two centre backs, Steve Bruce and Gary Pallister. However, it was marked for Roy Keane getting a red card for stamping on Gareth Southgate, who was playing for Palace, his first club. In the same minute Darren Patterson, soon to join Luton, got sent off as well for fighting with Roy Keane. Apparently, the atmosphere was rather tense, especially after earlier in the season that "kung-fu incident" at Crystal Palace. Of course, Cantona was suspended for both semifinal matches. Incidentally, United lost 1-0 to Everton in the final. A Paul Rideout header and several great saves by Neville Southall decided the match. Colin was an avid collector of programmes and would be very upset if, for whatever reason, he was not able to get one at a particular match. If I was going to a match without him, he always asked me to get him one as well. I have to say that it was depressing to see how the prices went up constantly, and personally, when a Wembley programme reached £10, I decided enough was enough. I feel really sorry for whoever had the task of sorting out and disposing of Colin's programmes after his sad demise in 2020. The same can be said about my extensive programme collection!

Chapter 87 - Season 1995/96

1995/96 was a disastrous season on the field, with the Town finishing in bottom place and relegated to Division 2 (3rd tier). A small consolation was avoiding defeat in the two drawn matches against Watford, who were also relegated with us. That ended 26 years in the top two divisions for Luton. The relegation was, of course, blamed on owner David Kohler for not spending enough money on players.

David Pleat had left for Sheffield Wednesday, and his role went to one of the coaches, Terry Westley totally inexperienced as a manager. He only lasted five months before being sacked, and Lennie Lawrence replaced him and at least stayed for five years, quite a good innings for a manager at Luton who have had over 30 different managers since the war.

We suffered some big defeats, for example, 5-0 at Stoke and 4-0 at Portsmouth and Birmingham. I was glad I didn't go to many away games! Notable additions were full-back Graham Alexander who came from Scunthorpe, and centre half Steve Davis from Burnley. Bulgarian Boncho Guentchev and Dwight Marshall were joint top scorers with a meagre nine league goals each. Another foreigner Norwegian Vidar Riseth came from Kongsvinger in his native country on loan but only played in 12 games and, in spite of being played as a striker, failed to score a single goal before moving on to Linz in Austria. The acumen of Lennie Lawrence brought in £500,000 by selling players. In spite of this, he also managed to bring in Sean Dyche on loan from Bristol City and Tony Thorpe from Leicester City, who were both to be very successful. In the FA Cup 3rd round, we had a humiliating 7-1 defeat at Grimsby! We entered the Anglo-Italian Cup in 1995/96, played four matches and lost three of them, the sole victory being a 5-0 at home over Ancona. I didn't go to any of them, surprisingly, in view of my attachment to Italian football. Maybe the fact that the Italian sides were from Serie B (2nd league) lessened the attraction, plus fans fighting was rather frequent.

There was a Luton fans group in the wings known as FLAG, Fans of Luton Action Group, who were keen to follow an example set by Bournemouth for the fans to own 51 per cent of the club. In 2000, Flag had been given a supporter's place on the board. In matches, if we scored, the fans famously sang, "We're bust, and we're 1-0 up." Over the years, three of our managers had two separate spells with the club, David Pleat, Mick Harford and Nathan Jones. Striker David Oldfield had two spells at Luton, making 39 league appearances between 86 and 89 and a further 140 between 95 and 98. He scored all the three Town goals in the 96/97 play-offs and, in total, scored

32 goals. Tony Thorpe was the top goalscorer with 30 goals in that season and a total of over 70 goals in his two spells with us. He was sold to Fulham for around a million pounds and later to QPR for a cut-price fee of £68,000. The low fee was after Thorpe threatened to invoke a rule where he could move to QPR for free. This made him very unpopular, especially as the club was in dire financial circumstances at the time, and he was never forgiven by the majority of fans.

Chapter 88 - George Best's 50th Birthday

May 22nd 1996, was the day of the European Cup final, and Juventus were playing Ajax Amsterdam in Rome. Juve had beaten Real Madrid in the quarters and Nantes in the semis. They were a notable team including Peruzzi in goal, a back four of Torricelli, Ferrara, Vierchovod and Pessotto, Conte, Paulo Sousa and Deschamps in midfield and Ravanelli, Vialli, and Del Piero upfront. In the Ajax team, there were also well-known names, including goalie Edwin van der Sar, Danny Blind, the captain, Winston Bogarde and Ronald de Boer. The most charismatic Ajax player has to be Edgar Davids, who later, after a short spell at AC Milan, had a long spell with Juve. He was nicknamed the Pitbull by Louis Van Gaal, which summed up his style well. He was characterised by his dreadlocked hair and the wearing of protective goggles as he suffered from glaucoma (high pressure in the eye). Very surprisingly, he finished his playing career at Barnet and also had a spell as their manager. I wasn't sure where I could watch the match with a crowd but chose a relatively new venue in Haymarket in London, which I think was called Football Football. Being early and taking a quiet pint in a bar next door, I found myself chatting to a man who turned out to be a journalist. It emerged that he was also going to Football Football but in a private room where a 50th birthday party for George Best was about to take place. Would I like to join him as he had no doubt he could get me in, which indeed he did. I have always admired the ability of some to gate crash anything and anywhere. I could never succeed and so never really tried! The party was vibrant, with lots of famous United players like Denis Law and Nobby Stiles coming and going. George's second wife, Alex, was there to protect him from the many admiring people. They had married in 1995 but divorced in 2004 after accusations that he was violent towards her. The little boy in me again made me get his autograph. His 50th was a great occasion for a football fan, but it meant that I missed the majority of Juventus's final, which ended 1-1 with a Fabrizio Ravanelli goal later equalised by Litmanen and, after extra time, went to penalties. Juventus won the shoot-out 4-2, scoring all their penalties, and hence won their first Champions League title (2nd including the European Cups), 11 years since the Heysel stadium one, which should have barely counted. Another George Best landmark was the Phene Arms in Chelsea. He always called it his office and would spend long days in there, mostly imbibing white wine. It is sad to say that he had become almost a tourist attraction! Of course, Best's failure to combat alcoholism resulted in his tragic death, aged 59 years, after a failed liver transplant.

Juventus followed up their win over Ajax by beating River Plate 1-0 with an 81st-minute goal by Del Piero in the Intercontinental Cup played in Tokyo. They reached the next two Champions

League finals but lost first to Borussia Dortmund 1-3 and then to Real Madrid 0-1. They have reached the final on four further occasions but sadly lost them all. The signing of Cristiano Ronaldo in 2018 was a desperate attempt to win it again, but it has not succeeded, and Ronaldo has gone back to Manchester United.

Chapter 89 - Foreigners in English Football and Another Turin Trip

The year 1996 was one noted for an increasing number of foreign managers and players in the premier league. Ruud Gullit was player-manager at Chelsea and had signed Gianluca Vialli on a Bosman free, while Bryan Robson took Fabrizio Ravanelli to Middlesbrough. The two came face to face at Stamford Bridge at the beginning of the season, and I was keen to go. I had not got a ticket but thought I would try my luck on the day. I cannot recall another occasion when there was not a ticket tout in sight, presumably because they had already sold their collection. I can only imagine that the whole of the London Italian community had come and snapped up all the tickets. So I went home with my tail between my legs and had to make do with the result 1-0 to Chelsea, thanks to another Italian, Roberto di Matteo scoring a late winner. Vialli had the unusual accolade for a footballer to have a pasta dish named after him in a very fashionable Italian restaurant San Lorenzo in Beauchamp Place, London. Apparently, it was one of Lady Diana's favourite restaurants.

Vialli stayed at Chelsea till he retired in 1999 from playing and went on to become manager till 2000 when he had a spell at, of all places, Watford! Indeed in 1997, Chelsea won the FA Cup, their first trophy for 26 years. In this final, Roberto di Matteo scored for Ruud Gullit's Chelsea in the first minute as they went on to win 2-0 over Bryan Robson's Middlesbrough, with Ravanelli still playing for Middlesbrough. Eddie Newton scored the clinching second goal in the 83rd minute, quite surprising as I think he only scored seven in his 214 appearances in his nine-year Chelsea career!

In September 1996, I took Colin to Turin to see a champions league group match against Man U. We stayed in one of my favourite hotels, the Gran Mogol, conveniently near the station and the tram stop and set off for the stadium in the tram. The Stadio delle Alpi still struck me as a horrible stadium not really suited to football with that large athletic track separating the fans from the action. The game finished 1-0 to Juve with a goal from Croatian Alen Boksic in spite of United having such stars as Peter Schmeichel, Gary Neville, David Beckham, Ryan Giggs and Eric Cantona. On this occasion, the tickets had come from Man U sources which meant that we were, as usual, locked in for a while at the end and then were faced with a barrier of police there to keep all the United supporters away from the locals. Although we wanted to go back into town, the police would not let us pass their cordon. In spite of my attempts to explain our needs in Italian, there was no way we could get back to the trams, and so finally, we got a local bus which at least took us away from the ground. In the end, we safely got back to the centre and the sanctuary of our hotel. The Manchester leg also finished 1-0 to Juve with a Del Piero penalty. It was the year Juve got to the final where they would meet and beat Ajax, already described. Zinedine Zidane, best known as Zizou, joined Juve from Bordeaux in 1996 for a fee of 3 million pounds and became one of the great Juve imports, often compared to Michel Platini. He must be ranked among the real soccer superstars. He stayed in Turin until 2001 when he was transferred to Real Madrid, where he was also a real success. He was crucial in France later winning the 1988 World Cup and the 2000 Euros. Zidane stopped playing professionally in 2006 and raised large amounts of money playing in a huge number of charity matches. Later in 2010, he became coach of Real Madrid, where he has been very successful, winning four Champions League finals.

Chapter 90 - 1996 European Championships

The year 1996 was the one when the European Championships were awarded to England, rather surprisingly in view of our history of crowd disturbances and violence. Six matches were played at Wembley, the first being the opening match of the tournament against Switzerland, which ended in a disappointing 1-1 draw. After taking the lead in the 53rd minute through Alan Shearer, we conceded a penalty in the 78th minute, from which the Swiss equalised. The next England match was against Scotland on June 15th. We had tickets for that match but were not sure what to expect in view of the fierce rivalry between the two nations. In the end, everything went well, England taking the lead with a 53rd minute Alan Shearer goal. In the 77th minute, Tony Adams gave away a penalty which David Seaman saved well. Within a couple of minutes, Paul Gascoigne scored one of the most memorable goals flicking the ball over Colin Hendry with his left foot and, as it dropped, volleying it forcefully into the net with his right. The celebration with him lying on his back with his head up, arms out to the side and mouth wide open was not the most elegant but seemed to fit in perfectly with Gascoigne's personality as a party animal and serious drinker. It was always known as the "The Dentist's Chair" celebration and included some of the other England players squirting water into his mouth. More importantly, it ensured the 2-0 victory, which restored some hope that we might indeed do well. Unusually for me, I didn't get to any other matches, although there were four more at Wembley. I can't tell you why I didn't go to the others, but I managed to see most of them on TV. One I regret missing was England's last group match when we beat the Netherlands 4-1! By the time Kluivert scored the Dutch goal, we were already 4-0 up, Alan Shearer and Teddy Sheringham having scored two goals each. The Scots drew with the Dutch and indeed beat Switzerland, but they were eliminated by the Dutch on goals scored, being tied on their head to head result (0-0), and on overall goal difference. Minor surprises were the elimination of Italy and Russia by Germany and the Czech Republic. Although the latter two were to be the ultimate finalists. So on to the quarter-finals, where France beat the Dutch 5-4 on penalties after a goalless draw, the Czech Republic knocked out Portugal 1-0, and Germany beat Croatia 1-0. The last quarter match was England v Spain which was goalless, and guess what, England actually won the penalty shoot-out 4-2, scoring all their penalties while Spain missed two. So that led us to the semifinals, the first being France losing to the Czechs after another goalless draw and a 5-6 penalty shoot-out. We played the Germans and an early goal by Shearer in the 3rd minute gave us real hope. Not for long, the Germans equalising in the 16th minute, and the game progressing to the inevitable penalties and a Gareth Southgate miss gave the Germans their place in the final. A final between the Czechs and the Germans didn't really excite me, but I still planned to watch it on TV. To my surprise, I had a call in the early morning of the match from Giampiero to say he didn't want to come over, maybe sharing my feelings about the match, and would I like to use his ticket? Too good an opportunity to miss, of course, so on my way to Wembley, I had to go via the Royal Gardens Kensington hotel to pick up the ticket. So on to the match, and I had great difficulty feeling any favouritism for either side! A crowd of 73,611 saw the game, rather low for a final in a stadium that held nearly 100,000 spectators. A goalless first half didn't help, but when Berger scored a 59th-minute penalty, I remember being pleased. After all, the Germans had won so much and the Czech Republic inevitably so little, being a relatively newly formed country indeed only three years old. The Czechs had stars like Pavel Nedved, Karel Podborsky and Patrick Berger in their team. Pavel was to become a legend in his country with 91 international appearances and at Juventus, both as a player who was with the club for eight years and later as vice-chairman. So I now felt hopeful for them, but inevitably the Germans equalised through Oliver Bierhoff about 15 minutes later. So on to extra time, and the only interesting thing was that the "golden goal" sudden death system was in operation in extra time for the first time in a match of that importance. In the 95th minute, Oliver Bierhoff scored his second, and anticlimactically the game stopped there and then, with Germany obviously declared the winners. The golden goal being decisive gave me a very strange and unhappy feeling, and I was pleased that I never saw another one. A little later, we had the silver goal, which meant that the team leading after the first period of extra time was declared the winner. Now happily, neither system is used, and we continue to use the penalty shoot out to decide matches drawn after thirty minutes of extra time or, in some cases, at the end of 90 minutes. A minor consolation for England was that Alan Shearer finished as the top goalscorer with 5 goals, two ahead of any others.

Chapter 91 - Season 1996/97

August 1996 saw the arrival of centre back Matthew Upson as a trainee, but he only played one senior game for Luton before being snapped up by Arsenal. Later he was to earn 21 caps for England. After retirement, he has become a successful pundit featuring in Match of the Day and the BBC's World Cup coverage.

In 1996/97, we had a good season, but after being top in late march, we could only finish 3rd. We lost to Crewe in the playoffs semifinal 4-3 on aggregate. The first leg away ended 2-1 to Crewe, with us having to play a part of the game without Julian James sent off early in the second half. At Luton, they drew 2-2 to knock us out. Tony Thorpe had got us there with 28 goals in the league and a further three in the Cups. In fact, Crewe beat Brentford in the final to play in the championship for the very first time in their history. Crewe had the same manager, Milan born Dario Gradi, for a record 24 consecutive years, and the club was famous for bringing on outstanding young players such as David Platt, Danny Murphy and Dean Ashton. Gradi's record was, of course, beaten by Alex Ferguson with 26 but all well behind Guy Roux, who was manager of Auxerre in France for 36 years.

In Italy, 1997 marked the retirement of one club man Franco Baresi, who had played 532 league games for AC Milan as well as 81 internationals for Italy. He was considered to be one of the greatest defenders, indeed sweepers, of all time. He was honoured with the Order of Merit of the Italian Republic in 1991. The sweeper, along with Gaetano Scirea, were two of my favourite Italian players. Gaetano came to Juventus from Atalanta, played 377 league games for Juventus and earned 78 international caps between 1975 and 1986. Amazingly for a central defender, he did not receive a single red card, and his leadership qualities made him the obvious choice as captain for club and country.

In 1998 I attended a meeting in Vigo in the north of Spain. Luck would have it that the Aston Villa team came to stay in our hotel, preparing to play Celta Vigo in the UEFA Cup. I made a beeline for Gareth Southgate and had a chat and a photo taken of him. No selfies in those days! I remember the hotel staff was warned about Villa owner, Doug Ellis, and to treat him with the greatest respect! He always had the reputation of being rather formidable and irascible.

Unfortunately for me, my commitments to the meeting prevented me from going to the match, in which Villa won 1-0. However, they lost the second leg at home 3-1 and were eliminated. Vigo came into my story again in March 2000 when Celta knocked Juve out of the UEFA Cup in the round of 16. Juve had won the first leg at home 1-0 but lost the away leg 4-0. My lasting memory of Vigo was of the small square populated by older ladies preparing and selling the most delicious oysters! Also, a great variety of other seafood was sold in the various restaurants, which were delicious but, according to Spanish custom, eaten very late and well lubricated! A variety of shellfish called in Spanish "percebes," roughly translated as goose barnacles, was new to us. They seemed to taste a bit like clams or lobster. Celta were sponsored by Citroen, a make of car that I have favoured for a long time. It has been my slightly strange habit to have a favourite team in all the countries with which I have connections, so I added Celta to the list, which already had Luton, Ajax, Juventus and Nice on it. You can imagine that with the blanket television and internet coverage of all the leagues that are now on offer, I must be heading for any or even all of the health issues associated with excessive screen exposure. If nothing else, it limits the time available for more healthy pursuits such as exercise. It also means less time for family and friends. Is there such a word as soccerholic? Should it be classified as an addiction?

Chapter 92 - Season 1997/98

In 97/98, a major disappointment was the sale of Tony Thorpe to Fulham for £800,000 in midseason. Although we had David Oldfield, who scored 11 goals, we were saved by David Pleat, who was by then Spurs Director of football, offering us the loan of 20-year-old striker Rory Allen. His goals, six in eight games, helped us to hang on to 17th place. Sadly Rory had to quit football at the age of 25 due to multiple injuries and subsequent surgery to his knees and ankles. That season was also marked by several major injuries. In late September, it was so bad that our bench was composed of three players who did not have a first-team appearance between them! Even Trevor Peake, employed mostly in a coaching role, got a game on September 20th (incidentally my birthday) to become the oldest player at 40 to play for the club since Dally Duncan in 1947. Some future stars came to the Town's first team, including Gary Doherty, Liam George and especially Matthew Spring. In early 1998 we got to the area semifinal of the Associate Members Cup, where we lost to Bournemouth 1-0. Could it be a rehearsal for the next season?

Chapter 93 - 1998 World Cup in France

1998 was a World Cup year, and this one was to be played in France. At that time, one of the leading figures in French politics was the far-right Jean-Marie Le Pen, who had huge support. He was hoping to be elected president, and unfortunately, at that time, there were many instances of obvious racism. Undoubtedly winning that World Cup in 1998 was important and led to a large improvement in the acceptance of coloured players by other French players and by the country at large. One only has to think of the impact that Zinedine Zidane, originally from Algeria, and most recently Kylian Mbappe, originally from Cameroonian stock through his father and Algerian through his mother, had on multiracial acceptance. Kylian was brought up in Bondy, a suburb of Paris sadly well known for rioting and social strife.

Obviously, I planned to go to that World Cup, and the only disappointment pre-tournament was that Nice was unsurprisingly not amongst the chosen venues. Their stadium, Le Stade du Ray, was rather old and dilapidated, having been built in 1927 and with a relatively small capacity of only about 17,500. Without too much prompting, Richard with his French wife decided to take a leaf out of our Tuscan book and rented a villa in Bonnieux, a beautiful hill village in the Luberon hills in Provence. Peter Mayle's best selling "A Year in Provence", published in 1989, had put Provence on the map and had really opened it up to British and other tourists. I don't remember the exact dates we were in France, but I know the first part of the tournament was spent in our Nice flat with Colin and another small part was spent with some other friends outside Marseille. Certainly, I was in the villa that Richard had rented for the later stages, including the final.

So Colin and I went first to the Nice flat, and the first thing was to buy a television so we could watch most of the early matches. We bought the cheapest of Turkish manufacture, which had the smallest screen you could imagine. Luckily in those days, we all had perfect eyesight, so it was not a great problem. Michel Platini was, as expected, the chairman of the organising committee. The Stade de France, a name coined by Platini, was newly built for the tournament. The stadium was constructed in two years and was all covered with a capacity for football of 80,000. It was built with excellent public transport links to discourage people from driving there.

The opening match there featured the World Cup holders Brazil against the underdogs Scotland. Not surprisingly, Brazil got off to a flying start with a goal by Cesar Sampaio, playing that year in Japan, in the 5th minute. Contrary to all predictions, the Scots equalised with a John Collins penalty in the 38th minute and held their own until the 76th minute when a really innocuous ball struck Scottish defender Tom Boyd and found its way agonisingly into the Scots net. So a game that had been surprisingly very clean and fair did give the holders a 2-1 victory. It should be considered probably the outstanding match of all time for the Scottish team, and the support they had received was truly amazing. The only other slightly surprising result in the first phase was Spain being beaten by Nigeria 2-3 and failing to qualify for the knockout phase. Otherwise, there didn't seem to be any outstanding results in the first Group matches up to England's first match, which was against Tunisia in Marseille. Colin and I had tickets for that match but were a little apprehensive as the reputation of the England supporters was still worrying, and the town of Marseille had frequent racial issues with its large North African population. The day before the match, there were indeed large disturbances involving England fans which continued on the match day as well. It was claimed that there were 48 injuries and 50 arrests which did not bode well for the match itself. The police were forced to use batons and tear gas to control the violence. Normally we would have gone the day before to visit the sights, especially the exciting port area. But as that was the centre of the trouble, we decided to go only on the day of the match, setting off early by train from the Nice station. The journey took almost 3 hours but is very scenic as the line is mostly close to the Mediterranean sea. From the station, there was a convenient metro line to the stadium. We had to queue a while to get in, and there were plenty of police, but otherwise, it was an uneventful journey. Similarly, as expected, the security at the stadium was very heavy, but we safely reached our seats, and I have to say during the match, I don't remember any real trouble. The Stade Velodrome was a wonderful bowl-like stadium, mostly uncovered and about 40,000 England supporters inside a 60,000 capacity stadium made for a great atmosphere. From the 2.30 kick-off, it was the Tunisians who started brightly, but England effectively took over, and it was no surprise when Alan Shearer typically headed in a cross from Graeme Le Saux in the 42nd minute. The second half continued with England on top, and it would have been no surprise that Paul Scholes hit the decisive goal, a screamer from outside the penalty area, in the 89th minute. Sadly fearful of getting caught up in any post-match violence, we had left five minutes from the end and only saw Scholes's goal later on TV. The match is also remembered for the fact that David Beckham was surprisingly left out by manager Glenn Hoddle and for Michael Owen coming on as a substitute at 18 years of age. An unusual fact was that there was not even one offside decision in the whole 90 minutes. Our journey back to Nice was uneventful. We reflected on the controversial ownership since 1986 of Olympique de Marseille by a certain charismatic Bernard Tapie, about whom many articles and books have been written. Suffice it to say that he was one of the most prominent French personalities of his era. Many wanted him to be President of France, and famously he was voted the man most French women would like to go to bed with at the time!

Tapie presided over Marseille in their most glorious days when they won many league titles and the Champions league in 1993 1-0 over AC Milan, having been runners up in 1991 to Red Star Belgrade on penalties. But he Tapie was sullied by bribing opponents and match-fixing scandals. The best known was bribing Valenciennes players to underperform in the league match preceding the Champions League final, and he received several prison sentences, only one of which he actually served, five months in Marseille. At the same time, he was declared bankrupt. The club was, as a result, relegated to Ligue 2 and not able to play in the next Champions League, the European Super Cup, or the Intercontinental Cup. He was known as an owner who interfered with coaching matters all the time, which made many top players and managers want to move on. He was forced to resign in 1994.

One of the most politically charged matches of all time in that 1998 tournament was the Group match between the USA and Iran played in Lyon. The relations between the two countries had been very hostile since the overthrow of the Shah in 1979. The Iranian team was told not to go toward the USA players nor shake their hands. In the end, they all formed a group with players from both sides. A terrorist organisation was reputed to have purchased 7000 tickets to stage a large protest. This was foiled, and plan B had been to stage a pitch invasion, but this was also foiled this time by the French riot police. In the end, the Iranian players all came onto the pitch with white roses, a symbol of peace. The match itself went well and peacefully, and the Iranians won 2-1, their first-ever victory in a World Cup finals match. It was said that this historic match did more in 90 minutes than the politicians had done in 20 years and showed how sport could overcome even the most intense political strife.

In the next group match, England lost 1-2 to Romania, but the two both qualified for the knockout stages. This as David Beckham did come on as a first-half substitute for Paul Ince but to no avail. The Romanians had some who had played in England, such as Dan Petrescu, who will be familiar especially to Chelsea supporters, having played there for 5 years. They also had Gheorghe Hagi as captain, having played for Real Madrid, Benfica and Barcelona.

So the time had come for Colin to return to England and for me to set off in our minuscule bright yellow Fiat 126 to our friends, a fellow anaesthetist and her husband in a house just along the coast from Marseille and called Sausset-les-Pins again very scenic. Mine was not the ideal car to negotiate a long distance on a French motorway. It contrasted dramatically with my host's powerful motorbike, where I spent quite some time as his pillion passenger! They were not football fans, but I was at least allowed to watch the highlights programmes. A compensation was especially the fabulous cooking of my hostess, and I particularly remember her Loup de Mer en croute de sel (salt-crusted sea bass). In the last series of group matches, Brazil surprisingly lost to Norway 1-2, but again, both qualified. So on to the knockout stages and the round of 16. Undoubtedly from our point of view, the most dramatic match of the last 16 matches was the England Argentina clash. Two things will always be remembered. Firstly Michael Owen's amazing solo run through their defence and perfect finish. Secondly, Beckham was sent off for kicking Diego Simeone in retaliation. Unfortunately for Beckham, the referee was only a few yards away and had a perfect view of the incident! Simeone remained in the public eye amassing 106 caps for Argentina and having a very long and successful spell as manager of Atletico Madrid. There were three penalties in open play, and then the match was decided by a penalty shoot-out after a goalless extra time. While Crespo missed for Argentina, Ince and crucially Batty missed for England, and so we went out.

It was quite difficult to find my way to the Bonnieux villa that my friends had rented, being very cross country and there, of course being none of the modern satellite navigation aids, only paper maps! I found it finally and was warmly greeted by Richard and family and how nice it was to see a much larger TV screen! Now I was among football fans, including Richard's son Thomas who had come to Rome with me in 1990, and our life was arranged around the matches.

Two matches stand out from the matches in the last eight. Firstly, France versus Italy, which pitted together the hosts and one of the powerhouse football teams who were especially renowned for their very strong defence. So one was not surprised when it finished 0-0 even after extra time! The penalty shoot-out went the way of France. While Lizarazu missed for the hosts, both Albertini and Di Biagio also missed to put Italy out. Very surprisingly, Croatia, only an independent nation since 1992, knocked out star-studded Germany 3-0. The Croatians had, amongst others Davor Suker who scored the third goal and one who later played and managed in England, central defender Slaven Bilic. While not otherwise worthy of mention, England supporters were pleased to see Argentina beaten by the Netherlands 2-1. Kluivert scored the first, and the winning goal was scored by Dennis Bergkamp in the 90th minute. Dennis was at that time a formidable striker in the middle of a very successful period with Arsenal.

So we were down to the semifinals a few days later. That gave us plenty of time to explore the beautiful Luberon hills, and we spent lots of time sampling and enjoying the local cuisine and wines. The Brazil Netherlands semifinal ended 1-1 after extra time, with Brazil winning 4-2 on penalties, scoring all their four while Cocu and Ronald de Boer missed for Holland. There did seem to be a lot of penalty shoot-outs in that tournament. The second semifinal between France and Croatia the next day ended with a France victory by 2-1. France scored first through Thuram, but a minute later, Suker equalised. How often does a goal for one team be followed immediately by one from the opposition? Finally, Thuram got his second to see France into the final. The third-place playoff ended with a victory for Croatia over the Dutch by 2-1, leaving the final next day between France and Brazil. The drama before that match centred around the Brazilian Ronaldo, probably the best player in the world at the time. He had been omitted from Brazil's starting lineup after apparently suffering from a convulsion in the hotel but was curiously re-instated by the coach Mario Zagallo three-quarters of an hour before kick-off. However, he was only a shadow of his normal self and, with today's protocols, would never have been allowed to play. Maybe it was a bit of a surprise that the hosts France won 3-0 over Brazil, Zinedine Zidane scoring two of the goals and Petit the third in the last minute. It was France's first World Cup title and maybe confirmed the undoubted advantage of home soil!

Chapter 94 - AS Monaco

Having the flat in Nice meant that AS Monaco was also a nearby club. They had a fairly new stadium opened in 1985 but of very small capacity at a modest 18,000. It is characterised by the nine arches at the away end of the ground. An oddity was that the pitch was directly over a large car park. The team is a member of the French league and also forms part of the France international system, not having its own international team. Amazingly Monaco has won the league 8 times and been runner up 7 times more, as well as many Cup wins, including the French Super Cup on 4 occasions. Could it be that the profits from the famous casino and luxury hotels and clubs help to pay for the team?

In March 1998, Manchester drew Monaco in the Champions League quarter-finals, and it was another occasion to go with Colin to see his team in European action. Our seats were right by the broadcasting area, which allowed us to have a chat with ITV's Brian Moore and Ron Atkinson before kick-off! They were both very busy making notes and presumably deciding what they might say during gaps in the action. It always surprises me the number of facts and records commentators and pundits can bring out. It was to be Brian Moore's last season before passing the baton on to Clive Tyldesley. That was the highlight for us as the match ended in a drab 0-0 draw. Incidentally, the second leg in Manchester finished 1-1, so Monaco progressed thanks to that away goal.

As well as Monaco matches, from 1998, Monaco hosted the UEFA Super Cup matches between the Champions League Winners and the Cup Winners Cup Winners. The Cup Winners Cup was later replaced by the UEFA Cup and later still the Europa League. In 1998 the match was between Chelsea Cup Winners Cup holders and Real Madrid, the winners of the Champions League. We had some good friends who had a wonderful villa in St Paul de Vence, and he was a very keen Chelsea supporter. Getting tickets for such a small stadium by remote control was going to be difficult, but luckily a man who worked for one of the Monaco antique dealers we knew through my father had a hotline to someone in the Monaco ticket office, so with my usual luck, it all fell into place. I had sussed out a nice Italian restaurant close to the stadium, and it was obvious that we should go there together and then on to the match. Happily, Chelsea won 1-0 with a late 83rd-minute goal from Uruguayan Gus Poyet. Chelsea were managed at that time by Gianluca Vialli and had eight foreign players in their team. Real Madrid were managed by Guus Hiddink and were also with eight foreigners, signs of the way the game was going.

The next year 1999, was another final with particular interest to us. This time it was Champions League winners Manchester United and UEFA Cup winners Lazio of Rome. So again, I had reason to get tickets knowing that Colin would be keen to come. We repeated the formula of the previous year with dinner at the same Italian restaurant before the match. The walk from the restaurant to the ground was lined by many stern-looking policemen with their even more fierce alsatians. The Monaco police had been reinforced by many from neighbouring France. It seemed incongruous in a principality renowned for law and order, but I am afraid it reflected the bad behaviour of the United supporters earlier in the day and their bad reputation generally. The match itself was characterised by the teams having very eminent managers. Alec Ferguson knighted that year and Sven-Goran Eriksson. The Lazio team was full of superstars. Suffice it to mention Alessandro Nesta the captain, Sebastian Veron, Pavel Nedved, Roberto Mancini and Simone Inzaghi, brother of Filippo. United also had their share, including Jaap Stam, the Neville brothers, David Beckham, Roy Keane, Paul Scholes, Teddy Sheringham and Ole Gunnar Solskjaer. The latter went on to manage United from the end of 2018. Lazio won 1-0 with a goal by substitute Chilean Marcelo Salas in the 35th minute. Colin, never a good loser, was keen to storm out of the ground at the final whistle and before the presentation, so we did just that.

I didn't find a reason to see any of the later matches, which was a pity. The fixture was played in Monaco until 2012, after which the matches have been played in a variety of different and often far-flung venues.

I had some interesting motoring/parking experiences attending Monaco matches. I rarely used the car park for two reasons. The first, I guess, is called meanness, and the second is being fearful of the time it took to exit the park at the end of the match. I usually found somewhere on the road from Cap d'Ail into Monaco but on two occasions found someone with a hostile attitude waiting for me when I got back to the car! The first was when I parked outside a small gate certainly not big enough for a car to enter, but on my return was greeted by an inmate of the building, which turned out to be a psychiatric institute. Having an English registered car made it possible to claim not to understand French, but I would often forget and weaken at some point in the discussion, and that made them even angrier. The end result was a small fist induced dent in the roof of my beloved Fiat 126. The second episode was when I parked in a layby outside a pizzeria on the same street. Again there was an issue because the owner of the pizzeria felt that those two spaces were for the clients of his restaurant and not for the likes of me! However, I was let off with a severe warning. I learnt my lesson and used the car park from then on!

The other episode was being stopped by the police on the road back from Monaco to Nice and being invited into their van. They threatened me with the breathalyser but apparently, feeling kind to foreigners, did not use it and let me continue my journey. In fact, my sole alcohol intake had been one 25cl bottle of Kronenbourg beer some two hours before, so I had nothing to fear. They were obviously satisfied with the state of the car, the registration document ("carte grise") and the up to date "controle technique" (the equivalent of our MOT test) only done every two years as compared with our one yearly.

Chapter 95 - Season 1998/99

In 1998/99, Juve dismissed Lippi and replaced him with Carlo Ancelotti, another manager going strong today! Del Piero suffered a bad knee injury keeping him out for over a year, and they had sold World Cup winner Didier Deschamps to Chelsea and Thierry Henry to Arsenal. The final day of season 1999/2000 meant that Juve had to beat Perugia to win the Scudetto. A deluge in Perugia caused top referee Pierluigi Collina to suspend the match at half time for about an hour. In the second half, finally played, Perugia scored, and it meant that Juve had blown a nine-point lead and given the title to Lazio. It was Lazio's first Scudetto since 73/74 and their last to date.

The Agnellis had won the bid for Turin to host the 2006 Winter Olympics, and a new stadium was a top priority. In fact, the Comunale was to be rebuilt and renamed the Stadio Olimpico. It allowed Juve to reside there while the hated Delle Alpi was rebuilt as a purpose-built football stadium that belonged totally to Juventus.

We played a pre-season friendly at Hendon and drew 1-1. Hendon was particularly convenient for me because their Claremont Road ground was less than a mile from where we lived, so I had good reason to go and watch Hendon if there was nothing better! I liked the contrast between their very primitive ground and the top football league ones. I think at the time it was £3 for admission and an extra £1 if you wanted to be in the main stand seated area! I was very sorry when they sold the site to a developer who put up a large residential complex there. Hendon football club has an interesting history that can be traced back to 1908. Only in 1946 and after four name changes was the club called Hendon. In 1963 the club was accepted into the Isthmian League. During the amateur era, Hendon reached the final of the Amateur Cup on 5 occasions, winning it in 1860, 1965 and 1972. Plenty of successes in the FA Cup proper can be described. They have reached the 1st round 21 times, the second round 6 and the third once when they drew 1-1 at Newcastle before losing the replay played at Watford 4-0.

Surprisingly in spite of everything that was going on with Luton entering administrative receivership in March 1999, we finished that season in a respectable 12th place in Division two. That in spite of rather meagre goal tallies of eleven by Stuart Douglas, a former apprentice and local boy and thirteen by Phil Gray. Phil earned 26 caps for Northern Ireland. Phil aroused different feelings but, unusually, was the central figure of the poem "A Gray Day" by John Hegley, relating to John's attendance at a 1-1 draw at home to Reading in that season.

The only highlight was a good Worthington Cup run, only losing at Sunderland 3-0 in the quarter-finals. An excellent new player was defender Emmerson Boyce who started as an apprentice at Luton and went on to make 212 appearances. Although born in Aylesbury, he was eligible to play for Barbados through his parents and earned 12 caps. After leaving Luton for Crystal Place, he later went on to captain Wigan to FA Cup final victory over Manchester City in 2013. That match was decided by a 91st-minute goal by Ben Watson. The Wigan side was managed by Roberto Martinez, City by contrast by Roberto Mancini. Martinez is a Spaniard who had played for Wigan for 6 years, later managing them for 4 years. Mancini had played 424 times for Sampdoria, scoring over 130 goals. After a short spell with Lazio, he became a manager and spent four years with Manchester City from 2009 to 2013. He has been the Italian manager since 2018, while Martinez has been the Belgian manager since 2016. Graeme Jones, later to have a one year spell as Luton manager, was his assistant in many of Martinez's posts. These facts emphasise the ever-increasing influence of foreign players and managers on our domestic football again.

Michael Mcindoe came through the youth system and seemed very promising but sadly developed a serious alcohol problem. With a change of club and help from many people, including Arsenal legends Paul Merson and Matthew Upson, he got over it and, in spite of being with many different clubs, played until 2018. He was also involved in the running of West End nightclubs but sadly was declared bankrupt in 2014. Sean Dyche came on loan from Bristol City but made only 14 appearances before moving on to Millwall. Of course, he has really made his mark as manager of Burnley since 2012.

Chapter 96 - Season 1999/00

That season ended with us one place lower in 13th position, with Liam George and Phil Gray topping the goals list. The colours were back to orange shirts with a new sponsor SKF on the front and blue shorts. SKF was a well established Swedish company making ball bearings with a presence in Luton since 1910. It was hard times with the club still in receivership and efforts ongoing to make major creditor Cliff Bassett the new owner. We were relying on youngsters and short term loans. We had two goalkeepers, Nathan Abbey and Ben Roberts. The former was coming to the end of a 6-year spell while the latter did two loan periods. After retirement, Roberts earned a first-class degree in Sports Science and wrote a dissertation entitled "A Bio-Mechanical Analysis of a Football Goalkeeper's Jumping Technique."

A landmark addition to the senior squad was Matthew Taylor, who came up from the youth team at the age of 17. He was always very talented, and three years at Luton were followed by six at Portsmouth, three at Bolton, three at West Ham, and two at Burnley, Northampton and Swindon Town. This added up to 750 appearances and 84 league goals, not bad for a 5 foot 10 inches midfielder. I believe he is now managing at Walsall. In October, thank goodness we exited receivership.

I remember meeting Ruud Gullit by chance in a Dutch hotel lobby around 2000 at a time when he was between managerial posts, and when I asked him what work he was doing at the time, he replied, "I am just enjoying myself"! In 1987 he won the Ballon d'Or, and I think it is fair to say that he had a stellar career as a player, manager and pundit. In 2004 he went back to managership at Feyenoord, the Rotterdam club he had played for in three seasons and that he had always supported.

Chapter 97 - Season 2000/01

That season was not memorable in terms of results. In July, Lennie Lawrence was dismissed as manager. Unusually three managers were then employed in quick succession, Ricky Hill, Lil Fuccillo and finally Joe Kinnear, who did survive into the following season. Sponsors SKF stayed faithful, but the colours reverted to white and black. During Ricky Hill's short reign, the club was in crisis. Some of the best players, such as Matthew Upson and John Hartson, were sold and commanding centre half Steve Davis returned to Burnley for a fee of £800,000. Mark Stein returned from Bournemouth but only managed four goals in thirty-six appearances before moving on to Dagenham and Redbridge. Ricky wanted to appoint Chris Ramsey as his assistant, but as he was also black, he felt it necessary to ensure that it would be acceptable to the board, which, of course, it was. Chris was appointed later a Member of the British Empire (MBE) in the 2019 Birthday Honours for his services to football and diversity in sport. A big signing was centre forward Steve Howard from Northampton Town in march at a bargain fee of £50,000. He could be described as a typical old fashioned centre forward who, as they say, "put himself about a bit". In 228 games, he scored 103 goals and helped the Town to two promotions. Sadly for us, in 2006, he went to Derby County for a million pounds and later on to Leicester.

We went to Thomas's wedding (yes, the same one who had come to Rome with me during the 1990 World Cup). It was a splendid occasion in September 2000, but sadly my wife went down with a high temperature. We had planned to go to Rome for a meeting and on to Nice on holiday and persisted with it, although Gillian spent the majority of the days in bed. When we got back, I was contacted by Abbott Laboratories, with whom I had done some research on new local anaesthetics, to deputise for a colleague and to give his lecture in Santiago, Chile. Never having been to Chile before, I was determined to go and leave my ailing wife in the hands of a general practitioner who I had known since my school days. While flattered to be asked, I don't think he really appreciated the responsibility, especially as she didn't seem to be getting any better. On my return, prior to a Wembley match that we Olympic Gallery foursome were on our way to, we were lunching at the Sea Shell, the Fish and Chip restaurant in Marylebone close to the station. We often went there as the train from Marylebone to Wembley Stadium often seemed the most convenient way to get to the stadium. The subject of my wife's continuing ill health came up in the conversation, and Peter, the Vet, threw out the line that it sounded like something his pigs got and that it responded well to an antibiotic called "Klaricid" (Clarithromycin). Transferring the news to my doctor friend, he was pleased to prescribe it, and my wife never looked back. I know the doctor felt humiliated that it took a vet to know what he obviously didn't! Obviously, having a variety of health professionals in our group had really paid off!

Sadly we finished in 22nd place and were relegated to Division Three, the 4th and bottom tier of the football league, once more. Only Liam George, with nine, contributed much to the goals tally. The 3rd round FA Cup tie at home to QPR had ended 3-3. The replay was notable for me in that it was the first time that I went to a match with my new son in law, David. He was and still is a Hull supporter, although his first love is Rugby Union. We got in behind the goal at the School end just as an unknown Luton youngster Lee Mansell was putting the ball into the net at the other end! However, it was not enough as we lost 2-1 and were eliminated. A memorable home match was against Swansea where we won 5-3 in spite of an unknown Venezuelan international Giovanni Savarese scoring a hat trick for the Swans while Lee Mansell was getting two for the Town. We had lost the away match 4-0, so it was a sort of revenge! Lee never quite made the grade at Luton and spent most of his career at Torquay.

Chapter 98 - Season 2001/02

2001/02 was one of my favourite seasons when Luton were promoted from the 3rd division as runner ups behind Plymouth. Manager Joe Kinnear assisted by Mick Harford had assembled a great squad with captain Kevin Nicholls ably assisted by such as Matthew Taylor at left wing-back, who chipped in with goals and went on to have a glittering career.

Steve Howard did finish up in that season with 24 goals, including a hat trick in a 4-0 win at Hull City. The only blemish on Steve Howard's 2001/02 season was a bizarre "penalty episode" when in spite of Kevin Nicholls being the designated penalty kick taker, Howard insisted on taking one at York, missed it and when it was ordered to be retaken, after an infringement, he missed again! He stayed until 2006, when he was sold to Derby County for £1 million.

The most memorable and charismatic player in that team for me had to be Jean-Louis Valois, a mercurial Frenchman who came from Lille and scored 6 goals in 34 appearances. Not so many, you might think, but most of them were pile drivers from a considerable distance. Sadly he apparently fell out with Joe Kinnear and left for Hearts in Edinburgh. We had an amazing run in with 13 wins and a draw from the last 14 matches. We finished up with 97 points but failed to catch Plymouth, who had gained 102 points. New arrivals included Australian central defender Chris Coyne who also, in seven seasons, made 252 appearances and won 7 caps for the Socceroos. Goalie Carl Emberson came from Walsall and played in 60 games over two seasons.

There was a Champions League match at Arsenal's Highbury stadium with Juventus on the 4th December 2001. I went with members of the Juventus Club Londra, which I had joined just before, and was struck by three things. Firstly no one took their designated seats but sat just where they fancied, and they were not going to be moved. Secondly, most people stood in front of the seats throughout the match and thirdly, if they felt like smoking, they did. Interestingly there were five Frenchmen involved in the two teams; Juventus had Thuram and Trezeguet. Arsenal, being captained by Thierry Henry, who was ex Juventus, also had Patrick Vieira, who four years later was transferred to Juventus. Vieira came to my notice much later as manager of Nice from 2018 to 2020. The Gunners were managed by Arsene Wenger, by then five years into his 22-year spell. The game was exciting, ending 3-1 to the Gunners with two goals from Freddie Ljungberg and one a sumptuous free-kick by Henry. Juve's lone goal was an own goal by the Gunners goalie Stuart Taylor. A very young 23-year-old Gianluigi Buffon and 27-year-old Alex Del Piero, as well as newly arrived Pavel Nedved, were in the Juve team that managed to earn three yellow cards during the match. Nedved had effectively replaced Zinedine Zidane, who had been sold to Real Madrid for a record fee of 150 billion lire, equivalent to 77.5 million euros. Buffon went on to become the most capped Italian goalie ever and was only second to Del Piero for the Juve appearance record. The team was managed by Marcello Lippi, already in his 12th managerial position and second in charge of Juve. Of course, he went on to famously manage the Italy World Cup winning team of 2006. As Juve only won the return leg 1-0 with a Uruguayan Marcelo Zalayeta scoring the goal, they finished bottom of the group and were inevitably eliminated.

In that season, Giraudo, the Juve executive, was banned from football for life after match-fixing offences, including influencing refereeing assignments and getting key players booked ahead and suspended for matches against Juventus. The club was stripped of its 2005 and 2006 titles and relegated to Serie B with a 9 point penalty but managed to win promotion back to Serie A at the first attempt.

Moggi was also involved in the refereeing scandal and also expressed unwelcome views about gay footballers. As a result, he resigned in 2006 and gave up all involvement in football administration except for some media work.

Juve were about to enter the blackest period in their history. Two officials, managing director Antonio Giraudo and club doctor Riccardo Agricola were accused of supplying drugs to several players. The drugs were theoretically legal but used in such a way as to be performance-enhancing. One such drug was creatinine which is muscle building. Another substance was Erythropoietin (EPO) which stimulates the production of red blood cells and therefore improves oxygen carriage to the muscle cells, making them work more efficiently. Amphetamines were also used with the effect of increasing energy. The main years of suspicion of systematic drug-taking were from 1994 to 1998. Agricola was given a 22 month suspended prison sentence in 2002 and other charges that died under a statute of limitation by 2007. But famously, a banner was exhibited in the stadium saying "Lippi spacciatore" (Lippi the drug dealer). Lippi was to leave for Inter to be replaced by the unpopular Carlo Ancelotti. He was unpopular on account of his defensive and unattractive style of football. Italian football was having a lot of crowd troubles at the time, but no one expected that Inter supporters would be able to set alight a Vespa that had been stolen from Atlanta supporters in Bergamo. They had smuggled it into the top tier of the San Siro and then dropped it from the top tier onto a luckily empty stand below. The club was punished unsurprisingly by having to play their next two home games away from the San Siro. The event reminded me of the time when I was an undergraduate at Cambridge, and the students got a pre-war Austin 7 onto the roof of the

Senate house. The only difference was that that event with the Austin 7 wasn't likely to cause injury or endanger life. The 2000/2001 Italian season was won by Roma for their third Scudetto. Everyone was excited to know whether actress Sabrina Ferilli a committed Roma supporter, would keep her promise to go topless at the Circo Massimo if Roma were triumphant! In a dance called Celebration, she got close, stripping down to a very scanty and provocative bikini! She has been described as the typical Italian beauty. She has appeared several times at the world-famous San Remo song festival. A recent poll in which Italian males from 15 to 34 yrs were asked to indicate one of the famous Italian women they loved the most showed that Ferilli was that woman.

Zidane's replacement at Juventus when he left for Real Madrid was effectively Pavel Nedved, a Czech international who cost about £30 million. One would not have expected that 20 years later, Nedved would still be seriously involved with Juve as vice-chairman. Another surprise was the signing of goalie Gianluigi Buffon from Parma for €52 million. Like Nedved, he is also still there, although he went recently to PSG for one season. Buffon is finally threatening to retire at the end of the 2020/2021 season! It all seemed to be happening as Filippo Inzaghi went to AC Milan. He didn't seem to get on too well with Del Piero and, anyway, had largely been sidelined by the presence of David Trezeguet. Importantly Marcello Lippi returned to Juve two years after leaving for Inter.

In April 2002 we were in Nice and went to see them play Martigues in Ligue 2. On arrival at my seat, I found that my neighbour reclining on a smart cushion was a black and tan Dachshund! In the Nice team, then in Ligue 2 was Patrice Evra, later, of course, to make his name at Manchester United and with the French National team, both of whom he captained. He later earned a runner up medal in the 2016 Euros. He had been converted from a forward to a very successful left-back. Another unusual feature was his ability to speak five languages. An exciting match ended 1-0 to Nice with a goal from local boy Laurent Gagnier. They went on to be promoted to Ligue 1 for the first time since 1997, while Martigues were relegated. Famous players who had come through Nice on their way to English teams are Goalies Hugo Lloris and David Ospina and outfielders Pierre Lees-Melou, Allan Saint-Maximin and Neal Maupay.

In May 2002 we attended a conference in Barcelona. It wasn't possible to see a game there, but we did find the time to do the stadium tour. Louis Van Gaal had returned for a second spell as manager, and our young lady tour guide wasted no time in telling us how unpopular he was with both the fans and the press. Of course, one was struck by the beauty of the Nou Camp stadium and its huge capacity of 99,354. An unusual feature was the chapel on the route from the dressing rooms to the pitch, occasionally frequented by a few players on their way out! The museum was inevitably full of trophies and would have warranted a much longer visit. However, both my wife and I were able to be photographed holding aloft the "Big Ears" Champions league trophy, a real treat! A sad incident on the Barcelona metro resulted in one of our colleagues being pickpocketed while we were being distracted by someone trying to clean off some powder from our anoraks. Other places where we have had a pickpocket or bag snatch attempt were Heathrow and Nice airports, the Colosseum area of Rome and the Turin tram! Luckily I hope we have learnt our lesson and are especially careful when travelling anywhere.

Chapter 99 - 2002 World Cup South Korea/Japan

2002 was a World Cup year, and the tournament was co-hosted by South Korea and Japan, the first to be held in Asia. There was no way I could think about going, but I had a good friend, an avid Wimbledon supporter, who did go with his wife and thoroughly enjoyed it.

So much so that he has been to every World Cup since but assured me that he was going to make an exception with Qatar. 32 teams had qualified, and South Korea reached the semifinal, having beaten Portugal, Italy and Spain. They were two very different cultures, but the highlight in South Korea was the start of fan fests, public viewing areas where fans could gather to watch matches for which they didn't have tickets. Indeed nearly 7 million Koreans (1 in 7 of the population) watched the semifinal between South Korea and Germany.

In the group matches, France were eliminated, having got but a miserly one point. Other notable exits were Portugal, Poland, Argentina, and Russia. So on to the round of 16 with an exit for Italy at the hands of South Korea and Japan by Turkey. The quarters saw victories for Germany over the USA, South Korea over Spain, Brazil 2-1 over England, and Turkey over Senegal. On to the semis with victories for Germany over the South Korean hosts and Brazil over Turkey, both 1-0. In the final, Brazil beat Germany 2-0 in Yokohama with 2 goals from Ronaldo (yes, the Brazilian one!) while the third place went to Turkey. Ronaldo won the Golden Boot award with 8 goals. Oliver Kahn won the Yashin award, and Belgium the Fair Play Trophy. Incidentally, it was the last World Cup to use the golden goal sudden death system. The last match in which it featured was Turkey beating Senegal in the quarters.

Chapter 100 - Season 2002/03 Including Nantes

It was a time when every year, I lectured on a course on ophthalmic anaesthesia in Middlesbrough. Many times we were put up in a lovely country house hotel called Craythorne Hall. It was a hotel where away teams due to play at the Riverside Stadium were often lodged. I remember two episodes. Blackburn were there, and some of their coaching staff were at the next table having breakfast and obviously relaxed and enjoying themselves. In came manager Graeme Souness, and the atmosphere changed dramatically. Respect and obsequence were now the order of the day. Graeme later became a very successful pundit, also characterised by his fiery nature and very strong views.

The other occasion was when Leeds, then in the Premier League, were the visitors. Many of the players were relaxing in the lounge, and I took the opportunity to chat with one of them, a certain 22-year-old Rio Ferdinand! I found him to be extremely articulate and well informed, and he was soon to be transferred to Manchester United for £30 million. I was not at all surprised when after his retirement from playing, he has also become a very successful pundit, especially for BT Sport's soccer coverage. Later on, he sadly lost his wife to breast cancer at the unbelievably early age of 34. He was then involved in the production on BBC of an excellent if moving documentary entitled Rio Ferdinand: Being Mum and Dad.

On 20th February 2002, Colin and I went to Nantes to watch the hosts play Manchester United. We went with a rather VIP group which I remember included David Beckham's parents. It was much more relaxed than many continental visits, and we partook of the local white wine Muscadet and bought several packets of Petit Beurre biscuits, also a famed product of Nantes. Interestingly Manchester United had three Frenchmen in their team, Fabien Barthez, Laurent Blanc, and Mikael Sylvestre. They also had many other stars, including the Neville Brothers, David Beckham, Ryan Giggs, Roy Keane, Paul Scholes, Juan Sebastian Veron and Ruud Van Nistelrooy. Nantes, by comparison, had a team of relative unknowns, at least to us. Perhaps Mickael Landreau, the French international goalkeeper, was the best known. Others were Marama Vahirua, a Tahitian and Viorel Moldovan, a Romanian who scored the 9th minute Nantes goal. Vahirua, who had come through the Nantes Academy, was later transferred in 2004 to Nice, where he stayed a further 3 years. Moldovan won 70 caps for Romania, scoring 25 goals. In front of over 38,000 spectators, it took a 94th-minute penalty from Van Nistelrooy to earn United a 1-1 draw after they had been kept at bay by a string of Landreau saves. Forlan and Solskjaer had come on as substitutes.

I remember the next day we took the tram to the stadium to purchase some memorabilia from the club shop! The need to behave like a little boy acquiring souvenirs wherever I can has never left me, and one day some poor relative is not only going to have the task of sorting out hundreds of programmes and World soccer magazines but pennants, stamps, mascots and keyrings as well!

That season at Luton was unremarkable, with us finishing in 9th place with Steve Howard scoring 23 goals, including one away at Watford in the Worthington Cup. The other goal in that 2-1 win there was a thunderbolt from 30 yards by Matthew Spring. Unfortunately, there was a degree of crowd trouble before and during the match, which I found very frightening. From my point of view, the only good thing about the Vicarage Road ground was that it was next door to the hospital where due to being a doctor I was always able to park! The next round was against a strong Aston Villa managed by Graham Taylor. At the time, Villa were in the Premier League and doing well while we were in Division 2 (third tier), so it seemed a match well worth seeing. Rather than driving to an evening match up the M1/M6 to the Midlands, I took my place in one of the supporters' coaches. There was a choice between the well established Bobbers Travel Club and the more newly formed Town on Tour, which was a little more upmarket! I chose the latter, and it was relaxing and fun to be among fellow supporters. Unfortunately, we lost 3-0, the league positions prevailing. Ulises de la Cruz, an Ecuadorian, scored the first, and then Dion Dublin scored twice, so another depressing journey back.

Chapter 101 - Football in Bucharest

In October 2002, I attended a conference in Bucharest. It was my second visit to Bucharest; the previous one had been when it was still a member of the Warsaw Pact and behind the Iron Curtain. The contrast was enormous. The street lights and shop windows were brighter, the people more colourfully dressed, and the old East German Trabant cars were largely replaced by Dacias, a Romanian manufacturer later taken over by Renault. On our first visit the supermarkets had had everything but only one type of each product! By now, the supermarkets were stocked with the variety of things you would expect in the West. I discovered that by chance, Romania were playing Norway in a European Championships qualifier and thought it might be fun to go. Many of the Norwegian players were known to me as being or having been England based, including Ole Gunnar Solskjaer with Manchester United, Henning Berg with Blackburn, Thomas Myhre with Sunderland, and Jon Arne Riise with Liverpool. Also, John Carew, who at that stage was playing in Valencia and Steffen Iverson of Spurs. The Romanians had Giorghe Popescu ex Tottenham but by then back with Dinamo Bucharest and Adrian Mutu then with Parma. My hosts thought I was indeed mad to want to go to a football match, but I guess they felt they had to accommodate the requests of their guests, however bizarre they might have seemed to be. I remembered that only four years before, in the 1998 World Cup, Romania had beaten England in the group stage by 2-1. In spite of that result, they both qualified for the knockout stages! Norway had also reached the same stage thanks in part to a very surprising win over Brazil.

Who could I go with? I settled on a Scots colleague who liked football almost as much as he liked girls and a Frenchman who had never been to a football match in his life. Tickets were no problem. The lady anaesthetist Cristina who was hosting the meeting was friendly with the Romanian goalkeeper Bogdan Vintila of FC National Bucharest, who had conveniently been a patient of hers. Cristina and her husband, Mihai, offered to drop us off at the stadium. They were not football fans either and were worried about letting us loose amongst so many Romanians. To prove how little they knew about it, they first took us to the wrong stadium and only realised their mistake when there was no sign of any crowd! Finally, we got to what was called the Steaua stadium from the name of the team that played there. It was a very old stadium with cover on only one side. We were on the opposite side, open to the weather and of course, as we were in sight of the stadium, the heavens opened. At the turnstiles, did I say turnstiles, there was only a flimsy gate manned by a solitary steward who checked tickets and let us in. Amazingly in a low economy country, they were handing out free plastic full-length disposable macs, which kept most of us fairly dry. It still seemed to be a standing area, although many did sit on the very wet steps on the terracing. We were close to the pitch and had a very good view. The atmosphere was great, with blue, yellow and red Romanian flags everywhere. The match watched by 21,000 seemed largely uneventful without a score in sight, and as our hosts had promised to be waiting for us nearby where they probably wouldn't have been able to park, we felt we should leave about 10 minutes before the end. Of course, typically, Steffen Iversen scored the only goal for Norway in the 83rd minute, which we missed completely. Not for the first or last time did I leave a game early and miss something crucial or exciting. So we found our hosts and were duly escorted safely back to our hotel. There is no doubt that the experience would not have encouraged our hosts to attend matches, and I am sure our French friend equally had seen his first and last live match.

Chapter 102 - Another Turin Visit

In February 2003, we worked out a trip to Turin to see Juventus play United in the Champions League second group phase. For once, our wives came with us, lured by a few days in Turin and the fact that we knew people there. I particularly remember us being taken out to dinner in a very elegant restaurant in the Parco Valentino. Our hostess, Elsa, a fellow anaesthetist, was dressed in a most elegant long scarlet coat and, with a lady friend, entertained us not only with an excellent meal but with a rendering of some well-known Italian songs! Elsa sang in the church choir and had a lovely voice.

On the day of the evening match, we took the tram to the stadium, and the girls were horrified by the behaviour and foul language of the United supporters crammed into it. At the stadium, we had trouble finding our entrance by walking the long and wrong way around the perimeter of the Stadio Delle Alpi. The tickets once again had come courtesy of Boniperti! How spoilt could I be! By the time we got to our seats, substitute Ryan Giggs had replaced Diego Forlan in the 8th minute and had already scored a 15th-minute goal. He went on to score another in the 40th minute. Together with one from Ruud Van Nistelrooy in the 61st minute, it resulted in a 3-0 victory. In goal for Juve was Gianluigi Buffon, who at the time of writing had finally retired, having held the Serie A appearance record with 648 games beating the now also retired Paolo Maldini. Also of note was the fact that Pavel Nedved, the Czech, was playing for Juve. After a stellar playing career in which he scored 110 league goals, in 2010, he went on to become a director and later, in 2015, became vice-chairman of the board of directors. We were a bit apprehensive about the return tram journey, but as we had been sitting in Juve seats, we were allowed to go straight to the tram. It all passed peacefully, and we got to our hotel uneventfully.

At the back of my mind was the fact that the final was to be played at Old Trafford and how wonderful and convenient it would be if Juve got there and even won it! They got out of the second group phase as runners up behind Manchester United and on goal difference from Basel and Deportivo La Coruna. Indeed I was getting quite excited when they beat Barcelona in the quarters 3-2 on aggregate in spite of Edgar Davids being sent off in the second leg and got to the semifinal where they had to beat Real Madrid. Real had won three of the previous finals and had a star-studded side, including Iker Casillas, Roberto Carlos, Luis Figo, Zidane (ex Juventus), Raul, and Ronaldo. The first leg was in Madrid, in which Real won 2-1, and the return in Turin was won 3-1 by Juve, qualifying them for the final on aggregate. So they had indeed fulfilled the first part of my dream. Incidentally, the other semifinal was a dour all Italian affair with the two Milan sides.

(AC and Inter) in opposition. An interesting anomaly was that although they both play in the same San Siro stadium, AC were designated as the away side. When the aggregate scores were 1-1, Milan qualified on "away goals"!

2003 was a year when a major financial scandal was unveiled in Italy. Parmalat was a highly successful company with chairman and CEO Calisto Tanzi at the helm. It included the football team Parma among its assets that were declared insolvent when the company collapsed. The chairman was later to be indicted for fraud, declared bankrupt and arrested. His bankruptcy was with debts of about £10 million, the highest recorded in Europe, and in 2010 he was sentenced to 18 years in jail. He largely served his sentence under house arrest at his villa outside Parma. The honour that he had received from the Italian state, the Cavalieri di Gran Croce was later forfeited. Palma FC had a decade of success with some famous managers such as Carlo Ancelotti and Nevio Scala and many stellar players that included Herman Crespo, Fausto Asprilla, Lilian Thuram, Gianfranco Zola and Gigi Buffon. Buffon, together with Dino Zoff, must be considered two of the greatest goalkeepers, although many would definitely also put Russian Lev Yashin, our own Gordon Banks and German Manuel Neuer on the list. Zoff made 642 leagues and 112 international appearances, Buffon a total of over 1100 appearances, including 176 internationals. Buffon was born in Carrara, a city famous for the exceptional white marble that is quarried there. He spent his first 6 years playing for Parma, then 20 years at Juventus, interrupted by one year at Paris Saint Germain. To everyone's surprise, at 43 years of age, he returned to Parma in Serie B, presumably to end his playing career there. We met him once in a restaurant where we were all having lunch on one of the Juventus Club Londra trips. I remember him telling us that he had received a great deal from Adidas, but it depended on him learning English. I don't know if he ever did?

Chapter 103 - 2003 Champions League Final

Surely after beating the two Spanish giants, being Serie A champions and heading for the next Scudetto for the 27th time, Juve surely had a good chance of beating AC Milan and finally lifting the trophy once again.

Juve were managed by Marcello Lippi, who had led them before to the Champions League final, winning in 1996 but losing in 1997 and 1998. The Juventus team was lacking their star midfielder and playmaker Pavel Nedved, having received 2 yellow cards in previous matches, including one in the semifinal. AC Milan were managed by Carlo Ancelotti, so one knew they would be very defensive. I went up in a minibus organised by the Juventus Club Londra, and there seemed to be an unexpected number of both Milan and Juventus supporters on the M6. The match itself was very tense, with both sides concentrating on defence. So there was little goalmouth action and no surprise then when it finished 0-0 after 90 minutes. If one didn't know what catenaccio (door bolt) meant, you definitely knew after watching that ninety minutes. So on to extra time, and there was no change after the first period, which meant that according to the silver goal rule, the tie went straight on to a penalty shoot. It was a bit of a relief as one had the distinct impression that no goal would be forthcoming in open play, however long they played. The penalty shootout was more exciting, with Del Piero and Birindelli scoring for Juve, while Trezeguet, Zalayeta and Montero did not. Milan were successful through Shevchenko, Nesta, and Serginho, with only Seedorf and Kaladze missing. Controversy, not for the first time, was caused by the fact that several of the unsuccessful kicks were associated with the goalie advancing off their line before the ball was struck, which was against the rules. So we were very disappointed to see Juve lose, and once again, when you have just lost a match, it's a long way home.

Paolo Maldini, one of my favourite players of all time, was selected as the man of the match. My feeling that he was an outstanding player meant that when in 2005 AC Milan were playing Liverpool in the Champions League final, I felt like having a small bet. I wouldn't call myself a betting man, but very occasionally, I had moments of inspiration. One result was that a bet was placed on Paolo Maldini, scoring the first goal. Of course, he did and after only 52 seconds! What a final that turned out to be with Liverpool coming from 3-0 down to force penalties which they won! My second and to date last betting triumph was a small sum placed on Unai Emery to be the next Arsenal manager in 2018.

Chapter 104 - Season 2003/04

Much of the Luton income in the 2003/04 season was channelled to the Trust in Luton, which had been recently formed. It was a merger with the Supporters Club following the controversial takeover of the club by John Gurney. At the time, supporters had been discouraged from buying season tickets as it was not clear who the owners were!

Trust in Luton was founded in June 2003 following the club's takeover by John Gurney. The Trust devised a strategy and began to acquire shares in the club's major creditor, Hatters Holdings. Hatters Holdings was an offshore company that the club owed several million pounds. The majority was owned by a combination of Trust in Luton and prominent supporters spokesman Gary Sweet, a former senior executive at Siemens. They successfully forced Gurney out after a reign of 55 days by placing the club into administrative receivership on the 14th of July 2003. Hatters Holdings later sold the club in May 2004 to a consortium headed by Bill Tomlins, and he brought the club out of administrative receivership. On 14th July 2003, Luton entered administrative receivership once again and only exited from it on the 26th May 2004. At the time, we had a very small playing squad, did not have a reserve team and were under a transfer embargo.

That season ended with us safely in 10th position thanks to Steve Howard, again top scorer aided by Gary McSheffrey and Enoch Showumni. A special match was the away 2nd round Carling Cup tie at Charlton, which ended 4-4 after extra time, and then we went on to lose 7-8 on penalties. Chris Coyne's penalty was the only one saved after 15 had been successfully struck.

So another consortium headed by Bill Tomlins, who had previously been a popular head of the administrative staff, took over in December 2003, with the acquisition completed in May 2004.

Off the field, a former bank clerk Cherry Newbery, employed by the club for over 30 years and having been appointed as Luton club secretary in 1994, proved very capable and went on to steer the sinking ship through troubled waters with considerable effort and no little skill. Players had to be sold to keep the club afloat, including the ever-popular Matthew Spring to Leeds and Emerson Boyce to Crystal Palace. Cherry Newbery, after leaving Luton, went on to become a trustee of Signposts, a local charity helping the homeless. Tomlins was fined £15,000 and suspended from all football activity for five years.

Hatters Holdings had sold the club on to a consortium headed by Bill Tomlins in May 2004, and he brought the club out of administrative receivership.

We had also fallen into administration again, and the administrator decided to sell, amongst others, Chris Coyne, Dave Edwards and Jaroslaw Fojut. At this point, the club was taken over by a fan-backed consortium called Luton Town 2020 Ltd, with popular media man Nick Owen as frontman and lifelong fan Gary Sweet as chief executive.

The name 2020 was taken because that was when it was hoped that the club would be restored to its former glory and would have a new stadium. It all seemed rather optimistic after three successive relegations.

The Trust became more involved with the club, and it was agreed that they should be present at quarterly meetings with the directors. It also became easier for fans to acquire shares in the club via the Trust. The loss of 30 points in two seasons, along with large fines, seemed extreme, to say the least.

So came a spell in the Conference which lasted much longer than predicted. Trust in Luton became a major influence, and in 2014 had been given the legal right to veto any changes to the club's identity regardless of who owns the club. This included the name, nickname, colours, club crest and mascot. The membership of the Trust tripled in one day. Later that year, the Trust merged with the long-established Luton Town Supporters Club.

The Trust had bought shares in the club's major creditor, Watson-Challis's Hatters Holdings, which then became majority-owned by a combination of Trust in Luton and prominent supporter spokesman Gary Sweet. Hatters Holdings sold the club to a consortium headed by Bill Tomlins in May 2004, and he brought the club out of administrative receivership. He remained at the helm until near the end of the 2006/7 season. Surprisingly in view of everything that had been going on, the club gained promotion to the Championship in season 2004-05 under manager Mike Newell. Tomlins had previously been a popular head of the administrative staff aided by the very capable Cherry Newbery, a faithful club secretary for over 30 years, but who lost favour when she blew the whistle on the financial activities. Newbury had been secretary since 1994 and was implicated as the employee who drew the Football Association's attention to former directors paying agents through the club's holding company. She was widely respected for her integrity and detailed many of the illegal payments to player agents that chairman Bill Tomlins was transacting. Sadly she lost favour when she blew the whistle on Tomlins, but he was forced to resign in April 2007.

Bill had got into trouble over irregular payments to incoming player's agents by the club's parent company, Jayten Stadium limited and was forced to resign in April 2007. He was fined

£15,000 and suspended from all football activity for five years. The club was fined £50,000 and had the points deducted for irregular payments to agents.

Chapter 105 - A Champions League Match in Monaco

In the autumn of 2003, we were in Nice when Monaco were due to play Deportivo La Coruna in the Champions League. My younger daughter Esther, not normally a football fan, came with me and as it turned out was a very good decision for us both. There was a great atmosphere in the small Monaco stadium, and the home team, coached at the time by Didier Deschamps, won 8-3, the biggest aggregate score in any match I have ever attended. I remember the very hi-tech electric scoreboard ran out of space to add the goalscorers! The star for Les Monégasques with four goals was a relatively unknown Croatian called Dado Prso, playing on his 29th birthday. He spent 8 years with Monaco before finishing his career with Glasgow Rangers. That year Monaco got to the Champions League final for the first time, where they lost 3-0 to Porto in Gelsenkirchen. Les Monégasques have been well supported by the Monaco royal family, firstly Prince Rainier and later Prince Albert, who were often seen at their matches. However, the owners now seem to be largely Russians. The president since 2011 is Dmitry Yevgenyevich Rybolovlev, a Russian businessman and investor. Rybolovlev owned the potash producer Urakali.

Chapter 106 - FIFA 100

In March 2004, FIFA held a gala in London to commemorate FIFA's 100th anniversary. It included an announcement of the best 100 players, half retired and half still active, as chosen by Pele. Pele finished with 125 names, saying it was too difficult to keep the retired to 50. The list was controversial with, for example, the choice of 14 from France and Italy and 13 from the Netherlands compared with only three from Spain. Not surprisingly, Brazil topped the list with 15 players.

A surprise was the inclusion of two female players, the first time they were mentioned in the same breath as men in football matters! Would anyone have predicted the progress they would make to be widely recognised both as players and media folk at present? From my point of view, it was very pleasing to see Boniperti on the list and that he was able to attend in person. Unfortunately, I was out of the country coming back that evening and could not accept the invitation he had got for me. The next morning I spoke to him on the phone to congratulate him. I also spoke to his elder son. He said Giampiero had been very emotional to be on the list and to reunite with lots of those he had played with and against. It was a sad day in April 2004 when Umberto Agnelli died, and that meant that for the first time in two generations, there was no member of the Agnelli family directly involved with Juve.

Chapter 107 - A final in Cardiff

The FA Cup Final in 2004 was between Manchester United and Millwall. Colin obviously wanted to go, and I reluctantly agreed despite loathing Millwall after what they had done to Luton in 1985.

The match was the 4th Cup Final at the Millennium Stadium Cardiff as Wembley was being rebuilt. Manchester United were the strong favourites, having won the cup 10 times out of 15 appearances compared with this being the first FA cup final ever for Millwall. The tickets came through the Wiltshire FA, and all the FA councils were allocated tickets. Luckily we were in one of the United sections and row 6, which was quite low and close to the pitch.

Millwall was also in a lower league and had amazingly reached the final without meeting any premier league club.

Seventy-one thousand three hundred fifty saw United win 3-0 with a Ronaldo goal and two by Ruud Van Nistelrooy, one of them was a penalty. Millwall had Denis Wise as player-manager! An advantage of Cardiff for us was the proximity of the stadium to the station and the direct fast rail connection to Swindon, near where Colin lived.

For the 2005/6 season, the second tier was renamed the Championship, had 24 clubs and was also a very lucrative league. To give an idea of the struggles a team like Luton Town would have to stay there, look at the size of our gates which were at least 8000 less than any other club in the league. It seemed like a preview of 2019/2020!

Then came the next two tiers, now called Division 1 and Division 2. It remains very confusing that Division 1 is still the 3rd tier and Division 2 is the 4th tier!

2004 was the year of a very exciting and surprising 16 team European Championships played in Portugal.

At age 19, Cristiano Ronaldo featured in his first International championships and scored two goals, including a penalty. Germany, Spain and Italy were eliminated at the group stage and France at the quarter-final stage. Greece beat the hosts in the opening match. But after beating England in the quarters 0-0 (6-5 on penalties) and the Netherlands 2-1 in the semis, managed to qualify for the final. The final was a repeat of the opening match and had the same result, a win for Greece over Portugal, this time by 1-0. The goal was scored by Angelos Charisteas, until then relatively unknown outside Greece. He was playing for Werder Bremen at the time, where he scored 18 league goals in 66 appearances. That was an amazing result because it was only the second time that Greece had even qualified for a major tournament, and Portugal had a team of international superstars.

Apart from Ronaldo, who was already starring for Manchester United, they had Luis Figo, Rui Costa and Helder Postiga, among others! The top scorer in the tournament was the Czech Milan Baros with five goals. He is probably best remembered for his skills as a striker and for being arrested in France between Lyon and Geneva for driving at 271 km (168 mph) in his black Ferrari. It was the fastest ever recorded in the region. Not surprisingly, it resulted in his car and licence being confiscated, and he had to return in a taxi to Lyon where he was playing!!

Chapter 108 - Season 2004/05

Next season (2004/05) in league one, we finished 12 points above 2nd placed Hull City! We won ten and drew two of the first twelve games, and that season featured some big home wins such as 4-0 over Bradford City, followed in the next match by 5-1 over Wrexham. Later in the season, we had a 5-0 win over Bristol City and a 4-1 win away at Torquay.

The season ended as it had started with six wins and a draw in the last seven matches! That season, Mike Newell received awards for the manager of the month and Steve Howard player of the month for August.

On the 26th of May 2004, we finally exited administrative receivership. Tomlins remained at the helm until near the end of the 2006/7 season. In April 2007, Tomlins was replaced by David Pinkney, a former saloon car racing driver, at which time we were relegated to League One.

Cherry Newbery was widely respected for her integrity and detailed many illegal payments to players' agents that chairman Bill Tomlins was transacting. Sadly she lost favour when she blew the whistle on Tomlins, but he was forced to resign in April 2007. She left by mutual consent after a period of suspension on full pay. The money, maybe £150,000, was paid to agents from the club's parent company Jayten Stadium Ltd.

On the 23rd of July, Colin and I went to Luton to see Luton playing Ajax, managed by Ronald Koeman, in a pre-season friendly. Ajax were, of course, previous European Cup winners and very attractive opponents.

Ajax, Dutch league champions and former European Cup winners, played the total football, which had been popularised in Dutch football at that time. It finished Luton 0 - Ajax 4. Unsurprisingly the status of Ajax drew a crowd of over 7,500. Two players stood out; one of them was Van der Vaart, an attacking midfielder, and second was Zlatan Ibrahimovic who replaced him at half time, marked by our youth graduate Curtis Davies. It was Zlatan's last season with Ajax before his transfer to Juventus in 2004.

Fabio Capello tells a great story that when he signed Ibra for Juventus, he told him that he didn't score enough goals and gave him a pile of videotapes of Marco Van Basten's scoring feats to study. Maybe they helped as he scored over 500 goals for many of Europe's top clubs and LA Galaxy and over 70 International goals for Sweden! Despite his height of 6'5", he showed wonderful skill and athleticism, and one could see that he was destined for the top.

Curtis also went on to have a stellar career, and when he left in 2005 for West Bromwich Albion for a fee of £3 million, at least the fee seemed an adequate reward for such a promising 20-year-old. In 2020 he was still playing, latterly for Derby County. For Luton, the sad news had been the transfer of Matthew Spring to Leeds and Emerson Boyce to Crystal Palace, both on Bosman free transfers.

The Bosman transfers arose from a ruling in a Belgian court in 1995. It banned restrictions on the number of foreign players that could play for a club in the EU. It allowed any number of players to move at the end of their contracts without paying the fees. Maybe two of the most high profile Bosmans were Edgar David's move from Ajax to AC Milan in 1996 and Steve McManaman from Liverpool to Real Madrid in 1999. The Bosman ruling was a major factor in players' rapidly escalating transfer value and the salaries they could command.

Surprisingly, given everything going on, our club won the league, gaining promotion to the Championship in season 2004-05 under Mike Newell. Mike had become a manager when Gurney sacked the popular team of Joe Kinnear and Mick Harford. A fan's phone poll on a premium line was supposed to have been held, but Mike Newell was appointed before the results had been announced.

We finished on top spot of League One, won by 12 points from Hull City and therefore promoted to the Championship (second tier). Steve Howard headed the goal tally with 18 leagues and 4 Cup goals, including a hat trick at Milton Keynes. The next was Croatian Ahmet Brkovic with 16 and Kevin Nicholls with 14 in the 87 league goals scored and only 48 conceded. Another player Rowan Vine scored 9. Although nominally a striker, Rowan provided many assists, making him very valuable. He must hold some sort of record, for including many loans, he has played for about 21 different clubs. We beat Swindon twice, 3-2 away and 3-1 at home.

The celebrations that greeted our first place can be imagined. That Swindon team was noted for the presence of Andy King, Luton born, in his 4th year as manager and Mick Harford as assistant manager. Both got a very warm reception from the Luton faithful. Other exciting games were the 4-3 win at Barnsley, three successive games in October/ November where we scored 13 goals, and a 5-0 home win over Bristol City.

To my delight, Juventus drew Liverpool in the Champions League quarter-final in April. Another reason to go with the Juventus Club Londra and witness the Anfield stadium with its special atmosphere. There was some apprehension as it was the first time they had played each other since Heysel. Any tension was defused to some extent by the Liverpool supporters on the Kop, unfurling a long banner reading Amicizia (Friendship).

Sadly Juve lost 2-1 with early goals from Sami Hyppia and Luis Garcia, followed by a second-half reply from Fabio Cannavaro. The return was a goalless draw meaning progress for Liverpool.

They beat Chelsea in the semis and won the competition with that amazing win over Milan, where they came back from a 0-3 half time score to win 3-2 on penalties.

In 2005, we went to that year's FA Cup final and played in Cardiff between Arsenal and Manchester United. Arsenal became the first team to win the FA Cup in a penalty shoot-out, despite being outplayed throughout the game, after neither side managed to score in the initial 90 minutes or in 30 minutes of extra time. The shoot-out finished 5–4 to Arsenal, with Patrick Vieira scoring the winning penalty after Arsenal goalkeeper Jens Lehman saved Paul Scholes' shot. After the match, I remember getting to the station to discover that no trains were leaving soon for Swindon. It seemed that nobody had told British Rail that there was to be extra time played and all the extra trains put on for the match had already left empty earlier!!

Finally, we got back much later than planned, having had to change at Newport and wait a long time on the platform there.

Chapter 109 - Season 2005/06

I didn't miss the last Millennium stadium final although I had to get there from my course in Middlesbrough. I had lunch with a Cardiff based anaesthetist friend, and we went to the match together. It was a very exciting 3-3 draw followed by a penalty shoot-out between Liverpool and West Ham United. Liverpool won the shoot-out 3-1. Zamora, Konchesky and Ferdinand all failed for the Hammers, while only Hyppia missed or rather had his shot saved for the Reds. My companion was a true red Welsh rugby fan who never missed a home 6 Nations international. He was struck by the much more hostile and aggressive atmosphere at a big soccer match, although both attracted the same full houses. Of course, the alcohol flowed freely for rugby, whereas it was largely banned at soccer matches. In return, I was hoping for an invitation in the future to a Welsh rugby international, but it never transpired.

For the 2005/6 season, the second tier was renamed the Championship, had 24 clubs, and was also a very lucrative league ranking 4th highest in the list of European league attendances, ahead of Italy's Serie A and France's Ligue 1. The next season we were in the Championship! The league was the top wealthiest non-top flight league and attracted huge sponsorship, ahead of Italy's Serie A and France's Ligue 1.

Below the Championship came the next two tiers, now called Division 1 and Division 2. It remains very confusing that Division 1 is still the 3rd tier and Division 2 is the 4th tier! Again, the top scorer was Steve Howard with 22 goals, including a hat trick at Milton Keynes.

Ahmet Brkovic ably assisted him with 15 and Kevin Nicholls, the captain with 12, and another striker Rowan Vine with 9. Brkovic started his career in Dubrovnik, Croatia and came to England to play for Leyton Orient in 1999. In 2001 he joined the Town, where he played for seven years, scoring 31 goals in the league.

Nicholls had come in 2001 from Wigan and spent two spells with the Town. He was a very successful and immensely popular captain, always gave 100%, and led very much by example. He was the regular penalty taker and rarely missed. He carried the Town to two promotions and victory in the Football League Trophy. Sadly he was plagued by knee injuries and had to retire from playing in 2010.

Juventus were drawn against Arsenal in the quarter-final of the Champions League. The first leg was played on the 28th of March 2006 in London and resulted in a 2-0 win for Arsenal. I went with my good friend Richard and son in law David, and again we were among the Juve supporters behind the goal. Fabio Capello was the Juve manager, but Arsenal scored through a very young Cesc Fabregas and captain Thierry Henry, but for Juventus Camoranesi, a fiery Argentinian and Frenchman Zebina both received second yellow cards. Two others, Trezeguet and Vieira, both got yellows. I was not proud to be a Juve supporter on that occasion as they were a really ragged and an angry mess by the end and showed nothing of the flowing football that had taken them eight points clear at the top of Serie A.

The Town finished safely in 10th position. After 14 games, they were in 3rd place, and we thought that we might be promotion contenders again. A game at home to Crystal Palace pitted us against our ex-striker and now manager of Crystal Palace, Iain Dowie, and Emerson Boyce our ex-defender. Howard and Vine were again the top scorers.

A 3rd round FA Cup tie against Liverpool at the Kenny ended 5-3 to Liverpool, making for an exciting game even if the wrong result. I remember it particularly for at 4-3 to the reds, Marlon Beresford, our goalie, came up for a corner which was cleared. Xavi Alonso picked up the ball and drove it into the net from within his own half! Sadly Curtis Davies, a local boy and cultured central defender was sold to West Brom for 3 million pounds, a new Luton record. At the time of writing, he is still playing for Derby County. Luckily we had signed a Finnish international centre half Markus Heikkinen in his place, and he made 77 appearances for us and earned 61 international caps.

Chapter 110 - Why do I go to away matches?

In 1994, Millwall moved into a new stadium called the New Den. I had been to the old one in "Cold Blow Lane" once before, but I don't remember the circumstances. I don't recall any adverse incidents. Indeed what I do remember was finding the club shop, which was at the time behind the goal populated by the infamous home supporters. By the time I left the shop, the game was about to start, and so I stayed where I was among the notorious hooligans, but by keeping quiet, I survived it quite well!

In March 2006, we were playing away at Millwall again, and for some reason, I decided to go to it. It was a season when we went on to finish in 10th place. I naively thought crowd behaviour and movement were largely under police and stewards' control. I wanted to go with the excellent Town on Tour, but by the time I got round to booking, the coaches were already full and even subject to a waiting list. So the next best thing was to go by train, the stadium being close to South Bermondsey station. The Millwall website described a walkway link to the stadium and called it "a cage". The first thing that surprised me was the number of policemen at London Bridge station, which was repeated at the South Bermondsey station. There were clear signs for us away supporters to enter the walkway. It was obvious that this cage-like structure would not allow exit in the event of any crowd pressure or surge. However, I dismissed such thoughts as I took my seat on the upper tier of the north stand on a lovely sunny day. The usual supporters' songs were heard, especially from the home fans "No one likes us, we don't care. We are Millwall, super Millwall. We are Millwall from the Den". The less said about the game, the better! Luton played as badly as I can remember in the first half and were a goal down at half time.

They only slightly improved in the second half and scrambled an equaliser through Chris Coyne, but it was no surprise when the Lions struck a late 90th-minute winner. So the exit from the ground led us into the infamous walkway where we all marched briskly towards the station. However, the march was halted because a couple of rows of policemen barred the way. To be charitable, I suggest that their role was to only let a certain number of people onto the platform. I realised the potential risk immediately as more supporters came on from behind and became restive and aggressive. In the end, they charged the police. Several people were knocked to the ground, luckily to my knowledge, without serious injury.

Police reinforcements only served to make for more serious skirmishes. The atmosphere could only be described as very angry and hostile, and the risk of injury remained. I remember clearly that a kind man, probably twice my size offered to protect me from whatever lay ahead. It was a replica of the exit from Juventus when we went to the Manchester United match in 2003. The short train journey to London Bridge was uneventful, but we were again stopped by rows of policemen along the platform to the exit. Once the fans were assembled the police walked slowly backwards (something I have never seen before or after), along the concourse, upstairs, along a walkway and downstairs onto the Thameslink platform.

Then we were all ushered on to a Thameslink train heading for Luton and Bedford whether that was where we wanted to go or not! Luckily for me, the first stop was Farringdon, where I alighted. I was relieved to find the sanctuary of my car, feeling physically unscathed but mentally scarred. Maybe my readers, many of whom have attended far more away matches than me, will wonder why I bothered to include this, experiencing similar happenings rather frequently. Maybe they take them in their stride as part of the experience of attending high profile away matches. A small minority may even seek and enjoy such experiences, but it all seemed sad to me. Also, I feel that we have to acknowledge the sad contribution of the "supporters" as, without their extreme behaviour, none of this would be necessary. The average supporter would be able to enjoy a pleasant afternoon of football free from the fear of violence. After that experience, I cancelled my plans to go to Watford when they next played Luton five weeks later.

Chapter 111 - Keith Keane

Keith deserves a special mention. To my mind, every club needs a Keith Keane. He was a local boy, came up through the youth system and made his first-team debut at 17 in the 2003/4 season. He could and indeed did play in any position except goalkeeper and striker. He was one of the few players to play in all four divisions. In 2004/05, he was part of the promotion-winning squad making 19 appearances in all.

Keane won many awards, including Player of the Season, Players' Player of the year, and Internet Player of the Season.

In 2008 under Mick Harford, he was elected club captain, but that was the year that the club was in administration, and we had been docked those 10 points for financial irregularities and a further 20 for exiting administration without a CVA (Company Voluntary Arrangement).

Keith made 40 appearances in season 08/09, but we were relegated from the Football league for the first time in 89 years. However, he was part of the victorious Johnstone's Paint Trophy team and was elected man of the match playing in midfield. His performance over that season earned him another Player and Internet Player of the Season awards. Under Richard Money, Keane was placed on the transfer list after contract disagreements, but luckily nothing came of it. He will be remembered especially for a very special goal direct from a corner against league leaders Oxford United in 2010. It was the last minute of the match, George Pilkington had just equalised, and Keith's goal earned the Town a 2-1 victory on their way to a playoff position. He was shown a red card for excessive celebrations with the Luton fans, having already been given a yellow one. It won the goal of the season award. Unfortunately, they lost the playoff against York City, both legs ending 1-0 to York, so we remained in the conference. In 2010 Keith signed a new two-year contract, having made 33 appearances in that season.

In 2011/12, he made a further 42 appearances in his final season for the Town before going to Preston North End. Signed by a former manager at Luton, Graham Westley and then on to Cambridge, also managed by a former Luton one, in this case, Richard Money. He finished his career at Rochdale.

He won the player of the season award on two occasions. He played the full 120 minutes in the 2011 Conference playoff final against Wimbledon at the Etihad stadium. Sadly Wimbledon beat us on penalties after Jason Walker had headed against the bar for us in the dying minutes of normal time.

Season 11/12 was to be Keith's final one at Luton and included "outstanding" accolades from then-manager Gary Brabin. So why do I single Keane out? Simply because of his upbringing as a footballer, his undoubted all round skill, enthusiasm and versatility, longevity at the club, and loyalty, all with a very modest demeanour.

Chapter 112 - Season 2006/07

In 2006/07, Luton, in an unhappy season, were relegated to League One, having finished in 23rd place with only Leeds United below us. The season had started badly with the sale of Steve Howard to Derby. Although it earned us a healthy one million pounds, to replace his 105 goals was always going to be difficult! In October, we were 5th, but only Rowan Vine got into double figures with 12 league goals in his 26 games which speaks for itself!

Sadly he left for Birmingham City halfway through the season, and captain Kevin Nicholls went to Leeds for £700,000. Kevin did return for another spell in 2008.

The club was fined £50,000 and had 10 points deducted for those irregular payments to agents.

There were also new problems with manager Mike Newell who refused to deal with agents, saying corruption was rife and caused controversy with his adverse comments about one of the first female assistant referees, Amy Rayner. After only three wins in 24 games, he was dismissed in March, with Brian Stein taking on a caretaker role. He only managed Luton for one match, a 2–0 home defeat to Ipswich on 17 March, and was replaced after only two weeks. Kevin Blackwell came from a struggling Leeds United by now owned by Ken Bates. Matthew Spring came back to Luton controversially from Watford, played for us, and stayed for two more years, contributing ten more league goals.

The England team at the time was to be managed by Fabio Capello. He had managed several top Italian and Spanish teams, including Juventus and Real Madrid, in two separate spells. On one visit to Turin with friends, we met Claudio Ranieri in the hotel lift at the time he was managing Juventus. He had left Chelsea a few years before, so that was the obvious topic of conversation! His English was limited despite his time in England, but it was enough for the short time we were together in the lift! The Italians were, I think, one of the first to realise the importance of keeping the players away from temptation on the nights before games! Many years later, of course, in season 2015/16, Ranieri managed Leicester City to the Premier League title, one of the great surprises and achievements of that or any other season. He is still active and has managed to date a total of 20 other clubs, but that may not be the final total!

Our club, by then, was at serious risk of being declared bankrupt with the Football League withholding TV and league sponsorship money.

Chapter 113 - A French League Cup Final

Nice had qualified for the Coupe de la Ligue final to be played at the Stade de France in Paris on the 22nd of April 2006. What a great excuse for a few days in Paris! We stayed in a hotel, the Franklin Roosevelt, just off the Champs-Élysées that had been recommended to us by a French lady friend and it didn't disappoint! However, it was dangerously close to Cartier jewellers, whose prices were, needless to say, way above anything we might have contemplating spending, so stuck to window gazing! In the afternoon, we visited a fabulous Monet exhibition in the Grand Palais, also close to the Champs-Élysées. Wonderful to once again be able to mix football with culture!

The night of the match, we took the train to Saint-Denis Porte de Paris, very close to the stadium, and made ourselves comfortable in our seats. With scarves above our heads, we listened to and even joined in the Nice anthem, which was well known to us and awaited the eagle's arrival. We didn't see it; presumably, it was too far for a mere Nice eagle to fly! The match was quite exciting, played in front of 76,830 spectators. I didn't know any of the Nancy players, while Nice had Hugo Lloris, a star French goalkeeper of the future with over 139 caps. Nice also had Marama Vahirua, a Tahitian forward who we had seen before playing for Nantes. Zerka opened the scoring for Nancy in the first half, but when Vahirua equalised at the start of the second half, we were confident that Nice would win.

However, our hopes were dashed when Kim, a Brazilian, won the match for Nancy. So a short journey back also seemed much longer than it was.

The next day we were queuing to eat at one of our favourite restaurants, L'Entrecote. The restaurant serves a fixed menu consisting of a simple green salad of lettuce topped with walnuts, and a mustard vinaigrette was offered as a starter, followed by the steak with butter sauce. The steak is cooked to your taste and served with chips (pommes allumettes, meaning matchstick potatoes). As usual in my life, full of coincidences, also in the queue by chance was an anaesthetist colleague I knew well with her family celebrating a birthday.

The Paris newspaper Le Monde let out the secret that the sauce is made from livers, fresh thyme and thyme flowers, full cream, white Dijon Mustard, butter, and water, plus salt and pepper.

You can have as many top-ups of the steak and chips as you can eat! On a non-football occasion in Geneva, we found another L'Entrecote, which had the same queues and formula and was well worth the visit!

Chapter 114 - Calciopoli scandal

Calciopoli, translated as "football gate," was a major scandal of Italian football match-fixing disclosed in May 2006. Italy had a bad reputation for financial and match-fixing football scandals for many years, so no one should have been too surprised. Many conversations were cited between team managers and referee organisations suggesting attempts to influence the choice of referees. Several clubs were implicated, particularly Juventus, who were stripped of their 2004/05 title and downgraded from title winner to last place in 2005/06 and relegated to Serie B for the first time. They started there with a nine points deduction, reduced from an initial figure of 30 points. Four other teams, including AC Milan, Fiorentina, Lazio and even Reggiana of Serie B, were also punished. Juventus general manager Luciano Moggi was the lead figure in the scandal and was forced to resign along with others, such as Chairman Antonio Giraudo. Moggi was given a life ban from football and a 20 months prison sentence. However, the statute of limitations came into play so that neither went to prison. A journalist for La Stampa, the Turin based daily, described it all like the eruption of a volcano. It was the biggest sporting scandal that Italy had seen.

What happened to the Juventus players in view of the effectively forced relegation? Several key members of the Juventus squad left. Still, several real stars, including Buffon, Chiellini, Nedved, Trezeguet, Camoranesi and Del Piero, stayed loyal and decided to stay and help the old lady back to Serie A. Del Piero famously commented that "a true gentleman never leaves his lady."

Others left, including Zlatan Ibrahimovic and Patrick Vieira (both to Inter Milan for a combined £23million), Fabio Cannavaro and Emerson (both to Real Madrid for a total of £13m), Lilian Thuram and Gianluca Zambrotta to Barcelona for a total of £13m and lastly Romanian Adrian Mutu (to Fiorentina for 5.5m). They were all picked off by those other elite European clubs.

Unsurprisingly because of the calibre of the players who remained and the appointment of ex-player Didier Deschamps as manager, Juve went straight back up to Serie A at the end of the 2006/7 season, only losing four games all season.

It must be noted that Juventus had always been a club that divides Italy more than any other but always had great power backed as they were by their majority owners, the Agnelli family. That family is often known as "the Kennedys of Italy".

Agnelli owned the Fiat Empire, among many other things. Fiat stands for Fabbrica Italiana Automobili Torino. The Agnelli assets were deputed to be about 4.4% of Italy's GDP! It was feared that the scandal and punishments would have a detrimental effect on the National team's chances in the 2006 World Cup in Germany. On the contrary, Italy went on to win it under Marcello Lippi. The Agnellis asked Boniperti to return as honorary president of Juventus and he accepted after persuasion from the then FIAT CEO Sergio Marchionne. It was assumed that Boni was the one person who would restore respectability to the Juventus structure and image. The club has regained its reputation as the foremost Italian club by winning nine consecutive Serie A titles from 2011/12 to 2019/20. One of the leading figures in that amazing run was Antonio Conte, an ex-player (1991-2004) and later manager (2011-2014).

Chapter 115 - 2006 World Cup in Germany

2006 was a World Cup year, the tournament to be played in Germany. The hosts had won the right to hold the tournament over South Africa. Not for the first or last time there were allegations of bribery and corruptions in the choice of venue. However it wan't the first time FIFA faced such allegations, and it surely was n't going to be the last.

England won Group B, which included Sweden, Paraguay and Trinidad and Tobago.

Italy was in Group E with Ghana, who they beat 2-0, but both went on to the next round in spite of the USA holding Italy to a surprising 1-1 draw and the presence of the Czech Republic, who Italy beat 2-0. The elimination of Poland and the Czechs was the only small surprise.

England beat Ecuador 1-0 in their first knockout match and got to the quarters, where they lost on penalties 1-3 to Portugal after finishing 0-0 after extra time. This time the failures from the spot were Frank Lampard, Steven Gerrard and Jamie Carragher. This continued a poor run of penalty shoot-out results that had started in our famous semi-final against Germany in Italia 90.

Netherlands and Spain came as surprise eliminations in the round of 16, while Italy beat Australia by one goal to nil. The remaining eight had made it to the quarter-finals, whereas Brazil, Argentina, England, and Ukraine were all eliminated.

So the semifinals were Germany versus Italy which was won by the Azzurri 2-0 after extra time and France versus Portugal. France won that one 1-0 to book their place in the final. Italy won the tournament beating France 5-3 on penalties after extra time had ended 1-1. The flawless Azzurri scored all their penalties and won the shootout 5-3, thus winning their 4th World Cup title.

An extraordinary event was when Zidane was sent off in extra time for head butting Marco Materazzi in the chest. It followed a highly personal remark by Materazzi to Zidane. Despite that, Zidane was elected player of the tournament. Interestingly, the goalscorers in the open play had been both the said Materazzi and Zidane. Germany beat Portugal 3-1 to earn 3rd place, which meant that teams from UEFA had dominated for the twelfth time, compared with South America nine. Brazil led the nations with five wins, followed by Germany and Italy with four. An unfortunate statistic from that tournament was a record number of 345 yellow, and 28 red cards dished out! The golden boot went to Germany's Klose with five goals. The Yashin Award for best goalkeeper, named after the wonderful Russian keeper, went to Italy's legendary Gianluigi Buffon.

It was the first time that I had heard of Fan Fests, public viewing areas where supporters without tickets could congregate and watch matches on giant screens. Food, alcohol and other goodies were available. In fact, they were introduced in South Korea in 2002. They mostly passed very peacefully, were deemed a great success, and continued in all subsequent World Cups and European championships. Fifa, of course, offers many sponsorship and partnership opportunities with the Coca Cola Company prominent.

Chapter 116 - More Drama

From Italy came a very sad story with the near-death of Juventus international defender Gianluca Pessotto in June 2006. He was known to the fans as il Professorino ("the little professor") on account of him wearing glasses, an interest in philosophy and literature and having obtained a law degree. After ending his playing career, he was a popular coaching staff member. He survived a fall from the 4th floor of the Juventus headquarters! He was holding a rosary, so it was surmised that he had attempted suicide in the wake of that Calciopoli scandal which had seen Juventus stripped of two titles and relegated to Serie B for the only time in their history. He survived multiple fractures and internal bleeding but made an amazing recovery so that he could, in due course, resume his coaching role.

I believe that he is still the sporting director of the club's youth academy. He was awarded the 5th Class / Knight: Cavaliere Ordine al Merito Della Repubblica Italiana in 2000, a very high honour.

Around that time, there was the passport scandal where false passports were issued to players so they could become "European" and therefore eligible to play without exceeding the number of non - Europeans rule. The best known was Argentinian Juan Sebastian Veron, who was a member of the Lazio squad. Lazio had won the scudetto in 2000, thus qualifying for the Champions League.

Chapter 117 - New Wembley Stadium

On the 9th of March 2007, the new Wembley Stadium built on the old site was handed over. The first formal match was the 2007 Cup Final between Chelsea and Manchester United. The stadium held an opening ceremony before the match, including the official opening by Prince William, a flypast by the Red Arrows and a parade on the pitch of nearly fifty former players and winners at the old stadium. Colin, by now an executive member at Old Trafford, had got the tickets. It was a very tight match but won by Chelsea 1-0 with Didier Drogba's late extra-time goal.

Chelsea had already won the League Cup that season by beating Arsenal 2-1 and got to the Champions League semifinal, where they lost to Liverpool on penalties. They also had to settle for 2nd place in the Premier League, which went to Manchester United by 2 points. Jose Mourinho managed the Chelsea team at the time in his first spell. Colin was very displeased that a team with the likes of Scholes, Carrick, Ronaldo, Rooney and Giggs could not even muster one goal in 120 minutes! A twice life-size statue of Bobby Moore sculpted by Philip Jackson had been unveiled earlier by Bobby Charlton. The famous Wembley arch, 133 metres high, is visible right across London and has replaced the twin towers as a characteristic landmark. It can be lit in a whole variety of interesting ways.

Chapter 118 - Season 2007/08

A highlight for me was the away match at Swindon at the beginning of the season. Swindon had just come up from League two by earning third place, so that club was buoyant! At that time, the top three clubs got an automatic promotion. Thanks to Colin, we sat in the Director's Box and had access to the accompanying lounge, which was very splendid. Sadly for me, the Town lost 2-1.

In April 2007, Tomlins was replaced by David Pinkney, a former saloon car racing driver, at which time we were relegated to League One and were again in administration. The administrator decided to sell among others Chris Coyne, Dave Edwards and Jaroslaw Fojut. Luton were then relegated to League 2. If that was not enough, they were relegated to the Conference League at the end of 2008-09, having been deducted a further 20 points to add to not one but ten for failing to satisfy the League's insolvency rules. Not much hope if you need ten wins before becoming positive.

The Trust wanted answers from the football authorities as to why the Town had been published so much more severely than other clubs guilty of similar financial misdemeanours.

Chairman Bill Tomlins and his consortium were fined £15,000 and suspended from all football activity for five years. Pinkney promised to fund the club's overheads. At the end of 2007, the club was deducted 10 points by the FA, being found guilty of paying agents via a third party. They had also fallen into administration in November. Jaroslav Fojut returned to Bolton having been on loan, and all loan players had to return to their parent clubs when we entered administration. We also saw owner David Pinkney's and manager Kevin Blackwell's departure, who Mick Harford replaced. One of the noteworthy players to pass through was Canadian international Paul Peschisolido, who made only five appearances and scored but a single goal. He had to retire after ankle problems failed to respond fully to treatment. However, he had accumulated 447 Football League appearances and 118 goals over 16 years, predominantly in the second tier of English professional football. He also made 76 Cup appearances, scoring 22 goals. In 1995 he married Karren Brady who became a baroness in 2014. She is, of course, one of the best known and most successful women in football administration and business. Luton were relegated to League 2, having finished the season in last place. If that was not enough, they were relegated to the Conference at the end of 2008-09, having been deducted a further 20 points for failing to satisfy the League's insolvency rules. Not much hope if you need ten wins before becoming positive on the league points table. There were endless arguments as to why the Town had been punished so severely compared with other clubs who had been guilty of similar misdemeanours. So came a spell in the Conference, which lasted much longer than anyone would have expected. Trust in Luton became a major influence, and in 2014 had been given the legal right to veto any changes to the club's identity regardless of who owns the club. This included the name, nickname, colours, club crest and mascot. The membership of the Trust tripled in one day. Later that year, the Trust merged with the long-established Luton Town Supporters Club.

Being in administration for the third time in less than ten years, we had to take a ten-point penalty. The future of the club seemed very precarious. A 1-1 FA Cup 3rd round home against Liverpool gave us a lucrative replay at Anfield worth around half a million pounds but a 5-0 defeat. In the same March, I was lucky enough to win a prize in one of the Luton club competitions. It included a club shirt signed by the player of my choice. In this case, I chose Chris Perry, who was a classy defender, although only 5 foot 9 inches tall. The other part of the prize was two places in one of those rather strange executive boxes. Of course, I took Colin, and we were greeted by two Luton players, Darren Currie and Steve Robinson, neither of whom could play due to injury, and we enjoyed the hospitality and a 3-0 win over Oldham. Talking of prizes, many years earlier, I had won the Golden Gamble, which offered a cash prize of 50% of the takings. I remember being rather concerned about leaving the ground with my cash which I had received by hand at half time, in full view of everyone. Rather than frittering the money away, I decided to buy something special and chose an old map of Bedfordshire by a very well-known 17th-century cartographer called John Speed and had it framed. Of course, since then, I have always bought two tickets at £1 each and never won again, so the profit and loss equation is certainly no longer in my favour!

My fascination with all things Italian kept me in contact with Italian Roberto Perrone, a presenter on BBC 3 Counties (Beds, Herts and Bucks) radio.

He also presented a weekly programme called Mondo Italiano for many years. He told me that there was to be at Olympia London on the 13th of May 2008 an Italian trade fair called La Dolce Vita. In the evening, the guest of honour was to be Marcello Lippi, who had, of course, been the manager who led Italy to victory in the 2006 World Cup in Germany and who was accompanied by a very glamorous Italian model. Marcello was presented with a trophy to mark his achievement.

It was a fascinating evening especially sampling the food and drink from the various stalls. Of particular interest to me was a stall called Gastronomica with a large selection of Italian produce and wines and which was to be found normally in Borough market. The Market was very close to the London Bridge Hospital and my work there nearly always ended with a visit to Gastronomica and a sampling of their products, mostly from my favourite area of Italy, Piemonte.

Chapter 119 - An 80th birthday outing

Colin McLaren was approaching his 80th birthday. He had given up his great seat at Old Trafford by now, finding the journey from Wiltshire too arduous. As a long time supporter and, more recently, executive member, I thought that the club and I might be able to do something for him to mark the occasion. On the 10th of February 2008, the Manchester derby coincided with the 50th anniversary of the Munich air disaster and was the day before his actual birthday. I wrote to the commercial department at United explaining that Colin was not only a long time supporter and, until recently, an executive member of United but also an ex-football league referee and politician at the Wiltshire FA. As I could have predicted, nothing was on offer except the commercial department suggested we pay for Match Day Hospitality which included closer-by car parking, sit-down lunch in a marquee and a visit from ex-United goalie Alex Stepney.

All this for a very large sum of money, which I reluctantly felt I had to pay. You have to look after your best football friend and give him what I hoped would at least be a memorable day on his special occasion. At least I had first-hand evidence of why United are one of the richest clubs in the world, to say nothing of the input of the American Glazer family, who had bought a controlling interest in 2005. The financial aspects do not bear a description.

So back to the day out, and we got there after the long drive from Wiltshire. Luckily Colin and Rosie had put us up for the night, but we had to leave early as it was a 1 pm kick-off. We found the car park and the marquee not without difficulty and took our places for what was quite a smart three-course lunch. A little memento was given to us to remember United and this experience.

As promised, Alex Stepney passed by in his role as club ambassador, and we all had a chat about various football-related things. I have to say that the waitresses had obviously been carefully selected to appeal to the largely male clientele. So then we made our way to our seats which were behind the goal opposite the Stratford end and were not ideal. On our seats were commemorative red and white scarves, and the teams lined up to stand for a minute in silence to remember those who lost their life in Munich. Quite surprisingly, City scored twice in the first half through Darius Vassell and Benjani Mwaruwari. Benjani was a Zimbabwean, and it was one of only four-goal league goals he scored for City in nearly two years!

We could have gone back to the marquee at half time, but we didn't think there was really time. In the 90th minute, Michael Carrick scored a consolation for United. While it was the commemorative occasion for United, it was a special occasion also for City as they had not won at Old Trafford since 1974, and it was the first time they had won both derby games in the same season since the 1969-70 season. We went back to the marquee for further refreshments hoping that by staying longer, we would avoid the traffic exiting the area. No such luck. It makes me think of which football ground has the worst access and exit difficulties from their ground. Without a doubt Wycombe Wanderers whose ground is up a long hill along a very narrow road. Anyway, we got out and finally left the traffic queues for the motorway back to Wiltshire. Was it worth it? After all, I had been lucky enough to be invited into many corporate areas and did not think this package was worth the money!

Chapter 120 - Season 2008/09

There was a pre-season tournament called the Emirates Cup played at Arsenal's Emirates stadium in August 2008. It involved Hamburg, Real Madrid, Arsenal and Juventus. It was over two days, and I went with friends from the Juventus Club Londra each day. The Juventus squad at the time included Zinedine Zidane, Thierry Henry, Antonio Conte and Alessandro Del Piero. Juventus beat Arsenal 1-0 with a David Trezeguet goal but the next day lost to Hamburg 3-0. Hamburg won the tournament, and Juventus came last! The Westfield shopping centre was packed with people, but we managed to find a suitable restaurant where we could continue the talk of all things bianconero.

It's difficult to identify highlights in a dismal season for the Hatters when you finish bottom of the table, so I'm only going to mention one match, an evening away game at Dagenham and Redbridge. It was of interest as it was a London club that I knew nothing about, had only been formed by a merger in 1992 and had only recently got into the football league. It was easy to get to being on the District Line, only 5 minutes walk from Dagenham East station. The manager was John Still, who was to come to Luton in 2013 and guide us back into the football league. Another of their players was a certain Paul Benson, who also came to us in 2013 and contributed 25 goals in 85 appearances in three seasons. He is remembered sadly for breaking his leg but more happily for linking up well with Andre Gray, who scored 57 goals in his 111 appearances in three seasons. The game at the Daggers is best forgotten as we lost 2-1! Luton's goal was scored by Ian Henderson, his only one for the Town. It is difficult to believe that the same player scored 178 goals for other clubs, especially Rochdale. The game attracted 2,310, including 733 from Luton, all obviously very loyal and faithful.

With the 30 point deduction, it was no surprise that needing more than ten wins before our points tally became positive, we finished at the bottom of the League, ensuring our 3rd relegation in a row, and this time to be out of the League and into the Conference. Most outside observers and, of course, the club and fans felt that we had been very harshly treated. We had only been allowed to play in 2008/09 if we waived any right of appeal. Littlewoods Cup winners in 1988 but relegated down to the conference at the end of 2008/09 must be some sort of record free fall. It was 89 years since we were last a non-league club. Surely we would bounce straight back into the League? The future looked better as the 2020 consortium fronted by Nick Owen took over.

Chapter 121 - Trophy victory

An unexpected bonus in a season of administration points deductions and relegation out of the League was getting to the final of the Johnstone's Paint Trophy in April 2009 at Wembley, where Scunthorpe awaited us. They were in a playoff position of League one and to be promoted to the Championship.

The JPT was a competition for League 1 and 2 teams only. After a bye in round 1, our campaign started with a 4-3 penalty shootout home win over Brentford after a 2-2 draw at 90 minutes, no extra time being played in that competition. The next rounds gave us 1-0 wins over Walsall away and Colchester at home. They brought us to a two-leg area final against Brighton. The first leg at the Goldstone ground ended 0-0, and the second leg finished 1-1 after Tom Craddock had scored in the 1st minute. But the lead was short-lived because Brighton had equalised in the 20th minute.

We had expected to do better after a Brighton player was sent off just before half time. However, the penalties went 4-3 to the Hatters again, on loan goalie Lewis Price making two great saves and the Town scoring all their four penalties. So we had got to the final after four wins, two of which were only after penalty shootouts. As expected, there were plenty of tickets available, and I mostly took members of the family plus, of course, the faithful Colin. I got £50 seats in the Club Wembley area as a special treat. The famous ground had been rebuilt, which was interesting to visit, and after all, I did not expect any more Wembley finals for Luton for a long time to come. The Wembley match attracted over 55,000 fans, of which maybe around 40,000 were from Luton, and it proved to be very exciting. There were various protests about the town's treatment, especially those addressed to Lord Mawhinney, League chairman, who was, of course, in attendance.

Scunthorpe took the lead after 14 minutes, but loanee Chris Martin equalised in the 32nd minute before Tom Craddock put us into the lead in the 70th minute. Just as we believed that victory was close, Grant McCann equalised for Scunthorpe in the 88th minute, taking the match into extra time, used only for the Final in that competition. Five minutes into extra time Claude Gnakpa, a Frenchman, who had come on as a substitute for Tom Craddock from the 85th minute, scored from Keith Keane's long pass with a long-range shot looped over the goalie and we held out to the end without further mishap. The stars of the day were undoubtedly recently returned captain and man of the match Kevin Nicholls and fellow midfielder, Keith Keane. The inspiration came from manager Mick Harford, and his undoubted attributes were transmitted to the players. It was a truly exciting match and some small compensation for all the club's problems.

We were the first club to win the trophy and be relegated from the football League in the same season. As defending champions, we wanted to defend our trophy the next season, but this was denied as we were no longer a football League club.

Chapter 122 - Conference years

I remained loyal despite having to watch Luton in the Conference in 2009 and visiting some unlikely venues. There were a few familiar names in that league, including Mansfield, Oxford United, Wimbledon, Rushden and Diamonds, Cambridge United and Stevenage. There were many more unfamiliar ones. Obviously, a striking feature was the much lower gates, especially at the away games. The lowest was to be 1218 at Gateshead! I made a trip to Hayes and Yeading, shades of that FA Vase final we went to in 1990!

We won there 3-2. Also, Grays Athletic won 2-0, Ebbsfleet, where we won 6-1, and Forest Green Rovers won 1-0. We also had an 8-0 home victory, 7-0 at half time, over Hayes and Yeading and I enjoyed a visit to Rushden and Diamonds (1-1), who had been founded in 1992 and was owned by the head of Dr Martens Max Griggs. Rushden were expelled from the Conference in 2011 but were reborn later. Mick Harford sadly left by mutual consent, temporarily replaced by Alan Neilson and then the long term appointment of Richard Money. So in our first season out of the league, we finished 2nd with 23 league goals from Tom Craddock and 16 from Kevin Gallen. We finished second behind Stevenage, meaning that we faced a two-leg semi-final playoff against York City, who had finished 5th. Sadly we lost both legs 1-0 and so stayed in the Conference.

Our new sponsors were Easyjet, and that coincided not surprisingly with us wearing orange shirts. I remember that Easyjet also sponsored Brentford and painted their orange logo on one of the stand roofs, which were on the final flight approach to Heathrow airport!

Chapter 123 - Chelsea versus Juventus

I always watched the Champions League draw with interest, hoping that Juventus would be drawn to play in England and even better if it was in London. To my delight, in the 1st knockout last sixteen round in 2009 Juventus were to play against Chelsea.

I knew that the American owned private hospital group HCA had executive facilities in Chelsea. I had never been invited despite working there for many years, and I must have been known as a football fanatic to anyone I had come into contact with! Mostly they showed hospitality to Physicians and Surgeons who brought in patients and hence income!

When the draw came out, I immediately contacted the Chief executive, who I knew reasonably well and invited myself to their facilities at Chelsea, to which he readily agreed. As well as numbers of doctors, many of whom I knew were two medical attachés from Middle Eastern embassies, other sources of an endless supply of patients! They were not known as prompt payers, so I was pleased to have some high up contacts in their health offices to help my secretary collect some long-standing debts. So the evening of 25th February, we all met at the ground and enjoyed a copious and excellent dinner, well-washed down with fine wines.

Our seats were in the West stand and, of course, provided an excellent view. Juventus were managed by Claudio Ranieri and Chelsea by Dutchman Guus Hiddink in his first home match at the helm. Chelsea went ahead with a Didier Drogba 12th minute goal, which turned out to be the only one. The match had been very well refereed by a Portuguese man with the wonderful but unpronounceable name of Olegário Benquerença. Chelsea only received one yellow card, but Juventus three, all in the second half.

So the tie was obviously well balanced, and I had to make plans to see the second leg 18 days later. Gillian was going to be on one of her South Africa trips, so I was free to plan my Turin trip as I wanted. I managed to precede the football trip with a short ski-ing outing to Cervinia with a couple of friends. Again very convenient being close to Turin and my having the use of an apartment belonging to a dear colleague and friend in Turin — another example of my amazing luck when it came to my projects. Four days before the match, I had a wonderful few days in Turin with cultural activities such as the opera, on this occasion Rossini's L'Italiana in Algeri, and visits to several museums. I may be biased, but I really love Turin. It has so much to offer and is a very aristocratic city. I have recommended it to countless friends, none of whom have been disappointed. Nietzsche, the famous 19th-century German philosopher, summed up Turin as "the city I loved most. Nowhere had better ice cream or more beautiful cafes. The Alps towered above its orderly streets". He loved to breathe the clear, bright air and walk through the high vaulted passageways of its arcades and porticoes. At one point, I even wrote a short article "a day in Turin". I have no idea why but on this occasion I did not get the ticket through Giampiero although I saw him and his family on several occasions. Rather I got it from a "tabacchaio" that my friend had located and probably paid an enhanced price! So I took tram number 5, which was inevitably very crowded. At one point, there was a disturbance around me which should have made me suspicious, but only when queuing to get into the ground did I realise that my camera had been stolen. More fool me for putting it in an obvious pocket in my coat.

I had difficulty finding the right entrance of the Stadio Comunale, in use in a ground share with Torino, while the Stadio Delle Alpi was being replaced by a new stadium on the same site. Getting in was a challenge, and it was the first time that I experienced detailed identity checks. By then, all tickets had one's name on them. No correct identity meant no entry. Luckily I still had my passport, which might also have disappeared on the tram. So on to the match, which was really exciting. An early blow for Juve was that Pavel Nedved had to come off with an injury in the 13th minute. However, Juve took the lead through Iaquinta, a surprise selection, but Essien equalised just on half time. No more goals until a Del Piero penalty on the 74th and a Drogba goal on the 83rd.

Chiellini had been sent off after a dubious second yellow card in the 71st minute. So Juve went out on aggregate 3-2!

This time a Spanish referee Alberto Mallenco did not cover himself with glory issuing four yellows to Chelsea and four yellows and a red to Juve. Maybe that's the view of a loser.

Chapter 124 - Watching Juventus on TV in England

Apart from the years of Gazzetta Football Italia from 1992 to 2002, when live matches were shown on Channel 4 on Sunday afternoons, Serie A was not shown on English TV until much later when it appeared on some of the pay channels, especially BT and Premier sport. This caused me a problem. How could I keep up with my beloved Juve? An Italian banker friend in London, Lorenzo, incidentally a Torino supporter, suggested that I try the Italian Church in Clerkenwell. It seemed an unlikely venue to watch a football match, even if Italy was a largely catholic country but also football crazy, but I decided to try it.

The priest greeted me on the church's steps upon my arrival and asked me if I had come for the Mass or the Match! I was directed to an upstairs room well-populated with football fans when I said the match. My visits there were fairly frequent till I discovered a club called Juventus Club Londra, which had been in existence for many years and ran largely by London based Italians. They organised tickets and transport to matches in England and Turin, and it was particularly pleasant to go on often long coach journeys with like-minded people. I was with them for several years until they became rather inactive. We went to many matches together during that time, including several European ties at home and abroad and league matches in Turin. The trips to Turin were very interesting and social, combining the match with good eating and some sightseeing. Contact with the players was often achieved to our delight. Of course, it was also a chance to see Giampiero and often his wife and one or more of his three offspring and grandchildren.

On 11th March 2010, I went to Fulham with season ticket holder Thomas to see the second leg of Fulham versus Juventus in the round of 16 of the Europa League. The first leg had been a comfortable 3-1 win for Juventus, and when David Trezequet scored for Juve after 2 minutes at Craven Cottage, it seemed all over.

We should have known that Roy Hodgson's teams don't give up easily. By half time, Fulham had scored twice, and then a successful penalty in the 48th minute brought the aggregate scores level. A goal by American forward Clint Dempsey in the 82nd minute won it for Fulham. It was a remarkable comeback. Because of that excitement, I was happy to be invited to the next round. It was the semi-final where Fulham were to play Hamburg. There was all to play for at Craven Cottage after a goalless first leg in Hamburg. Once again, Fulham had to come from behind to win 2-1 with goals from Simon Davies and Zoltan Gera. Two German supporters seated behind us (not sure how they got into the Fulham territory, but I suppose you could say the same about me) kept telling us how wonderful the Fulham support was and how it was so much better than that offered to the home teams in Germany! The other semi-final finished in a victory for Atletico Madrid over Liverpool, so the hoped-for all English final did not materialise. Atletico won the final 2-1 after extra time in Hamburg.

David De Gea was in goal for Atletico, while Diego Forlan the Uruyguan scored their goals, and Davies got the lone Cottagers goal. Other well-known figures for Atletico were Sergio Aguero and their manager Quiche Sanchez Flores who later had two spells as manager of Watford.

The Juventus team of that era was full of stars, but one who definitely deserves more than a passing mention was Claudio Marchisio, nicknamed Il Principino (the little prince). He came through the Juventus youth system and played 389 times for Juventus, scoring 37 goals as a very versatile and skilled midfielder. He played 55 times for Italy, scoring five times and was the captain on occasions. Despite his combative style, he only received one red card in his whole career. He was selected as part of the 2015 Champions League team of the season and in the Serie A team of the year in 2011 and 2012. His all-around performances and modest demeanour made him a joy to watch.

Another trip was to Manchester City on 16 December 2010 for a Europa League game against Juventus. I found myself interviewed on the Man City television channel pushed forward by the officers of Juventus Club Londra on the basis that I probably knew more about the history of the club than they did!

In that match, Filippo Boniperti, Giampiero's grandson and a promising midfielder, made his professional debut for Juventus, coming on in the second half. His Serie A debut came soon on 22 May 2011 in Juventus's final game of the 2010/11 season, in which he came on as a substitute for Simone Pepe at the start of the second half.

The 09/10 season was a success, with Luton finishing in 2nd place behind neighbours Stevenage Borough. Tom Craddock was the leading goalscorer with 24 goals, aided by Kevin Gallen with 18. So we had a two-leg playoff against York City but unfortunately lost both legs 1-0 and so had to look forward to another season in the conference.

Amazingly our gates in the conference were higher than those of some League 1 clubs.

Chapter 125 - 2010 World Cup in South Africa

2010 was, of course, a World Cup year and one to be played in South Africa, the first time ever on the African continent. My wife's favourite overseas destination was Cape Town, where we had lots of friends, and we went there quite frequently. We enjoyed the fact that it had southern hemisphere weather and that there was very little time change. Cape Town is, of course, one of the most beautiful cities lying in Table Bay on the Atlantic ocean side of the Cape of Good Hope. The architecture is very interesting with much Dutch influence, and the beautiful beaches, nearby wineries and diverse cultural life make it all fascinating and very attractive to tourists. The city is overlooked by the famous Table Mountain, often covered by a layer of cloud known for obvious reasons as "the table cloth".

Especially attractive to my wife was the fact that one of her best nursing friends from her early days lived there. We had also made good friends with several of the South African doctors and their wives that we had met at various international conferences.

Finally, John, a good friend, solicitor and keen Arsenal supporter, told us he was also going and had an English client and friend who had a luxurious flat in a block called Bordeaux in Sea Point, just along the coast from Cape Town. We took a British Airways premium economy flight out and sat just behind Roy Hodgson, around the time he was to leave Fulham to have a short spell managing Liverpool. Roy had managed in Italy, especially at Inter Milan, so I felt I had plenty as well as Fulham to talk to him about. The little boy in me felt the urge to get his autograph which later on I gave to my friend Thomas the Fulham supporter. That had possibly made me one of the oldest autograph hunters around! Hodgson was still managing by then, leaving Fulham for Liverpool and then on to West Bromwich, England and lastly Crystal Palace, his 22nd managerial post at the age of 73, although later he was replaced by Patrick Vieira, who had left Nice. This puts Roy ahead of Claudio Ranieri and Neil Warnock in the managerial record books of clubs managed and age still managing! The draw had included 32 teams. Between us, we had tickets for all the matches played in Cape Town during our time there. They were played at the newly completed handsome Green Point stadium close to the city centre and the famous Victoria and Albert Waterfront. The stadium had a capacity of 64,000 and was later renamed the Cape Town stadium. The 40-minute opening ceremony was on the 11th of June in Johannesburg and involved about 1500 performers, including several well known South African musicians and the Soweto Gospel Choir. So on to our matches. The first one for us involved England, and we had to queue for quite a while to get through the security.

So we were in for England's second match versus Algeria, which was seen as an easy one for England in a supposedly easy group including also the USA and Slovenia. Not so, the match was not memorable for any of the football although we had captain Steven Gerrard, Frank Lampard and Wayne Rooney in our team, and Fabio Capello managed it. It ended 0-0. Since England had managed to just beat Slovenia 1-0 with a 23rd minute Jermain Defoe strike, we finally went through in second place behind the USA, with whom we had drawn 1-1, both finishing with 5 points, similar goal differences but the USA had scored more goals! At the end of the Algeria match, Wayne Rooney famously had a spat with England supporters, saying into a TV camera, "Nice to see your own fans booing you, you football supporters".

The most striking feature of the tournament was the frequent blowing of vuvuzelas and horns, which produced a monotonous and very annoying noise. They were originally used to summon distant villagers to attend community gatherings but later became a symbol of South African football grounds. We also heard lots of Bafana Bafana, the boys in Zulu and the team's nickname. There was much honking of car horns and vast amounts of other noises. Everyone seemed to have permanent smiles on their faces, and there was street dancing and lots of provocative bottom shaking. There were many fancy dress outfits and wigs. Overall, it was the best party seen at a World Cup.

John's friends living in the Cape Town area took us to some of the best restaurants, and the food was always well lubricated with excellent wines. It was a pleasure to meet their daughter and her husband as well. John's daughter was also with him, and it was good to get to know her better. Everybody seemed very friendly, and several times we were offered lifts back to our B & B by complete strangers. Cape Town has changed a lot since our last visit. A great bonus was a new circular bus route around the city. From our point of view, there was a stop nearby, and that bus took us right into the centre. The whole central area of the city seemed much safer than it had been. The famous Long Street, normally a no go area after about 9 pm, was heaving with people long into the night!

And the security at and around the stadium was very effective. The Fan Fest would show all 64 matches on a giant screen and be open from 11:00 and 23:00 and show a lot of different entertainment with all musical tastes catered for. The purpose of the Fan Fest was to offer a safe, convenient and convivial alternative to being at the stadium so that even those without tickets could watch the matches live and enjoy the stadium atmosphere without actually being there. It was said that 162 different artists and groups performed, and another feature was a spectacular laser light display.

There were food and drink kiosks, and on offer were local favourites, including Malay chicken curry, lamb neck poitjie and biltong, as well as internationally popular dishes. Drinks included hot and cold ones, and wine and beer were on sale to the over 18s. Entry was closed, monitored and limited to 25,000, and each one had to pass through a security cordon. Any attempt to bring in food, alcohol, weapons or drugs is liable to confiscation.

Unruly behaviour of any sort was not tolerated, and the perpetrators ejected rapidly. The organisers said that their intention was to ensure that every visitor to the Fan Fest had a good and memorable experience. We stayed at a very nice B & B close to the Gardens shopping centre, another bonus for my wife. Normally we stayed at a smart hotel on the front in Sea Point, but it was unavailable, having been taken over completely by Sony! We knew another couple, keen AFC Wimbledon supporters who went to most of the World Cups up to and including the Russian one. They have already decided to give the 2022 Qatar one a miss! We went with them to visit the famous Kirstenbosch gardens, a special treat for my wife, who is a fanatical gardener. On a Saturday evening, we watched on TV as Cameroon lost to Denmark 1-2 in an exciting match, but Samuel Eto'o and his team were eliminated, finishing their group without a single point. The next day Italy could only draw with New Zealand 1-1, having already only drawn with Paraguay, also 1-1. They went on to lose 3-2 to Slovakia and were eliminated, finishing bottom of a supposedly weak group!

France and the hosts were also surprisingly eliminated. Our next live match was Portugal versus North Korea in Group G. It brought back memories of the 1966 World Cup when North Korea had eliminated Italy. The former beat the Italians 1-0 in Middlesbrough, resulting in the Italian squad being pelted with rotten tomatoes and other missiles on their return. In the next match in 1966, the North Koreans led Portugal 3-0 before losing 5-3, Eusebio scoring 4 of the five goals. Now it was pouring with rain to the extent that we had to buy pac-a-macs before heading to the stadium. We had lunch near the stadium and saw Arsene Wenger pass by. I was struck by how unexpectedly tall he was, and on this occasion, he was clearly not going to stop for a chat or an autograph. For me, the excitement was to see Cristiano Ronaldo live, then aged 25, and playing his club football for Real Madrid. He didn't disappoint, scoring the last goal in a 7-0 victory after generally being prominent throughout. Indeed he was given the man of the match award. Portugal qualified for the knockout stages finishing second to Brazil, with whom they shared a goalless draw. They then lost 1-0 to Spain after extra time, a match we saw live and were glad in hindsight to have seen the eventual winners of the tournament. We had seats very high up, and I remember a man came with us who had very recently had a heart transplant. He was clearly fitter than me as he bounded up the steps!

A couple of days earlier, in the round of 16, England had been beaten 4-1 by Germany. That game included a very controversial disallowed goal by Lampard where although the ball had clearly crossed the goal line by at least a foot, the officials and, in particular, Uruguayan referee Jorge Larrionda declined to award it. It would have been the equaliser just after Matthew Upson had scored to reduce the deficit to 2-1 to Germany. It was one of the major triggers for the introduction of goal-line technology in 2012.

30th June was, for us, a day without football. Instead, we were taken on a long and fascinating tour by two of my wife's friends.

The day after that we watched Brazil 1 - Netherlands 2 quarter-final on TV. The Netherlands came from behind with two goals from Wesley Sneijder to win and go on to be a finalist. Later the same day, we were invited to a friend's house for dinner and luckily were allowed to watch another quarter-final, this time between Uruguay and Ghana, which ended 1-1 a.e.t. Ghana, of course, had the whole of the African continent behind them. Ghana missed a 120th-minute penalty hitting the crossbar after Luis Suarez had handled the ball on the goal line, and then the penalty shoot out went the way of Uruguay by 4-2. The next day we had tickets for Argentina versus Germany. It kicked off at 4 pm, and we got there very early to soak up the atmosphere! Who does an Englishman support when Argentina are playing Germany? Argentina had always been on my black list since their antics in the 1966 World Cup and the behaviour of the Estudiantes players in that Intercontinental cup in Manchester. In that historic match, the second leg, two United players and one Argentinian were sent off. There was also the "hand of God" goal by Maradona in the 1986 Mexico World Cup.

So, in the end, I decided that it was one of those occasions when Germany was clearly the lesser of two evils. Two people stood out for Argentina. Firstly Diego Maradona is the manager, and Lionel Messi is already acknowledged as one of the greatest players in the world. Maradona was by now better known for his misdemeanours off the field, and I have to say he looked really unwell and overweight in the dugout. Messi, on the other hand, looked very fit but was not given much chance to shine. The Germans romped to a 4-0 victory with a team that contained such Bayern Munich contemporaries as Manuel Neuer and Thomas Muller. They scored in the 3rd minute through Muller, followed by Miroslav Klose with two easy goals, and the third one by Friedrich Arne. Bastian Schweinsteiger was chosen as the man of the match.

In the evening we all went to a nightclub called Pigalle where good food, dancing and an excess of alcohol was the order of the night! The next day we were invited to Stellenbosch, a famous university town and wine area, for lunch and ate snoek and venison washed down with excellent white and red wines. Snoek is a local fish of the snake mackerel family, which can be as long as 200 centimetres! It is often prepared in a manner similar to Portuguese bacalhau and is a Cape Malay speciality. That was the end of our World Cup venture, as the next day, we had to return to London and back to work. We watched the Dutch beat Uruguay 3-2 on TV in the first semi-final played in Cape Town.

A pretty close match until Sneijder and Robben pulled the Netherlands away into a 3-1 lead before Pereira scored an added-time goal for the South Americans. I am not quite sure why we didn't stay for that one as well, but I guess one can only take so much time off from one's work! The next day the other semi-final was a much more tense affair with Spain thanks to a 73rd minus goal by Barcelona central defender Carles Puyol narrowly defeating Germany 1-0 in Durban. So there was the 3rd place match won by Germany 3-2 over Uruguay. Both teams held interesting records relating to appearances in the third-place playoffs. Germany has the record (4) for 3rd place finishes while Uruguay holds the record (3) for 4th place finishes. So that only left the final, which was another very tense and close affair, Spain finally prevailing with an extra-time goal in the 116th minute by Iniesta. They broke another unexciting record by scoring the lowest number of goals, eight, by a World Cup winning team. In fact, the whole tournament had the lowest total number of goals ever, a hundred and forty-five.

Chapter 126 - Season 2010/11

In 2010/11, our second season in the conference, we finished in 3rd place behind Crawley and Wimbledon. During the season, both Tom Craddock and Kevin Gallen left. That season we had two managers, Gary Brabin, the assistant replacing Richard Money in March.

We had some big home wins, e.g. 6-1 over Forest Green, 5-0 over York, 4-0 over Darlington and Histon, and 6-0 over Southport. Away we won 6-1 at Ebbsfleet, a match I went to. So again, into the playoffs. Only this time against Wrexham, who we beat 3-0 away and then 2-1 at home, so 5-1 on aggregate. Matthew Barnes - Homer was the leading scorer with 19 goals. The final was to be against Wimbledon at the Manchester City stadium, and I went in one of the many Luton Town supporters coaches laid on, definitely the most convenient way to travel. It was a very close match with both sides striking the post, but even after extra time, it remained goalless and proceeded to a very nerve-racking penalty shootout. We managed to miss two by Alex Lawless and finally Jason Walker, who had come in from York and Barrow during the season. And so the long and very quiet coach trip back left us contemplating the 3rd season in the conference to come.

In May 2010, Andrea Agnelli became chairman of Juventus after cousin John Elkann left, becoming the chairman of Fiat. Andrea thus became the fourth Agnelli to run the club after his grandfather, father, and uncle. He took over at a difficult time with the Calciopoli scandal still warm and the construction of the new Juventus Stadium, now called the Allianz stadium, estimated to cost €155 million and threaten the club's financial stability. One of Andrea's first tasks was to appoint a new manager, and he chose former player and fan favourite Antonio Conte.

Antonio had already managed four different Italian clubs after a 13-year stellar playing career at Juve. He then managed Juve for three years before being appointed manager of the national team. Amazingly Juve set off on a run of nine winning scudetti and four Coppa Italias. An important figure at the time was the Czech Pavel Nedved. He had a very distinguished playing career in which he scored 110 league goals, mostly with Sparta Prague, Lazio and Juventus and 18 international goals. His position was mostly as a left-sided offensive midfielder, from where he shone and won countless awards. He was ever popular at Juventus, and after his playing career ended, he remained. Having been appointed to the board of directors later in 2015, he became vice-chairman of the club. His characteristic mop of blond hair is regularly seen on televised matches sitting next to Andrea Agnelli. On the 8th of September 2011, the beautiful new stadium was opened with a friendly against Notts County, the world's oldest professional football club, which had provided Juve with their first strip, hence the black and white stripes.

In March 2011, I went to Forest Green Rovers with Colin. He had been on the Wiltshire FA council for many years and had recently been elected President. That meant he had contacts at Forest Green, and after a scenic drive to Nailsworth and a long steep drive up to the New Lawn ground, we were entertained in the VIP areas. There I met Gary Sweet, Luton chief executive officer and David Wilkinson Vice Chairman, who was later to take over as Chairman, and of course, we all had a chat. Forest Green has an interesting history. On two occasions, they had been saved from relegation by irregularities by other clubs in their division. The club was owned by Dale Vince, the founder of Ecotricity, a former New Age Traveller known as the £100 million hippie. He made sizeable donations to both the Labour and Green parties. FGR was known for it being the first vegan football club in 2015. The aim was to improve player performance and to give supporters healthier, tastier food on match days. They also only used natural products on the pitch and were certified as carbon neutral.

It meant that our pre-match meal was unusual and interesting, to say the least. The game ended 2-1 to the Hatters with a Fleetwood goal and a last-minute penalty by Scott Rendell giving us the win.

Another interesting excursion was to Turin in October 2011. It was to show the city of Turin to younger members of my family and to see a match in the new stadium. It was for the 4th match in the stadium played between Juventus and Genoa which finished 2-2. I had gone to Turin on my own, and there was a fairly chaotic check-in at Stansted where having got to the front of a long queue discovered that it was the wrong one. I was luckily let into the right one at the front. Security was very slow, and my hand luggage was checked in the boarding queue to see if it fitted into a cardboard box! No marks for guessing that the airline in question was Ryanair! I got to Turin safely and took the bus to the main Porta Nuova station. The facade of that building was designed by Carlo Ceppi and is architecturally neo-baroque, very impressive and very central. It was a short walk to a B & B that had been recommended to me by a Turin doctor friend. I had lunch with Elsa's daughter and met her two children. I made myself useful by helping them with their English homework. It was the first time that they realised that English was a language that people actually spoke! In the evening, Giampiero and his wife took me to a very nice restaurant in the hills overlooking the city. On Sunday, my son in law Dave and eldest grandson Thomas arrived on time, and we did the tourist bit, walking down the Via Roma to Piazza Castello and having coffee at the famous Mulassano cafe. It is very old, dating from 1925, the present building being architecturally very interesting. One of the Turin specialities is Bicerin, a hot drink made of espresso coffee, drinking chocolate and milk served layered in a small glass. Thomas's main interest seemed to be to go in and out of all the shops, luckily without seeming to want to make any purchases! We had lunch in a restaurant on the scenic arcaded Via Po and then on to the Cinema Museum. The museum is housed in the most famous Turin landmark, the Mole Antonelliana. It had been built to be a synagogue, but when it was completed in 1889, it did not appeal to that community. They had a falling out with Antonelli, the architect! The views from the top, reached by a panoramic elevator, are usually spectacular but on that day were not very good due to misty weather. We walked back along the Via XX Settembre so I could show them two famous shops, one selling all sorts of pasta and the other a huge variety of cheeses.

We set off for the stadium by tram and bus and, as often, cut it a bit fine. I was very excited to see this new stadium, having seen many games at the Stadio Comunale, which was open till 1990 and covered the years of the fascist era, and then the Stadio Delle Alpi was built for the 1990 World Cup and used from 1990 to 2006. The Stadio Comunale became the Stadio Olimpico when refurbished to host the 2006 Winter Olympics and where both Juve and Torino played until Juve moved to the Allianz stadium, leaving only Torino to play at the Olimpico.

Many were surprised that a city in the plains could host a tournament that needed mountains and snow. However, of course, there were ski resorts nearby, especially Sestriere, Sauze d'Oulx and Cervinia. On arrival at the stadium, it took us a little while to find the relevant entrance G. We finally hot-footed it to our seats in the Club Omar Sivori with 5 minutes to kick-off and admired the fantastic view and the choreography of the spectators holding up coloured flags in blocks. Club Sivori was one of two upmarket enclosures, the other unsurprisingly being called Club Boniperti. Both offered much more than just the seat, including buffet/sit down catering which I didn't discover till my next visit! Normally access to these enclosures was only on a seasonal basis, so again, I put myself in the very spoilt and lucky category! Club Sivori was on the Anello due (the 2nd tier) and accessed by a long ramp rather than steps. It is a wonderful stadium, although sadly, the toilet was, on that occasion, a bit of a skating rink. The stadium had been opened by Andrea Agnelli, President of the club, on the 8th of September 2011, 6 weeks before. An unforgettable image was of Boni and Del Piero sitting together on a bench placed in the centre circle. It was one of only four stadia in Italy that actually belonged to the club rather than a third party. Its capacity was 42,147 seats, relatively small, but when compared to the old Stadio Delle Alpi with its athletics track, the new stadium had the first row of supporters just 7.5 metres from the pitch. The lighting system was very revolutionary, with all sorts of innovative features. There were three well-known architects involved, Gino Zavanella, a Turin born man well known for stadium design, and Hernando Suarez, leader of the Studio Shesa in Rome. And perhaps most surprisingly, Giorgetto Giugiaro, a local Piemontese man and world-renowned industrial designer much more famous for automobile design. All the seating areas were covered by a transparent roof allowing the maximum amount of light to get onto the grass. For the match. Juve had a strong team with Gigi Buffon in goal, the famous BBC (Barzagli, Bonucci and Chiellini) back three and Pirlo and Marchisio in midfield, amongst others. Matri had opened the scoring for Juve in the 6th minute, but Marco Rossi equalised before half time. In the second half, Juve took the lead again with another Matri goal, but Genoa took a point with an 85th-minute goal by substitute Andrea Caracciolo. Genoa missed a couple of late chances to win the game, and Juve lost the chance to go three points clear at the top. There was no problem exiting the stadium but quite a long walk to the 72 bus stop, where we joined an even longer queue. Conveniently an empty taxi passed by into which we leapt and so were safely and speedily back to the B & B. The next day was spent exploring the Lingotto shopping centre, which was a conversion from the old Lingotto Fiat works. We had lunch in the well-named Eataly and a tour of The Automobile Museum, founded in 1932 and home to over 200 cars. We were picked up by my great friend Elsa and taken to her house in Moncalieri for dinner, attended as well by her elder daughter and granddaughter, who was about Thomas's age. So next day, back to Stansted early in the morning and home. A great time was had by the three of us!

Chapter 127 - Season 2011/12

In pre-season, Luton played a friendly against a team completely unknown to me called Gabala. Where did they come from? They turned out to be from the Azerbaijan top division, but how did we come to be playing them? The only explanation was that the connection was that they were managed by Tony Adams of Arsenal fame and had several international players in their squad. Anyway, they gave a good performance beating us 3-2.

The season was noted for me by a home FA Cup draw against my neighbour Hendon a match which unsurprisingly we won 5-1. An exciting signing for us was Andre Gray from non-league Hinckley United. He immediately broke a Luton record by scoring in his first four games for the Town. The season was a bit of a struggle, but we finished in 5th place, 22 points behind the automatic promotion place, and so into the playoffs yet again. The 78 league goals were spread around, but only Stuart Fleetwood got into double figures. Manager Gary Brabin had been sacked at the end of March with the Hatters in 7th place and replaced by Paul Buckle. Coincidentally we met Wrexham in the semi-final playoffs once again, this time winning the home leg 2-0 with goals from Andre Gray and Stuart Fleetwood but losing the away leg 2-1. A Pilkington penalty, though, had clinched our place in the final where York awaited us at Wembley. I was disappointed not to be able to join the over 30,000 Hatters fans at the final as we were to be in the middle of a conference and social trip to Turkey.

The only football-related thing was that the Hilton hotel in Istanbul where we were put up overlooked the Besiktas stadium! Our room would have given us a good view if a match had taken place while we were there. Interestingly we were the victims of a ruse by a taxi driver who switched notes and then accused us of underpaying! Again we missed the clue that he had dropped us off outside the hotel gates rather than at the hotel entrance doors.

It was apparently a tense final, with Andre Gray scoring after only 71 seconds, but York replied with two goals to clinch their win. It was always believed that the winning goal was scored from an offside position but not granted by the assistant referee.

At the end of the season, Keith Keane left for Preston after nine years with Luton and, as I have already written, was always one of my favourites.

In October, Marc, my son in law, took me to see Spurs beat the Russians Rubin Kazan 1-0 in the Europa League. Paradoxically the Spurs goal was scored by their Russian Roman Pavlyuchenko direct from a free-kick. He spent four years at Spurs, where he scored 42 goals in all. I was always intrigued about that team as they bore my name translated as "Ruby" and Kazan the Town, capital of Republic of Tatarstan and the 5th largest in Russia. As a result, I have always followed their results and seen them on TV a few times! I know they were founded in 1958 and promoted to their Premier league in 2003. Twice they have reached qualification for the UEFA Cup. I tried to communicate with the club but didn't succeed.

On a trip to Nice in November 2011, I went to a match still in the Stade du Ray and played in the pouring rain. The opposition was St Etienne. I had foolishly got a ticket in the uncovered temporary stand opposite the main stand, presumably because it was quite a bit cheaper.

I bought a pair of Nice gloves in the club shop, but an umbrella would have been more appropriate! Nice lost 2-0 but unusually received three straight red cards, including one for goalie David Ospina, a Colombian international who was later with Arsenal and Napoli, and two more yellows. St Etienne received three yellows! The goalscorers were interesting being Sinama - Pongolle, a substitute for Aubameyang, who was later to join Arsenal and Kurt Zouma later with Chelsea. Another match on the next trip was Nice 0 - PSG 0 on a very cold night. It justified the purchase of an OGC Nice bobble hat!. This time I got my ticket from a lady close to the ticket office who offered it to me at a big discount! When I tried to enter the ground, it was pointed out that I did not appear to qualify for a junior ticket! With my usual luck, another lady saw my predicament and gave me a spare one she had free of charge!

Chapter 128 - Season 2012/13

In season 2012/13 at Luton, I was eligible for a further discounted season ticket rate called the Golden Senior (over 75s)! It was very welcome, and while most clubs have an OAP (over 65) rate, I didn't know of other clubs with an over 75 rate. In fact, they also have an under 22 rate and the usual junior one! At one of the home games, I met members of the Italian Luton supporters group who had come from Naples to see our Conference side. Indeed I believe we also had supporters groups in Ireland and Scandinavia and Greece, the Czech Republic, Canada and New Zealand! That's real dedication.

In the autumn of 2012, Juventus had drawn Chelsea again in the group stage of the Champions League. After seeing the first game at Stamford Bridge, another potentially exciting outing to Turin awaited me. On the occasion of the first match, I bumped into my friend Alex a colleague and keen Chelsea supporter. You don't expect to unexpectedly meet a friend among over 40,000 people and with seats in completely different parts of the ground. It always amazes me how often coincidences happen in my life.

Therefore, I went to that game with the Juve Club Londra and was in the Juventus section. There was their usual behaviour with standing throughout, but they created a wonderful atmosphere and support. I especially enjoyed the rhythmic jumping up and down, which had been a feature of the Nice support. Chelsea took a two-goal lead thanks to a brace from the Brazilian Oscar, but Juve got one back before half time thanks to the Colombian Vidal and got a late equaliser by Quagliarella. Of note was the performance of Andrea Pirlo and the fact that not one of the famous Juventus central defenders, Barzagli, Bonucci or Chiellini, got booked! On the team sheet, as he seemed to be for an amazing time, was goalkeeper Buffon! However, Alex del Piero was missing as he had by now left Juventus for his final spells with Sydney FC Australia. He made 48 appearances and scored 24 goals, and with the Delhi Dynamos, ten appearances and a goal! Chelsea, by contrast, had Lampard, Hazard the Belgian, and Torres the Spaniard, as well as Oscar. Roberto di Matteo managed the Chelsea team at the time, of course, an Italian international himself. After the game, we found a nice pizzeria on Fulham Road to refuel.

In October, we lost 2-3 at home to Braintree, and in November, we played at home to newly-promoted Dartford and lost 2-0. It dropped us to 6th place and out of the playoff places. With respect to Dartford and Braintree, how much lower could we sink? It is amazing to support a club that could boast matches against the likes of Manchester United and Liverpool, as well as those against Tamworth and Hyde! Rarely a dull moment! We finished in 7th place, our lowest ever finish in the conference, and missed out on the playoffs. John Still took over as manager from the end of February 2013 and gave us all a bit of hope as he had won promotions from the conference before with Maidstone in 1989 and Dagenham and Redbridge in 2007. Andre Gray was again our leading scorer with 20 goals in all competitions.

We did make history in January 2013 by becoming the first non-league team to win an FA Cup tie against a premiership team, in this case, Norwich City away by 1-0, a goal scored by Scott Rendell in the 80th minute. Sadly, we were brought down to earth in the next round by the dreaded Millwall, who won 3-0 at Luton to knock us out! John Still was appointed manager on the 26th of February 2013, replacing Paul Buckle. Writing about John Still reminds me of the many "meet the manager evenings" organised by the Luton Town Supporters Club that I attended. John was one of the most entertaining speakers, I would add Alec Stock, David Pleat, Joe Kinnear, and Mick Harford!

Chapter 129 - Alessandro Del Piero

No Juventus supporter could minimise the contribution of Del Piero to the club nor to the national side for whom he played 91 times, scoring 27 goals.

One could easily fill a book detailing Alessandro's achievements. Nicknamed Il Pinturicchio after the diminutive renaissance artist, he was signed by Boniperti from Padova in 1991 for € 2.5 million at the age of 19. Little did Boni know then that his young signing would ultimately beat his own appearance and goal records for Juventus.

Suffice it to say that he was a highly skilled supporting striker with an uncanny ability to score goals from almost anywhere and especially from free-kicks. He is considered to have been one of the best players of his time and certainly one of the best Italian players of all time. He played in 3 World Cups and 4 European championships and was in the victorious team that won the World Cup in 2006 and were runners up in Euro 2000.

For Juve, he won eight league championships, the Champions league in 1996, the super cup and the Coppa Italia. He recovered from a very bad cruciate ligament knee injury which kept him out for nine months. His loyalty to Juve when they were relegated as a result of the Calciopoli scandal was commendable. In spite of losing many of his teammates and turning down many lucrative offers, he remained faithful to the club that had developed him into the undoubted star he was.

Although he seemed to be rather shy, he served as the Juve captain for about ten seasons. He was included in Pele's choice of the 100 greatest alongside his mentor Boniperti! I have to say that he never really endeared himself to me. While admiring his skills as a footballer, I found him a bit characterless and hated his goal celebration of sticking his tongue out! However, he has to be praised for much very creditable charity work. He finally retired from playing in October 2015. He has since worked as a pundit for Sky Sport Italia and has appeared in many TV shows with and without his soccer colleagues.

He justly received awards from the Italian state, including the 5th Class/Knight: Cavaliere Ordine al Merito Della Repubblica Italiana in 2000 and the 4th Class/Officer: Ufficiale Ordine al Merito della Repubblica in 2006. They are the highest-ranking honours of the republic and may be seen to be equivalent to our knighthoods.

Chapter 130 - Yet another Turin trip

The return Chelsea match was in mid-November. I again flew Ryanair to Turin and took the airport bus at Caselle airport, but it only went as far as Porta Susa station because the Turin marathon had closed some crucial streets.

So I took the metro to Porta Nuova station and found my new B & B very close by on the main Corso Vittorio Emanuele II. The B & B belonged to the sister of Juventus Club Londra's president Paolo and was perfect for me! As I had a free afternoon, I took a train trip to Racconigi castle, including a very interesting tour of the house and beautiful landscaped gardens. Racconigi had been one of the residences of the House of Savoy and later for members of the Italian Royal family.

I had arranged to see Giampiero and some of the family members and was given my ticket, which was again in the Club Omar Sivori. The next day we met at Giampiero's house, was driven by his daughter to her house, where I was handed over to Filippo, Boni's grandson and a friend of his. Also, one of the younger of the grandsons and a friend of his came with us. Sadly Filippo was injured and so was not involved in the match. Not surprisingly, we had VIP parking at the ground, and I discovered that the Club Omar Sivori included a lounge and buffet supper, which you had to sign in for. I had missed that chance when I had come before with Dave and Thomas! It was a great match for Juve supporters. Chelsea was still managed by Roberto di Matteo who had played for Chelsea after Lazio. At 2-0, goals from Quagliarella and Vidal looked to have given Juve victory, and five minutes from the end, we left to beat the traffic and missed a third by the diminutive Sebastian Giovinco. Sebastian was 5 ft 3 in (1.60 metres) if he stood tall! He was, however, well ahead of the world's shortest player, Elton, a Brazilian who was 5ft 1in. Interestingly Lionel Messi's future as a professional player was threatened when, at age 10, he was diagnosed with a growth hormone deficiency, often called idiopathic short stature.

This condition earned him the nickname La Pulga (The flea in Spanish). The necessary treatment with injections of human growth hormone was very expensive and raised issues of taking illegal and performance enhancing substances. Possibly he made use of a therapeutic use exemption which can be granted if a treatment is considered medically necessary. So it is possible to say that without the use of this controversial medical treatment, Messi may never have reached the heights that he has.

He is listed at 5'7" by FC Barcelona, which is about average for an Argentinian male. At the time Messi's condition had been diagnosed, he was only 4'2". Messi may now be normal and average in the physical sense, but certainly not normal when it comes to talent! Like Maradona before him, his low centre of gravity gives him the possibility of special ball control and the ability to dribble past opponents easily. He is also a free kick and penalty taker with exceptional accuracy.

The next day I was invited to lunch by Luca and Laura, antiques dealer friends of my cousin Alan. Laura proved to be a wonderful cook, and some exceptional wines accompanied the food.

On the way back, we stopped at a spectacular chocolate shop called La Bocca del Leone (the mouth of the lion). Turin is one of the cities in the world famous for chocolate, and I purchased as much as I thought I would be able to carry back to England!

So back to Stansted with a full Ryanair flight and very slow immigration controls. I took the Victoria coach, which then broke down on the M11. The driver seemed unsure what to do with his passengers. First, he told us to get off and stand behind the barriers on the hard shoulder and then thought we would be safer back on the coach! After about a rather long hour in the cold, we were rescued by another coach.

Chapter 131 - OGC Nice and Season 2013/14

The 1st of September 2013 was the last match played at the Stade du Ray in Nice after an 85-year history. It was preceded at 13.30 by a huge gathering in Nice's main square, the Place Massena. All the assembled Nice supporters marched roughly 3 kilometres up the main Jean Medecin avenue and hill to the stadium. The match against Montpellier kicked off at 1700, and two evenly matched teams played out a 2-2 draw in an amazing atmosphere. The players obviously took it seriously as the referee dished out eight yellow cards, five of them to Montpellier players!

My first visit to the Allianz Riviera stadium was to watch a Champions (Heineken) Cup rugby match between Toulon and Cardiff on the 11th of January, 2014. It was a good opportunity to become acquainted with the stadium and see two of rugby's great fly-halves in opposition. They were Jonny Wilkinson playing for Toulon and Leigh Halfpenny for Cardiff. It was all very exciting, with both players contributing many points in a 43-20 victory for Toulon. Wilkinson kicked 23 points, Halfpenny 12 points, but four Cardiff players went into the sin bin. The sin bin in Rugby followed a yellow card with ten minutes off the field, while a red card would mean expulsion from the field for the rest of the match. I knew rugby was a great spectacle as well, but I couldn't really imagine finding the time to follow rugby and soccer at the same time! A group of us did, however, usually manage to get to the United Hospitals Cup final matches played at Richmond and the Cambridge - Oxford matches and occasionally international matches, all at Twickenham. The Hospitals Cup is the oldest rugby Cup competition in the world. The teams changed along with the amalgamation of Medical schools. For example, the joint Westminster / Charing Cross team, to which of course I owed allegiance, became a serious threat to the serial winners of the era St Mary's. We also had a group who went to Twickenham each year for the Varsity (Cambridge and Oxford) match. Obviously, I supported Cambridge, and in the early days, they were often several internationals on view. That outing progressed over the years from picnics in car parks, especially that of the South and West Middlesex Hospitals, to a splendid corporate outing based on Queen's tennis club. By this time, I was only a social member of Queen's, but glad that my membership still came in useful in that regard.

Well-known names in the Nice team were the Colombian goalie David Ospina and the Argentine centre forward Dario Cvitanich. Dario later acquired Croatian nationality as well. The Nice team was managed by Claude Puel and finished in a respectable 5th place. On the 22nd of September, the first match was played at the Allianz Riviera stadium west of Nice close to the airport when Nice hosted Valenciennes in front of a full house, and Nice appropriately won 4-0.

The stadium holds over 36,000 spectators and hosts the home matches of the soccer team and occasional matches of the rugby union club Toulon. The start of Nice games had always been marked by the arrival of a large eagle and the singing of the anthem, Nissa La Bella, things that were repeated at all subsequent home games! The anthem is sung in Niçard, the local dialect, and dates from 1903. Its role is comparable to "you'll never walk alone" at the Anfield Kop, a song made famous by Gerry Marsden of Gerry and the Pacemakers, a Liverpool group almost as famous as the Beatles. The Nice song was sung with the traditional scarves held above the head and moved from side to side. The flying of eagles was temporarily banned on health and safety grounds, but the ban has been largely ignored. It fits well with the club's nickname, Les Aiglons, the eaglets. It is a great attraction to those like my wife who are less passionate about football.

My son-in-law David and his father, as keen Hull supporters, were rather excited by an FA Cup semi-final match in April 2014 that saw Hull defeat Sheffield United (then in Division One) 5-3. David got the tickets through Hull sources, and it proved to be a very exciting contest that lived up to expectations and saw Hull through to their first-ever FA Cup final. Hull was in the premier league and managed by Steve Bruce at that time.

Nigel Clough managed Sheffield United, a Division three team, and the match had flowed from end to end, including a goal each in the 90th minute with Hull victorious by 5-3! So on the 17th of May 2014, there was the FA Cup final at Wembley against Arsenal. It was Hull's first-ever FA Cup final appearance compared with 18 for Arsenal. Hull took a 2-0 lead thanks to goals from James Chester and ex-Hatter Curtis Davies in the first 10 minutes. However, by the 90-minute mark, Arsenal has equalized through Santi Cazorla and Laurent Koscielny. In extra-time, Aaron Ramsey scored what proved to be the winner for the Gunners. Aaron was later to join Juventus in 2019. The City supporters were very vocal, chanting Steve Bruce's name and, unusually, 01482, which was the telephone code for Hull.

In the next season, 2013/14 under John Still, we finally won the conference title and re-entered the football league without the need for the playoffs.

We had won the league, 19 points ahead of Cambridge, the largest distance between first and second in conference history. Andre Gray had been very successful at Luton as a striker with good movement and an eye for goal, whether from foot or head. He scored 30 goals in that season. Unfortunately, his life outside football was rather sad, being involved with gang culture and homophobic and racial tweet issues before he moved on to Brentford. Luton records that season included a points total of 101, 23 clean sheets and only 35 goals conceded in total. It featured a record 27 match unbeaten run in which we scored 78 goals. Other prolific scorers were Paul Benson and Luke Guttridge. So we had made it after five seasons in the Conference and three playoff defeats.

Chapter 132 - Season 2014/15

In Luton's first season back in the football league, we had to do without the departed Andre Gray and for much of the season Paul Benson, who had sadly broken his leg. A hopeless run coincided with seven consecutive lost matches in March and early April. We still finished in 8th place, but only one place and 3 points below the playoffs.

Signings from Premier league academies included Cameron McGeehan and Pelly Ruddock Mpanzu. One name stands out; Pelly, a midfielder, came to Luton from West Ham United and played in the conference, divisions 1 & 2, and the Championship, and in 2021, was still the first choice with more than 299 appearances and over 19 goals. He is a real character with wonderful skill but sadly is rather inconsistent, often giving the ball away unnecessarily. However, he has received international recognition with DR Congo.

Only 50 goals were scored, with Mark Cullen, the top scorer with 14 and the only one to double figures. Attendances just above 10,000 were commonplace, with Portsmouth drawing a maximum of 10,071. One of the stalwarts of that period was Steve McNulty, a scouser from the Liverpool youth team who we signed from Fleetwood Town. At the end of the previous season, he was the lynchpin of a defence that kept 23 clean sheets. Following the departure of Ronnie Henry, he was made captain and led very much by example, his physical stature helping to keep opponents at bay. On the 24th of July 2014, I went to Brentford to see Nice play there, obviously in a pre-season friendly. I saw the Nice team with manager Claude Puel coming out from the Twickenham rugby stadium, which they had just visited. It was very hot. The Brentford Stadium, Griffin Park, was famous for having a pub on each corner of the ground. It was to be replaced by a new stadium in 2020/2021 in Lionel Road.

I was interviewed by OGC Nice TV and recounted how I came to be connected with their team. The Brentford team included Andre Gray, who just signed from Luton in the close season. Andre Gray had commanded a high fee of about £59,000, and there were additions to be had as he moved on from Brentford to Burnley for £6 million pounds with add ons for the Town of over a million pounds! More recently, Watford paid 18.5 million pounds coupled with an annual salary reputed to be about £3,640,000. Brentford beat Nice 3-2 in front of 2,168 spectators.

On the 22nd of November 2014, we saw our first soccer match at the impressive new Allianz Riviera stadium with Nice playing Reims, a famous French club that had seen better days. Nice were 11th and Reims 15th, so we didn't expect too much. For Nice, we noted Gregoire Puel, the right-back son of manager Claude and a typically skilled striker from Argentina, Dario Cvitanich! Unfortunately, the match did not live up to expectation ending in a goalless draw with each side getting two yellow cards! Another notable Nice player was the teenager Neal Maupay who has since starred at Brentford and Brighton. Reims had fallen on hard times since the 1950s when they regularly won the French league and got to two European Cup finals, losing both times to Real Madrid. Their best-known players were undoubtedly Raymond Kopa, who was sold to Real and Juste Fontaine, who had come from Nice and was the top scorer in the 1958 World Cup with 13 goals. Since then, Reims have only managed to be in the top flight for a few seasons and, at present, are up there (just!).

Chapter 133 - 2014 World Cup in Brazil

Fan Fests were a huge success attracting maybe 5 million people over the twelve venues. And there were many other things introduced for the first time during this World Cup. Goal-line technology, vanishing spray and cooling breaks were all used for the first time. Anti-doping measures were increased with all the players being tested before the tournament began and then two from each team after each game.

Surprises were the elimination of holders Spain, Italy and England in the group stages. England under manager Roy Hodgson were bottom of their group 36 years after their last elimination in the group stage. They were eliminated with Italy in favour of Uruguay and group winners Costa Rica. Italy finished 2nd bottom although they beat England 2-1, goals for Balotelli and Marchisio as against one from Sturridge. We also lost to Uruguay 2-1 (2 goals by Suarez, one by Rooney) and scraped a 0-0 draw with Costa Rica. Portugal and Russia were also eliminated. There were no real surprises in the round of 16. In the quarters, Brazil beat Colombia, Germany beat France, Argentina beat Belgium, and the Netherlands beat Costa Rica, but only after a goalless game and a 4-3 penalty shoot out. Costa Rica had undoubtedly been the surprise team of the tournament.

So there were the big two teams from South America and two European teams in the semis. A real shock was Germany beating Brazil 7-1 in Belo Horizonte with five different goalscorers, including Kroos and Schurrle, each scoring two goals. Argentina beat the Netherlands on penalties after a 0-0 draw. The German manager at the time was the long-serving Joachim Low. Germany had almost exhausted their goal supply by that semi but in the final against Argentina, managed 1 goal by Mario Gotze in extra time enough to win 1-0 and be crowned champions. The Dutch beat Brazil 3-0 in the 3rd place match. It was the first time that a European team had won the Cup in a South American country.

In retirement, I decided to take Italian classes to try and improve my command of the language and especially the grammar. A very friendly man in the class worked for the English National Opera and was a keen Swindon Town supporter. Inevitably we arranged to go to the next Luton Swindon match at Luton, which was a Football League round one Cup tie to be held on the 12th of August 2014.

We arranged to meet at the Bricklayers Arms on High Town Road—a pub mostly frequented on match days by away supporters. It was the first time I had been there and found it very pleasant and friendly and with a good selection of ales! We didn't sit together as he had got tickets together with a friend of his in the infamous Oak Road away end! That visitor's end is renowned for the lack of legroom, but it doesn't seem to matter as they all stand up anyway!

The match was quite close, but Swindon had the majority of the possession and won 2-1 with two goals in the last quarter of an hour.

Exciting news that came from Nice in 2016 was the signing of Mario Balotelli from Liverpool on a free transfer. He was another of those maverick players who had huge ability and charisma but regular disciplinary and off the field issues. Jose Mourinho tells a great story of his time at Inter when they were short of strikers and playing a Champions League match against Rubin Kazan.

Balotelli, who had already been booked around the 42nd minute, was the last striker standing with no others on the bench. At half time Jose spent most of the time with Mario stressing the importance of avoiding controversy and staying on the pitch. He was told: "don't touch anybody, play only with the ball. When we lose the ball, no reaction. If someone provocates you, no reaction. If the referee makes a mistake, no reaction. The unsurprising result was Mario getting booked again in the 46th minute and consequently sent off! In his first Nice season, he scored 15 goals in 23 appearances helping Nice to 3rd place and a Champions League place. The next season Balotelli scored another 18 league goals in 26 starts and a further seven more in Europe. In May 2014, he was recalled to the Italy squad. Patrick Vieira had replaced Lucien Favre as Nice head coach, and he fell out with Mario, who was not only late for pre-season training but in poor shape. In January, Mario moved on to Marseille. He lasted less than a year before signing for home town club Brescia on a free transfer! When I last heard of him was playing in Turkey for Adana Demirspor.

Chapter 134 - Season 2015/16

So in league two, we had players of note at the time. They included Steve McNulty in defence, Cameron McGeehan and long-serving Jake Howells in midfield. Jake was a local boy born in St Albans and who came through the academy. Jake played 334 times in the league for Luton scoring 31 goals. He also played for the England C team as well as Wales under 21 teams. He was a very popular figure who always gave his best. Then there were strikers Paul Benson and Jack Marriott. Jack Marriott, signed from Ipswich, was the top scorer with 16 goals in all competitions.

In December, John Still, who will always be remembered as the manager who got us back into the Football League, was sacked with us in 17th place in league 2 to be replaced as manager by Nathan Jones. Nathan had been a player making over 335 appearances for Brighton and Yeovil before taking up management. Before coming to Luton, Nathan was assistant head coach at Brighton under Sami Hyppia and later Chris Hughton. He guided the Town away from the relegation zone to an 11th place finish. Nathan is an interesting character, religious and bilingual, speaking good Spanish as well. He had played in Spain for Numancia and Club Deportivo Badajoz. I have the greatest admiration for Nathan as a man and a manager. The football he encourages is very skilled and depends on maximum effort from all the players. It is football well worth watching and mostly very effective. My only criticism is his moaning about sometimes having to play three times in some eight-day periods. I would dare to remind him of the days when at Christmas and Easter, they had to play three games in 4 days! And that was at a time when the players were probably far less fit than they are today. I was sorry to see Steve McNulty leave for personal reasons, going to the northwest to play for Tranmere Rovers. Good news for the Town was Gray's onward transfer from Brentford to Burnley, which with the latter's promotion to the Premier League meant nearly another 2 million pounds for the Town!

The European Championships were played in France in 2016, and the England versus Iceland match in the Round of 16 was played in Nice. It resulted in the most infamous result and England's humiliation, a 1-2 loss and elimination. The result led to manager Roy Hodgson being severely criticised for his selections and tactics, or rather lack of them. He resigned on the 27th of June after that Iceland game. The result was very badly received by the travelling England fans, which angered Wayne Rooney in particular. A real surprise was the progress of Gareth Bale's Wales with a 3-1 win at the expense of Belgium. But they lost to the eventual winners, Portugal, who won the tournament for the first time 1-0 after extra-time over the hosts France. Some consolation for the hosts was that Antoine Griezmann was the top scorer with six goals. We saw the final on television with one of our friends in France and drove back to our flat, and the roads were unsurprisingly very quiet!

World Soccer magazine goes from strength to strength. It continues to amaze me how they produce the necessary material so promptly and the high standard of their journalists. It has recently introduced a Women's Football section acknowledging the rise in stature and increasing popularity of that section of our most popular sport. They now have the opportunity to play on perfect pitches and receive coaching from the very best. They have their leagues and competitions just like the men.

Chapter 135 - Season 2016/17

In August 2016, Juventus were invited to play West Ham in a friendly to inaugurate the Olympic Stadium as a football venue. West Ham had won the right to play there in a battle with Spurs and Leyton Orient. They were apparently content to leave the charismatic Boleyn ground in Upton Park. At that time, Juventus included Paul Pogba and had Gianluigi Buffon in goal.

They also had Gonzalo Higuain, an Argentinian who recently arrived from Napoli, where he had been capocannoniere (top goalscorer) with a total of 36 goals. He came on as a substitute and was clearly far from his optimal fitness level. He made up for it with some stellar seasons making him one of the Juventus greats. His transfer fee of €90,000 paid by Juventus was a record for a South American footballer until Neymar's transfer to Paris St Germain in 2017 and the highest ever paid by an Italian team until Cristiano Ronaldo signed for Juventus in 2018. On the other hand, West Ham had signed central defender Angelo Ogbonna from Juventus the season before. An open game ended 2-3 to Juventus. Andy Carroll scored both the West Ham goals, but goals from Paolo Dybala, Mario Mandzukic, and Simone Zaza gave Juve the win. Striker Dybala was another Argentinian who had come from Palermo for €32 million in the previous season and went on to have a very successful career with Juve with to date 260 appearances and 103 goals. Dybala is sometimes the captain if others such as Bonucci and Chiellini are not playing. At one point there was a scuffle between rival fans just behind us, showing once again how little it takes to start trouble, and perhaps these matches should be more accurately called "pre-season" rather than "friendly". So it was another successful outing with members of Juventus Club Londra and was followed by a nice meal in a restaurant in the very crowded Westfield Stratford shopping centre.

Nathan Jones continued to re-shape the squad with ten new players coming in! Glen Rea is one who is still there. Our season started promisingly with a 3-0 win away to Plymouth Argyle and ended well with five wins and two draws in the last seven games.

So we finished in 4th place with 77 points but were knocked out in the playoff semifinals by old foe Blackpool. The first leg away ended in a 3-2 defeat. A very exciting 2nd leg end to end match finished 3-3 with the tie decided by the Luton goalkeeper Stuart Moore on loan from Reading, scoring an own goal in the 95th minute! The home leg attracted a crowd of 10,032, and just over 10,000 full houses became the norm from then on. So we faced another season in League 2. Danny Hylton, a free transfer from Oxford, was way out in front as the top scorer with 26 goals in all competitions, Isaac Vassell got 14, Jack Marriott 12, while Cameron McGeehan chipped in with 11. Danny was another player with outstanding attributes but a desire to provoke the opposition, usually ending in him receiving many cards and, therefore, suspensions. Indeed I think he has amassed 35 yellow and five reds during his Luton career.

Chapter 136 - Season 2017/18

We managed to see Mario Balotelli play against Monaco in a match on the 9th of September 2017 that started despite a seriously waterlogged pitch thirty minutes before kick-off. He scored two goals in a 4-0 victory. Once again, I was trapped by The Nice Club TV to give a few pre-match comments! When transmitted, they had amazingly linked it to the interview I gave at Brentford in 2014!

Big news from Luton was that Nick Owen, who had been in post since 2008, was standing down as chairman to become a Vice President. He had done a massive amount to steer a club which was close to its collapse to a position of stability and success. He was a great ambassador for the club, but he cited his media commitments preventing him from continuing to give Luton the time and effort required. He was followed by the appointment of lifelong Hatters fan David Wilkinson, who his fellow directors had voted in as the new chairman. Luton born David had been the club's vice-chairman and a founder member of LTFC2020. Together he and chief executive Gary Sweet have also been instrumental in steering the club to calmer waters and setting the scene for financial stability and a potential new stadium in the centre of Luton at Power Court. The stadium would initially hold around 15,000 spectators but could be expanded to a capacity of 22,500. The build would be financed by the sale of the Newlands Park site that the club owns at Junction 10 of the M1. The main opposition to the plans came from the adjacent Mall shopping centre, but ultimately they were defeated.

In his first full season as the manager, Nathan Jones put his mark on the playing staff with lots of comings, 12 in all, and ten outgoings. Benson went to Dagenham and Redbridge in May 2016, and McGeehan was later sold to Barnsley and Marriott to Peterborough. James Justin, a local boy, emerged, and the crowd would sing, "he's one of ours." He was a full/wing-back who could play equally well on both sides, and he began to make his mark. It was rumoured that big bids were starting to come in for him.

Another important signing was Jack Stacey, another full-back, this time from Reading. James Shea, a goalie, was signed from AFC Wimbledon and Harry Cornick, a forward from Bournemouth. The final piece in the jigsaw was James Collins, a striker from Crawley Town who later rose to win Republic of Ireland caps. We managed to keep most of our best players, which was important. The first match of the season ended in an 8-2 home win against Yeovil, which augured well. I went to both Barnet games with Stuart, a distant relative of my wife and a keen

Barnet supporter. He was always willing to come with me, and as I have become older and frailer, he is very helpful in driving me to Barnet or Luton games and generally looking after me!

The season's first away game was lost 1-0 at Barnet with a goal in the 90 + 1 minute, but we won the home game 2-0 with goals in the 2nd half from Hylton and Collins. Other amazing results included a 7-1 home win over neighbours Stevenage, 7-0 at home to Cambridge and 5-0 at home to Swindon. We finished in 2nd place behind Accrington Stanley and so were promoted directly to League One. Great to have avoided the play-offs, which could never be seen as our forte! So a season of real excitement for the long-suffering but very faithful Hatters fans.

Spurs were drawn to play Juventus in the Champions League round of 16.

The second leg on the 7th of March 2018 was to be played at Wembley as White Hart Lane was being rebuilt. So I went with my younger son in law, the Spurs season ticket holder, and we parked in the mews behind Wembley Park Drive, memories of our Littlewoods Cup finals against Arsenal and Nottingham Forest in 1988 and 1989. Spurs had drawn 2-2 in the first leg in Turin, coming from 2 Higuain goals down before the 10th minute, and getting the draw thanks to goals from Kane and Eriksen.

That meant that Spurs were the favourites to go through. In the second leg, Son opened the scoring for Spurs in the 39th minute, but two quick goals by Higuain and Dybala, the two Argentinians, in the 64th and 67th minute gave Juventus the win. It meant Juventus were going through to the quarter-finals 3-2 on aggregate. But they lost in the next round to Real Madrid, the eventual winners.

Later in the next season, Juve drew Manchester United in the group stages. Juventus won 1-0 with a Dybala goal at Old Trafford but lost 1-2 in Turin. A Ronaldo rocket had given Juventus the lead, but United came back to win with two goals in the last 5 minutes. The second one in the very last minute was a Leonardo Bonucci own goal. That left the records between those two heavyweights overall exactly similar, with six wins, two draws and six defeats!

On the 20th of September, 2017 was my 80th birthday which we celebrated by taking all the family totalling 12, including the two of us, two daughters and the two sons-in-law and six grandchildren, to the Club Med in Sicily. We went in advance of the birth date to fit in with the school holidays. The Club Med is a wonderful holiday destination for families and all ages with excellent food and wine/beer, a stage show every evening, tours to local places of interest and exceptional sports facilities, all managed by the staff who also effectively act as coaches. In view of my age, I had to decline participation in nearly all of the sports on offer. I was pleased to win a medal for my participation in Petanque (French metal bowls), a suitable sport for oldies! The only football-related activity was watching the Champions League final on the 3rd of June on the TV. It was held in the Millennium Stadium Cardiff, which meant I would probably have gone to watch it but the family outing had been booked long ago and just occasionally, I had to put family before football! It featured Real Madrid beating Juventus 4-1 and was very exciting if rather depressing for the predominantly Italian viewers. In central defence, the Juventus team had Buffon in goal and the famous BBC (Barzagli, Bonucci and Chiellini). It was one of the last games the BBC played together before Barzagli became the first of them to retire. The rest of the team were Dani Alves, Pjanic, Khedira, Alex Sandro, Dybala, Higuain and Mandzukic, a team very strong on paper. Juventus were managed by Massimiliano Allegri and Real by Zinedine Zidane, two of the top managers of the era.

Ronaldo scored the first for Real in 20 minutes, but on the 27th, Mandzukic, with a spectacular overhead kick, equalised. In the 2nd half, goals for Real from Casemiro on 61 minutes, Ronaldo again on 64th, and finally, Asensio on the 90th sealed a comfortable victory for the Spanish club. Real won without receiving a yellow card while Juan Cuadrado, Juventus's Colombian substitute, not for the first or last time, received two yellows, meaning, of course, a red. He reminded me of Camoranesi, who, like Sivori before, was an Argentinian who came to Italy and played for the Italian national team. He also managed to pick up an excess of cards. Among the top red card collectors in a Juve shirt was Paolo Montero, the Uruguayan central defender who played for Juventus from 1996 to 2005. He was fifth on the all-time list with 21 career red cards.

England has only Vinnie Jones, ex Wimbledon Crazy Gang, in the top 9 with 12 red cards. However, that's way below the record holder, the Colombian Gerardo Bedoya, who received 46! The list confirms what I have always believed, and that is that South American footballers are way ahead of the Europeans when it comes to the game's dark arts.

Luton finished the season in a very creditable 2nd place and was promoted to League 1. The attendance had regularly topped 10,000, and it was great to see the old ground heaving match after match. Again, the top scorer was Danny Hylton with 23 goals in all competitions, closely followed by James Collins with 20. However, in the last match, Danny typically ended the season with two yellow cards, both for minor but definite offences.

A major change in refereeing came with the introduction of VAR (video assistant referee) in England in 2018 and the same year for the 2018 World Cup. It was to be used for four issues, Goal/no goal, Penalty/no penalty, Direct red card, and mistaken identity. VAR is there to identify clear and obvious errors only and leads to three possible scenarios: the decision upheld or overturned, the on-field review recommended, or finally, the referee chooses to ignore VAR advice. The first VAR training centre in Italy opened in 2018 at Coverciano near Florence, complete with a simulator. Coverciano has been the site since 1957, where the national team trains and is the technical headquarters of the Italian Football Federation. To date, VAR is only available in England in The Premier League stadia. Still, it would undoubtedly have corrected major errors such as Maradona's "hand of god goal," Thierry Henry's handball goal for France against Ireland in the 2009 World Cup qualifiers and Frank Lampard's "disallowed goal" against Germany in the 2010 World Cup previously discussed.

Chapter 137 - Season 2018/19

Expectations were high with Nathan Jones getting the team to play really well. An exciting outing was to Newcastle for a 3rd round FA Cup tie in January 2019.

Normally I would not have gone because of the distance involved, but my neighbours in the main stand offered to drive me there, an offer I could not refuse. It was the first time I had been to any northeastern grounds, and I was very impressed with St James Park. We got there in good time and found a pub recommended to us by the locals. Like many in the north, this one was very large and filled with welcoming Geordies.

The match itself was exciting, although ultimately, we lost 3-1 in front of over 47,000 fans, of whom 7,500 were Hatters supporters. Newcastle had taken a 3-0 lead before Danny Hylton scored early in the second half and then had a goal dubiously disallowed for offside. If it had not been chalked off, it was felt that we might have got something out of the match. The long drive back was luckily uneventful, and I was really pleased that I had gone.

Disappointment came with the news that Nathan Jones talked to Stoke City, who he rapidly joined as manager in mid-season. He left Luton with the highest points total per game of any manager in our history to be replaced temporarily by Mick Harford. Mick successfully guided the Town to promotion to the Championship.

We only lost six games all season and amassed 98 points. We finished twelve points above second-placed Hull. James Collins, with 25, led the goalscoring. Harford was followed by Graeme Jones, who had made his name as assistant to Roberto Martinez with the Belgium national team but did not have any top-level managerial experience. So amazingly, we were to be a championship side next season, only ten years after losing our way and dropping into the Conference.

A surprise at Juventus was that highly successful manager Massimiliano Allegri appointed in 2014, was stepping down as manager after apparent disagreements with the hierarchy.

He had achieved an amazing record, winning five consecutive scudetti and four consecutive doubles. However, although he got the club to two Champions League finals, they were both lost to Barcelona and then to Real Madrid. The Juventus Stadium was later sponsored and named the Allianz stadium in July 2017. In July 2018, Cristiano Ronaldo was signed by Juventus for a fee of €105 million. It was by far the record paid by an Italian club for an over 30-year-old. He scored almost one goal a game during his spell with Juve. In the past, Ronaldo had played in three Champions League finals, two for Manchester United and one for Real Madrid. However, one of the motives of Juve signing Ronaldo was not only to go on winning scudetti but undoubtedly to help them add to their very meagre Champions league victory total of two. It was not to prove as easy as it may have seen, although Ronaldo kept his part of the deal by prolific goalscoring. In August 2021, he re-signed for Manchester United, leaving Juve a bit short of strikers.

At the same time, OGC Nice had been bought for 100,000 euros by English multi-billionaire Sir James Ratcliffe, chairman of Ineos, a Swiss-based British petrochemicals company. The Ineos group, aided by Ben Ainslie, was preparing to compete in 2021 for the 36th America's Cup, the most prestigious sailing trophy. Sir Jim is a Monaco based tax exile, so he lives fairly close to Nice. He also owns the Swiss soccer club FC Lausanne-Sport. His brother Bob became Nice club president in March 2019.

Sir Jim also owns the Team Sky, now known as Team Ineos, cycling team and became the principal partner of the Mercedes AMG F1 motor racing team. Unfortunately, the British boat was outclassed by the Italian boat and lost the series 7-1. The Italians looked forward to a final against New Zealand, but they were outclassed.

Chapter 138 - Season 2019/20

Luton versus Leicester in the Carabao Cup 3rd round on Tuesday the 24th of September 2019 was a special occasion for me. It was, of course, a repeat of the first match I ever saw at Luton in 1949, 70 years before, although in a different Cup competition. Far from drawing 5-5 as in 1949, we lost 0-4. We held out for 34 minutes before the floodgates opened. James Justin, Luton's ex full-back, scored the second goal and was kindly restrained in his celebration. Justin was a huge success at Leicester, having been bought for about £6 million. He was noted for his regular outstanding displays that took him to the brink of selection for the England team. Unfortunately, in February 2021, he tore the anterior cruciate ligament in his knee and would be out for a long time.

Leicester went on to the semi-finals when they lost to Aston Villa. The Luton match was an occasion when I contributed a piece to the Luton programme in the section "My Town" describing the events associated with that 5-5 draw in 1949.

We attended Nice versus Paris Saint Germain in October 2019. One of our Nice neighbours had got us the tickets, and I was a bit apprehensive as the tickets had his name on them rather than ours. Luckily, one only had to put them through the entrance machine, which was not clever enough to identify us. We used the city bus that was put on, especially for the matches and left from convenient stops in the centre. PSG had a team full of superstars, and I was particularly keen to see Neymar, Mbappe and Di Maria in the flesh. Di Maria did not disappoint, scoring twice, but Neymar was absent injured, and Mbappe only came on for the last few minutes but still had time to score, followed by a Mauro Icardi goal. Nice then lost their cool, and Cyprien got a second yellow to be sent off, as was Herelle. So PSG comfortably won 4-1. It was another occasion when leaving a bit before the end meant missing something important, in this case, the last two goals!! Finding the way to the buses proved quite difficult, and I remember seeking help from a lady steward who seemed upset that I hadn't said "Bonsoir" before starting my request. Despite spending so much time in France, I had never realised that it was impolite not to say bonjour or bonsoir as appropriate. Another bit of French etiquette that I only mastered later in life was which cheek to use first when greeting someone with the bise! It's not as easy as you might think, being the left cheek first in the south and southeastern parts of France and the right cheek elsewhere. Usually only two pecks, but in Belgium, it is three!

Two Luton matches worthy of mention were the away game at QPR lost 2-3 after 0-3 at 28 minutes. Memorable for me because I went with my elder daughter, who didn't come to many matches and with one of her old school friends who was a QPR season ticket holder and had a very smart car. It's not often that one is driven to a match in an all-electric Jaguar. I must say I would have been worried about parking such a car close to a football ground, but it proved to be alright. For some reason, the event was noted for a very large police presence due it was said to the presence of a well known far-right activist with Luton connections. The following week we played Hull. I took my son in law and his father, and they were pleased to watch Hull win 3-0, crowned by two late goals!

It was a hard season as we had lost 12, drawn two and won only 5 of the first 19 games. We were languishing at the foot of the table when on the 24th of April 2020, Coronavirus shut down all professional football. The Town was 6 points from safety, effectively seven because of a very inferior goal difference.

Mick Harford stepped in yet again when Graham Jones left by mutual agreement in April. Guess what? Gary Brabin, assistant manager, first-team coach Inigo Idiakez and technical goalkeeping coach Imanol Etxeberria had also had their contracts terminated with immediate effect.

On the 28th of May, Nathan Jones, apparently forgiven, was re-instated as manager, assisted by Mick Harford. Later they were also joined by Paul Hart. A few days later, the EFL suggested that the championship could restart on the 20th of June but behind closed doors. At the restart, there were nine games to play, including tough away games against Swansea City and top of the table Leeds United. The stadia were all closed to spectators, but we were able to watch the matches live on i-follow. The home and mid-week matches were free of charge as compensation for the inability to use our season tickets! Amazingly we got 16 points out of the last possible 27 achieving Nathan Jones's secret points target. Nevertheless, safety was only achieved at the end of the last match at home to Blackburn Rovers, which we won 3-2. Even that match was tense to the end, especially after we went a goal down in 8 minutes. There was also the factor that Wigan were facing a 12 point deduction, but that was subject to a possible appeal. In the end, the result of their appeal might have affected Barnsley but not us. It was an amazing last day, with 11 of the 12 Championship matches having a possible bearing on the final promotion and relegation positions. The tension was too much for me, inducing a migraine, something I only rarely suffered from.

So the bottom three were finally Hull, Wigan and Charlton. To my son in law's despair, Hull had lost seven and drew two of their final nine matches, including a 1-0 home defeat to a Lua Lua Luton goal late in the penultimate match of the season. We only lost two games in the last sixteen. For Luton, it was like winning a mini-league, and the celebrations at the end were equivalent. It was only a pity that it was all happening in largely empty stadia.

Chapter 139 - Season 2020/21

With my amazing luck, a family moved in near to us that included a husband and daughter who were Luton Town season ticket holders and went to most of the matches. During the COVID-19 pandemic, I often watched the matches in their house on ifollow TV. As I got to know them better, it seemed obvious that we should go together whenever possible. It meant that I didn't have to drive and park, and they were able to drive me to my disabled parking space very kindly provided by the club. The only disadvantage for them was the need to keep an eye on this increasingly decrepit old man with a stick as I went rather slowly up the incline of Hazelbury Crescent to the stadium. So on to the next season, and it was interesting to see how many changes were made to the squad, both in and out. Luckily we didn't have to sell two of our best players, as had been the case with fullbacks Justin and Stacey at the end of the 18/19 season. We finished the season in a comfortable 12th place, continuing our amazing upwards progress.

So as I think of putting my pen down, Luton are within range of the premier league, something that would have seemed impossible in those relatively lean years.

To add to my happiness, Juventus won their 9th successive scudetto thanks to Cristiano Ronaldo continuing to bang in 25 goals at the age of 35 and despite unhappiness over Maurizio Sarri's management and a poor end of the season with 3 of the last four games ending in defeat. Unsurprisingly being knocked out of the Champions League by Lyon spelt the end for Sarri. But who would replace him? No one could have forecast the appointment of Andrea Pirlo, whose only previous managerial experience was the previous nine days in charge of the Juventus under 23s!

The start of the season saw Juventus trail behind the two Milan teams. It looks as though their chances of winning the tenth successive scudetto were remote despite Ronaldo continuing to score, so far, 27 goals in 30 appearances. Their Champions league progress was also in some doubt as it depends on them overturning a 2-1 loss incurred at Porto. They won the home leg 3-2. So they failed on the away goals rule.

Finally, Nice, managed by Patrick Vieira, had finished in 5th position in the top French league, which was enough for them to earn a Europa League place for 20/21. Things can change very quickly in football. In December, after a run of 5 defeats and elimination from Europe, Patrick Viera was dismissed as Nice manager and replaced by his assistant Romanian Adrian Ursea. One of the factors in the decline of the results was an anterior cruciate ligament knee injury to a 37-year-old veteran captain and Brazilian central defender, Dante. He had been a leading figure since his arrival in 2016. He is particularly known for his flamboyant hairstyle and his great ability to defend.

Highlights, which of course the Covid crisis meant we had to miss, would have been watching Manchester United in the third round of the EFL Cup, which we lost 3-0, and away to Chelsea in the FA Cup 4th round, which we lost 3-1. There was more transfer activity, with seven coming in and eight going out. Notable departures included James Collins to Cardiff and Matty Pearson to Huddersfield.

Arrivals had included Elijah Adebajo, a young striker from Walsall who scored five goals in the last 15 matches. The season's stars were undoubtedly the loan midfielder Kiernan Dewsbury-Hall from Leicester, closely followed by Croatian international goalkeeper Simon Sluga.

OGC Nice finished the season in 9th place ending the season in style by winning 3-2 at Lyon. In the UEFA Cup, they lost to Bayer Leverkusen 6-2 and then beat Hapoel Be'er Sheva 1-0. They then lost 3-2 and 3-1 to Slavia Prague, 3-2 to Bayer Leverkusen and finally 1-0 at Be'er Sheva. So they were eliminated in last place in their group. Only Amine Gouiri, a young French striker, got into double figures of goals both 20/21 and 21/22.

And so finally to Juventus. After winning nine straight Serie As, they could only finish in 4th place behind Champions Inter and AC Milan and Atalanta, the latter the surprise packet of the season. They did, however, win the Supercoppa, beating Napoli 2-0 and the Coppa Italia beating Atalanta 2-1 in the final. Barcelona were playing Juve in the Champions League and Juve qualified for the next round. Although Juve had lost 2-0 at home, they won surprisingly 3-0 in the Nou Camp. So they progressed only to be knocked out by Porto on the away goals rule after the matches ended 4-4 on aggregate.

Ronaldo was again the star playing in a total of 44 matches and scoring 36 goals! His future was uncertain, but he did sadly ultimately go back to Manchester United. Watch out for Federico, son of Enrico Chiesa, who seems to me to be the new Juventus and Italy star on the block!

Chapter 140 - Season 2021/2022

Luton, having just survived in the Championship last season, finished this one in a very creditable 6th position. Sadly their playoff games ended 1-1 and 0-1 to Huddersfield Town. So near to another Wembley appearance, yet so far! In that season, Adebayo top scored with 17 goals. Odd results had been losses against Birmingham City, 0-5 at home and 0-3 away!

As I drift on, I will end with an update on my clubs as we enter the 2022/23 season.

Celta Vigo march on in La Liga, not being very near the top nor down near the bottom. Their star player is undoubtedly the Spaniard Iago Aspas, who has made over 370 appearances in two spells for the club, has scored over 165 goals, and has earned 18 caps for Spain.

Ajax continue to be regularly in the top three of the Eredivisie and qualify for Europe season after season. They have won the European Cup / Champions League 4 times. Their undoubted star at the present time is Brazilian striker Antony, who is being trailed by several top European clubs and indeed has just signed for Manchester United for £85.5 million.

OGC Nice have hung on to their Ligue 1 status for many years, actually finishing third in 2016/2017 and qualifying for the Europa Conference League. Familiar names in the team are the newly arrived Kasper Schmeichel and Aaron Ramsey, as well as the veteran Brazilian defender Dante.

Juventus had a bad season in 2021/2022, only finishing fourth after nine successive Serie A titles and just squeezing into the Champions League!

In the long absence of the injured Federico Chiesa, I have to note Dusan Vlahovic, a Serbian striker signed from Fiorentina in the close season and who's already scored 7 goals in 17 appearances.

So that leaves last but definitely not least Luton Town. They are continuing their steady upwards progress finishing in 6th place and reaching the Championship playoffs. Last season I would have to have singled out defender Kal Naismith as the star of the season, but sadly he left for Bristol City. New Scots international Allan Campbell appears to be the potential star of the team, reinforced by two new goalkeepers. One of them, Ethan Horvath, is a USA international. My personal favourite player is a right-wing-back, James Bree so accurate with crosses and set pieces.

Chapter 141 - In Memoriam

I will end on a very sad note accompanied by another of those coincidences that seem to crop up regularly in my life. For several years, I had phoned Boniperti regularly on July 4th, his birthday, to see how he was and to have a chat.

For some reason, this year, I chose to phone his younger son a couple of weeks earlier on June 18th 2001 and, for no particular reason, phoned on what happened to be the morning after Giampiero had died in the night at the age of 92. I was not aware that his father had just died, and probably due to my failing Italian, I did not immediately grasp what had happened, which was very embarrassing in hindsight.

I hope this publication, in which Boni features so largely, will be seen as a sort of obituary as well. Suffice it to say, I have lost a great friend and someone who played such a large part in my football story. I can only wish him to rest in peace and say that he and his family will always remain large in my memory.

Chapter 142 - My Favourite Quotes

Some people think football is a matter of life and death. I don't like that attitude. I can assure them it is much more serious than that. (Bill Shankly)

Some people are on the pitch. They think it's all over. It is now; it's four. (Kenneth Wolstenholme)

Vincere non e importante. E l'unica cosa che conta. Winning is not important. It's the only thing that matters. (Giampiero Boniperti)

Football is the most important of the unimportant things in life. (Arrigo Sacchi)

When the seagulls follow the trawler, it's because they think sardines will be thrown into the sea. (Eric Cantona)